FLIGHT 93

FLIGHT 93

The Story, the Aftermath, and the Legacy
of American Courage on 9/11

TOM McMILLAN

FOREWORD BY GOVERNOR TOM RIDGE

Guilford, Connecticut

An imprint of Rowman & Littlefield

Distributed by NATIONAL BOOK NETWORK

Copyright © 2014 by Tom McMillan
First Lyons Paperback Edition, 2015

British Library Cataloguing in Publication Information Available

The Library of Congress has previously catalogued an earlier (hardcover) edition as follows:

McMillan, Tom (Newspaper writer)
  Flight 93 : the story, the aftermath, and the legacy of American courage on 9/11 / Tom McMillan ; foreword by Governor Tom Ridge. — First Edition.
    pages cm
  ISBN 978-0-7627-9522-2 (hardback)
  1. United Airlines Flight 93 Hijacking Incident, 2001. 2. September 11 Terrorist Attacks, 2001. 3. Victims of terrorism—United States. 4. Aircraft accidents—Pennsylvania—Shanksville. I. Title. II. Title: Flight ninety-three.
  HV6432.7.M357 2014
  974.8'79—dc23

2014015137

ISBN 978-1-4930-0934-3 (pbk.)
ISBN 978-1-4930-1421-7 (e-book)

CONTENTS

In Memoriam

THE CREW AND PASSENGERS OF FLIGHT 93

Pilots

Captain Jason M. Dahl
First Officer LeRoy Homer

Flight Attendants

Lorraine G. Bay
Sandy Waugh Bradshaw
Wanda Anita Green

CeeCee Ross Lyles
Deborah Jacobs Welsh

Passengers

Christian Adams
Todd M. Beamer
Alan Anthony Beaven
Mark Bingham
Deora Frances Bodley
Marion R. Britton
Thomas E. Burnett Jr.
William Joseph Cashman
Georgine Rose Corrigan
Patricia Cushing
Joseph DeLuca
Patrick Joseph Driscoll
Edward Porter Felt
Jane C. Folger
Colleen L. Fraser
Andrew (Sonny) Garcia

Jeremy Logan Glick
Kristin Osterholm White Gould
Lauren Catuzzi Grandcolas
Donald Freeman Greene
Linda Gronlund
Richard J. Guadagno
Toshiya Kuge
Hilda Marcin
Waleska Martinez
Nicole Carol Miller
Louis J. Nacke II
Donald Arthur Peterson
Jean Hoadley Peterson
Mark David Rothenberg
Christine Ann Snyder
John Talignani
Honor Elizabeth Wainio

FOREWORD

by Governor Tom Ridge

Honorary Co-Chair, Flight 93 National Memorial Campaign

First Secretary, US Department of Homeland Security

43rd Governor of Pennsylvania

The Founders of the United States of America affirmed by their own words and deeds that preservation of liberty is more than an ideal but a way of life. They hoped that way of life would see the country and the greater world through inevitable challenges and the passage of time.

How proud they would be to know that the stand for liberty and freedom has long had a home in the American experience—as a group of forty courageous people demonstrated on September 11, 2001.

Every September 11 that has passed since that year, people have gathered to honor the nearly three thousand souls—citizens of the world from more than eighty nations—who lost their lives on that tragic day.

We miss them, but we also have worked hard to celebrate the contributions they made while they were here.

Among those contributions is the accounting we have of the last hard moments of "the fourth plane"—the plane that began to veer from course and speed toward the US Capitol, the plane that didn't reach that intended target, the plane that held the brave passengers and crew of United Flight 93.

The sweeping and inspiring story of Flight 93, of bravery that had no bounds, spoke volumes of people, brought together by chance, but bound together by courage.

Having learned of the fate of the other three planes and the terrorists' intentions for theirs, the men and women of Flight 93 rose up and fought back—collectively and intrepidly and at all costs.

Because of their sacrifice on that day, lives were saved, and thus heroes were made over the skies of Shanksville.

These extraordinary men and women have our respect, our admiration, our gratitude, and, with it all, our promise that future generations will know their names as well as their selfless and moving valedictory.

Through the devotion and hard work of the Families of Flight 93, the National Park Service, countless volunteers, and generous contributors, the Flight 93 National Memorial is now a beautiful and peaceful resting place for these forty precious souls. Visitors can come to this hallowed ground and learn of the people who fought the first battle against those who attacked our nation.

In this book, Tom McMillan wraps it all together—the moments and the memorial. But more than that, Tom shines a soft light on the lives of the passengers and crew. He takes off the generic label and, with the help of their family and friends, allows us to see the individual lives that the "40 Heroes" connected to while on earth, the depth of their goodness, the reach of their ambitions, and the many reasons that help us understand where their strength and bravery originated.

This book tells the story of people whose courage mattered, whose lives had great meaning, and who remain deeply missed. It's a story that will long be told, respectfully and gratefully, just as we find on the pages that follow.

—Governor Tom Ridge

Author's Note

We can never know every detail of what happened aboard Flight 93 when the passengers and crew staged their heroic revolt on September 11, 2001. But a number of sources, including the cockpit voice recorder, the flight data recorder, and reports of phone calls from the plane, provide valuable information about their activities—and the response of the hijackers.

As a result, it now is possible to piece together a reasonable step-by-step reconstruction of those final desperate minutes of their lives. I have attempted to do so in chapters 8 and 9, using the best information available thirteen years after the attack.

The National Transportation Safety Board (NTSB) created an animation of the Flight 93 flight path, based on the flight data recorder recovered at the scene. It enables us to know the altitude and direction of the plane throughout the flight. It also recorded the various turns made by the professional pilot and the hijacker pilot—including the "rocking of the wings" in the final five minutes.

Phone calls made from passengers and crew from Airfones on the United Boeing 757 offer a window into their thoughts and actions. Three of those on board left voice messages for loved ones, and there are direct transcripts of their words. Twelve other calls that got through to family members or coworkers on the ground have been recounted in various forms. The wives of two passengers involved in the counterattack, Deena Burnett and Lyz Glick, wrote books that included details of their phone conversations—as did Lisa Jefferson, the GTE/Verizon operator who took a call from passenger Todd Beamer.

Most of passengers and crew, however, did not make phone calls from the air that day. It is impossible to know their stories—and, therefore, the complete story. Were they part of the planning? Did they participate in the counterattack in any way? Would they have provided different perspective? It is an everlasting mystery.

The FBI released a detailed transcript of the cockpit voice recorder that gives us a specific chronology of the voices and sounds in the cockpit during the last thirty-one minutes of Flight 93. As of 2014, the audio recording has not been made available to the general public. Only family members, investigators, and those involved in related court cases had listened to its content and the various pitches and inflections. Still, the transcript provides significant insight as to what was said and heard in the cockpit that day.

The individual hijackers who were doing the speaking are never identified by name. However, because there were four microphones at strategic locations in the cockpit—including one described as "left seat cockpit" and another as "right seat cockpit," where the pilot and copilot would have been sitting on a normal flight—we can draw conclusions as to which hijackers were speaking.

Ziad Jarrah was the only member of the Flight 93 hijacking crew who was trained to fly an airplane. He attended flight school in Venice, Florida, in the summer and fall of 2000 and earned his private pilot's license. Al-Qaeda member Ramzi Binalshibh, the coordinator of the September 11 attacks, later confirmed that Jarrah was the pilot of Flight 93.

According to the transcript, the microphone located at the "left seat cockpit" is the one that picked up two messages from a hijacker attempting to communicate with the passengers shortly after the takeover. The first message began, "Ladies and gentlemen: Here the captain." In the second message, he also identified himself as "the captain." We can easily conclude that this is Jarrah. In addition to being the pilot, he was the leader of the hijacking team and would have been the one to handle communications and issue directives.

I have attributed the statements coming from that seat and that microphone for the rest of the flight to Jarrah.

Another microphone was located at the "right seat cockpit." Al-Qaeda never identified which of the muscle hijackers would join Jarrah in the cockpit, but Jarrah specifically addressed someone named "Saeed" on two occasions during the flight, referring to fellow hijacker Saeed al Ghamdi. Accordingly, I have attributed statements coming from the "right seat cockpit" microphone to Ghamdi.

There are several moments later in the flight when the transcript is unclear about the origination of a particular voice or statement. This is probably when sounds are jumbled from the chaos in the cockpit. The statements during those times have been attributed generically in the narrative to "one of the hijackers."

The transcript does make helpful distinctions for "Arabic-speaking male," "native English-speaking male," and "native English-speaking female." It also identifies "Translated Arabic text," "English text," "Unintelligible text," and "Shouting."

Telephone records and other data made available during the trial of al-Qaeda member Zacarias Moussaoui also have contributed greatly to our understanding of the entire September 11 operation, including the final moments of Flight 93.

I have done my best to create a fair and comprehensive depiction of the actions during the hijacking and the passenger uprising. Readers may draw their own conclusions.

—Tom McMillan
Pittsburgh, PA
March 2014

Preface

By any measure, September 11, 2001, was a strategic, symbolic, and humanitarian disaster for the United States of America.

Nineteen Islamic terrorists had infiltrated the country during a period of twenty months, successfully passing through immigration checks even though they'd all attended al-Qaeda training camps in Afghanistan. Four trained extensively as pilots at American flight schools. At the specially selected "Zero Hour," they proceeded through airport security and boarded four cross-country flights for the West Coast, armed only with small knives and a deep-seated hatred for American values. The 9/11 Commission later described their achievement in cold, terrifying terms: "By 8 a.m. on the morning of September 11, 2001, they had defeated all the security layers that America's civil aviation system then had in place to prevent a hijacking."

The horrific events that morning had been in the works for quite some time. Osama bin Laden, the Saudi exile who commanded the al-Qaeda terror network, had issued a religious fatwa in 1998 declaring war on the United States: *"The ruling to kill the Americans and their allies—civilians and military—is an individual duty for every Muslim who can do it in any country in which it is possible."* But no one outside a small core of the US intelligence community seemed to take the threat seriously. Operating mostly in the shadows, bin Laden's group mounted successful bombing attacks on US embassies in Kenya and Tanzania in 1998 and on the USS *Cole* in the port of Aden (Yemen) in 2000, but the scope of those events, though tragic, was only a hint of what al-Qaeda envisioned. Something else was in the works. Something that would leave no doubt who al-Qaeda was—and what it was intent on doing.

The terrorist teams succeeded in hijacking all four flights on September 11, violently assaulting the flight attendants and airline pilots in the cockpits and putting their own pilots in charge. Transforming large commercial airliners into missiles, they crashed the first two planes into the Twin Towers of the World Trade Center (WTC) and a third into the US military nerve center of the Pentagon, wreaking physical destruction and psychological chaos up and down the East Coast.

It must have stunned al-Qaeda, then, that a fourth plane never reached its target.

＊＊＊

The passengers and crew members of United Flight 93 could not have known that the terrorists in the cockpit were intent on slamming their Boeing 757 into one of the iconic symbols of US democracy—either the Capitol or the White House (the precise target has never been determined with 100 percent certainty, although with its prominent dome, it was likely the Capitol). But they knew the hijackers were on a suicide mission. Given the benefit of extra time—their flight had been delayed in departing from Newark International Airport—the people on board made Airfone calls to family members and learned of fiery crashes into three landmark buildings. That was all they needed. They were determined to have a say in their own fate.

They huddled, shared information, and hastily assembled a plot to reclaim control of the plane. As the planning reached a crescendo, they even paused for that most American of traditions—they took a vote.

Shortly before 10:00 a.m., a group of patriots as brave as any who had fought at Yorktown or Gettysburg or Normandy charged the hijackers and battered their way to the cockpit.

They didn't quite succeed in seizing control of the aircraft, but in many ways they won the battle in the skies over western Pennsylvania that morning. The ferocity of the counterattack so unnerved the hijacker pilot that he either lost control of the plane or purposely crashed it, plunging upside-down into a field in rural Somerset County. Citizen-soldiers from the United States had fought back, the Capitol still stood, and countless lives on the ground were saved.

In the days and weeks that followed, much of the narrative of the September 11 attacks focused on the tragedies in New York City and Washington, DC, which caused almost three thousand deaths, destroyed both towers of the World Trade Center, and demolished part of the outer rings of the Pentagon. Television networks were reporting live from the scene when the second plane hit the South Tower, capturing the impact in real time—the haunting approach of the aircraft, the stupendous fireball, the incomprehensible gust of smoke and dust and shattered concrete that engulfed entire blocks of the city. Video images were burned forever in the national memory.

By contrast, not as much was made of the smoking crater near little Shanksville, Pennsylvania, where forty heroes from all walks of life bonded together and defied the forces of terrorism. The plane crashed into an open field on the site of a reclaimed strip mine, and most of it had plowed deep into the earth. Famous buildings had not been struck. Innocent citizens working in their offices had not been slaughtered. The media coverage, at least in the immediate aftermath, was not as easily packaged with video or photo highlights for the daily news cycle. There was not much to see at all. Certainly this was part of the reason that the coverage was more muted—television needs the visuals to tell the story. But the story of Flight 93 lies buried in the earth.

In time, important parts of the story were pieced together and tugged at the nation's heartstrings. Jere Longman, a reporter for the *New York Times,* wrote an outstanding book the first year after Flight 93's crash. Several movies, including one major studio production, *United 93,* released in 2006, told and polished the legend of the passengers and crew. They made valuable contributions to our understanding of the event. But as a student of history, and as one who had visited the Flight 93 crash site on numerous occasions from my home in Pittsburgh, I still wanted more.

I discovered there *was* more.

In the thirteen years that have passed since September 11, reporters, professional investigators, and amateur historians gradually have uncovered many more elements of the story, piece by piece. The researchers at the Flight 93 National Memorial have interviewed hundreds of people directly involved in the day and its aftermath—family members, first responders, investigators, local residents, volunteers—and created an invaluable archive of oral histories. The 9/11 Commission published its groundbreaking report. The National Transportation Safety Board used information obtained from the flight data recorder to produce an animation of the entire Flight 93 flight path. Wives of some of the heroes wrote books and spoke to reporters. The trial of Zacarias Moussaoui, an al-Qaeda operative who was on the fringes of the plot, resulted in reams of documents and other evidence being made available to the public.

The goal of this book is to draw on many such sources of information and perspective—some fresh, some published but rarely seen—while building on the established storyline in an attempt to create a more comprehensive account of the story of Flight 93.

The full story cannot be told without an examination of the origin of the plot and the plotters. Flight 93 was a unique event in American history, but it did not take place in a vacuum. The roots go back at least as far as a terrorist's first attempt to bomb the World Trade Center in 1993. A concept that called for planes crashing into buildings was first proposed to bin Laden in 1996. The trail that led the hijacker pilots from their homes in the Middle East to the morning of September 11 is, in itself, a fascinating journey of historic happenstance.

It also cannot not be told without a closer look at the investigation and its aftermath, drawing on the contributions of regular folks from Somerset County who had their lives transformed forever by this national tragedy. Foremost among these is Wallace E. "Wally" Miller, the Somerset County coroner, who became such an integral part of the recovery effort and a de facto spokesman for the families. But there are many others.

Most of all, though, it cannot be told without attempting to achieve a more complete understanding of the passengers and crew and what happened on board in those heart-pounding minutes after the hijackers took control. We never will know everything. As with every hallowed battlefield, many of the facts are buried with the heroes. But in this book, I have tried to collect and weave together as much of the pertinent information as possible—long-established facts and recent revelations—to create an updated sequence of the events that took place against a backdrop of such unthinkable terror.

"We're going to do something," passenger Tom Burnett told his wife that morning—the last words she ever heard him speak.

They did.

And this is their story.

CHAPTER ONE

Morning

Flight 93 was late.

Almost forty minutes after its scheduled departure time of 8:00 a.m., with the spectacular late-summer sky above New York City already teeming with air traffic, the United Airlines Boeing 757 crawled along the snarled runway at New Jersey's Newark International Airport, waiting its turn.

For veteran business travelers such as Tom Burnett, seated in 4B, and Todd Beamer, a few rows back in 10D, it was an almost expected annoyance; the staggering volume of traffic at New York's three metropolitan airports meant that delays were part of the routine, even on a Tuesday morning, one of the lightest travel periods of the business week. We can't know whether this deviation from the schedule created sudden angst for the four Middle Eastern men scattered among the six rows of first class—the ones who hadn't bought tickets for a return flight.

The night before, they'd each read a four-page document, handwritten in Arabic, instructing them to tune out all distractions, to steel themselves for battle, to renew their oath to die, and to prepare themselves for eternal bliss. And to pray. Above all, to pray.

Be busy with the constant remembrance of God. God said: "Oh, ye faithful, when you find the enemy, be steadfast and remember God constantly so that you may be successful." When the (airplane) moves, even slightly, toward (unknown reference) say the supplication of travel. Because you are traveling to Almighty God, so be attentive on this trip.

Still, as the plane sat on the runway, and the minutes ticked away, it had to be disconcerting. For all their meticulous preparation, the al-Qaeda terrorists apparently never factored in a lengthy ground delay. Their plan had been proposed for the first time in the mountains of Afghanistan in 1996 and refined repeatedly in the intervening years. But it was dependent on precise timing for maximum shock effect.

Four transcontinental flights selected for hijacking were scheduled to take off within a tight time frame of twenty-five minutes, between 7:45 and 8:10 that morning. The hijackings were to start about fifteen minutes after each flight was in the air. If everything went according to plan, the four planes would be crashed into their targets in such rapid succession that US political and military leaders (not to mention the passengers and crew on the planes) would have no time to react. And the physical damage to the World Trade Center, the Pentagon, and the Capitol—devastating as it was sure to be—would be dwarfed by the massive psychological damage to the American spirit.

The clock ticked.

Do not seem confused or show signs of nervous tension. Be happy, optimistic, calm, because you are heading for a deed that God loves and will accept. It will be the day, God willing, you will spend with the women of paradise.

The four men assigned by al-Qaeda to the mission on Flight 93 could not have imagined what effect the delay in departure would have on their plan to seize control of the plane and steer it toward Washington, DC. Their target in all probability was the Capitol, whose giant dome was easily spotted from the air—and where a full session of Congress was scheduled. But if Ziad Jarrah squirmed in his seat in 1B, just outside the cockpit, or if Ahmed al Haznawi dabbed sweat from his forehead in 6B, directly behind Jarrah and in the last row of first class, it is unlikely that the thirty-three regular passengers or seven crew members would have noticed.

No ordinary traveler on a US flight in 2001 worried about the threat of hijacking, and certainly no one on board ever had conceived of Islamic terrorists commandeering airplanes in midair and turning them into missiles. This would be an ordinary weekday flight. The pilots and crew went about their normal preflight preparations; the passengers, such as Mark Bingham, a public relations executive who'd hustled to barely make the last boarding call before settling into seat 4D, sipped orange juice and waited for the six-hour trip to San Francisco.

Remind your soul to listen and obey (all divine orders) and remember that you will face decisive situations that may prevent you from 100 percent obedience, so tame your soul, purify it, convince it, make it understand, and incite it. God said, "Obey God and His Messenger, and do not fight among yourselves or you will fail. And be patient, for God is with the patient."

It was precisely 8:41:49 a.m., according to the records of the National Transportation Safety Board (NTSB), when an air traffic controller in the tower at Newark's airport told Captain Jason Dahl and First Officer LeRoy Homer: *"United ninety three wind three three zero at seven, runway four left cleared for takeoff."*

At 8:41:53 a.m., as the pilots prepared to send their Boeing 757-200 hurtling down the runway, the response came from the cockpit: *"cleared for takeoff four left United ninety three."*

At 8:42:41 a.m., from the control tower: *"United ninety three contact departure."*

Two seconds later, from the cockpit: *"going to departure, United ninety three good day."*

Passengers that morning were scattered through the first twenty-one rows of the plane, which had thirty-four rows in all. Kristin White Gould, seated in 21C, was a freelance medical journalist with deep, even historical, American roots. Kristin was a descendant of William Brewster, a passenger on the *Mayflower* in 1620 and the senior church elder at Plymouth colony. She was heading to California to visit friends. Colleen Fraser (seat 13A), a nationally known advocate for the disabled, was traveling to Nevada for a conference on grant writing. Just four-foot-six, Colleen carried a tiny copy of the Constitution with her to encourage the disabled to become their own advocates.

Retirees Donald Peterson and Jean Hoadley Peterson, the only married couple on board, seated in 14A and 14C, were leaving on the first leg of a trip to meet other family members at Yosemite National Park. Christine Snyder (seat 17A) was returning from her first-ever trip to the East Coast, heading home to Honolulu after attending a forestry conference in Washington, DC. Retirees Patricia Cushing (seat 19C) and Jane Folger (seat 19B), sisters-in-law from Bayonne, New Jersey, had been looking forward for weeks to vacationing in San Francisco, where Patricia would finally see the Golden Gate Bridge and ride her first cable car.

Up in first class, four men with something else entirely on their minds—Jarrah, Haznawi, Ahmed al Nami (seat 3C), and Saeed al Ghamdi (seat 3D)—said their quiet prayers and dreamed of paradise.

Then it takes off . . . Oh Lord, pour your patience upon us and make our feet steadfast and give us victory over the infidels . . . Give us victory and make the ground shake under their feet.

It was Tuesday, September 11, 2001.
Flight 93 was finally in the air.

—✦—

"Wally, get in here. Now!"

Shortly before nine o'clock that morning, Wallace E. "Wally" Miller, the coroner of rural Somerset County, Pennsylvania—eighty miles east of Pittsburgh—had reported for his day job as director of the Miller Funeral Home on Tayman Avenue in the borough of Somerset. The place was a family business started by his father, Wilbur, in 1953, four years before Wally was born. Wilbur went to college on the GI Bill, worked seven years as an assistant in a funeral home in nearby Indian Head, then struck out on his own—and, having boldly started a new business in a small town, promptly waited ten months for his first funeral. But eventually the enterprise began to thrive. Wilbur's personal touch with grieving families and others in the community earned him such a reputation that in 1973 he decided to run for coroner—and won.

Being the coroner in Somerset County didn't come with all the accommodations that larger counties offered; there was no secretary, not even an office. Wilbur ran the operation out of his own funeral home and handled things so efficiently that the farmers and coal miners of Hooversville and Confluence and Fairhope Township kept re-electing him for twenty-four years. Wally eventually took over the business and ran to succeed his dad as coroner, winning his first election after Wilbur retired in 1997 to make it a legitimate family dynasty. His down-home nature was a huge selling point in these parts; Wally, who still answers his own phone at work, likes to tell people that "when you call the Miller Funeral Home, you get Miller."

Despite retirement, though, Wilbur retained territorial rights to the place on Tayman Avenue. He and his wife, Wilma, still lived in the apartment above the funeral home—Wally and his two siblings grew up there—and even now, in the mornings, before the business opened for the day, Wilbur, age seventy-four, would find his way to the smoking lounge on the first floor to have a cigarette and watch television.

He rarely called out for Wally, but, when he did, Wally came running, especially when the old man said, "Now!"

"A plane hit the World Trade Center!" Wilbur shouted, in a voice so bold he seemed to be announcing it to the whole county. He was mesmerized, never taking his eyes off the screen.

"We're thinking the pilot must have had a heart attack or something," Wally recalled later. They were coroners after all. They dealt with death on a daily basis and in some ways thought they had seen it all. Wally's mind immediately went to a recent auto accident on a stretch of the Pennsylvania Turnpike that winds its way through Somerset. "We had a crash where the guy had a heart attack, ran off the road and died, but he didn't die of the crash—he died of the heart attack." They thought this might have been the same thing.

As the TV reports continued and 9:00 a.m. approached, Wally, age forty-four, ambled back to his office on the first floor to conduct the daily business of Somerset County. Though this was clearly national news, New York City was five hours by car and a million miles by pace and style from the world he inhabited. Wally was a native of Somerset, had been on the basketball and track teams at Somerset Area High, and, other than four undergraduate years at Washington & Jefferson College in nearby Washington, Pennsylvania, and one year at the Pittsburgh Institute of Mortuary Science in the big city just more than an hour to the west, he had spent his whole life in the county. He understood the slow tempo of life here, the rural nature of the people; in fact, he lived it. He knew most of his patrons—and all the firefighters and police officers—by their first names.

Sprawled across a mountainous region along the Pennsylvania border with Maryland, both rugged and picturesque, Somerset County had a population of just more than eighty thousand residents in 2001. The most common occupations were farming and coal mining—both deep mining and surface (strip) mining—but the area probably was best known to outsiders for the Seven Springs Mountain Resort. It was the kind of place where each little dot on the map had its own volunteer fire company, and the fire companies still handled the ambulance service—in many ways, a window back to a simpler time.

"Look! It happened again!"

The current coroner of Somerset County dutifully went back into the lounge where the former coroner kept watching the television coverage—and this time his jaw simply hung there. The footage showed an airplane, apparently a large commercial jet, plowing into a tower of the World Trade Center and sending a searing fireball spewing out of the other side. But this wasn't a replay of a plane striking the first tower, as some viewers originally thought—as some would naturally assume, considering the shocking rarity of the image. No, this was a *second* plane hitting a *second* tower.

"Holy crap," Wally said, as they stood there transfixed. These were men who knew death and were rarely rattled. "Is there a war going on or something?"

His mind raced. He thought of tragedies he'd handled in Somerset—a motorcycle crackup on the turnpike at high speed; a skier who'd slammed into a tree in the dusk; a domestic dispute gone horribly wrong—but he knew this was something so much larger, so much more destructive, almost beyond his comprehension.

Even before the towers crumbled, when authorities were dealing with billowing smoke and raging fires in two hundred-story buildings, the death toll was feared to reach the thousands. Wally felt especially safe to be in remote little Somerset County on this day of all days. What happened in New York was the type of large-scale trauma that could never take place in Elk Lick, Stoystown, Upper Turkeyfoot Township, or two other anonymous hamlets within his jurisdiction: Stonycreek Township and Shanksville. Or so it seemed

"Hey," Wally said to his dad, still watching in disbelief as the unthinkable scenes unfolded on his television, "how'd you like to be the coroner in New York City today?"

—◦—

Ed Ballinger was supposed to have the day off. After forty-three years in airline operations with United Airlines and nineteen years as a full-time flight dispatcher, he'd certainly earned the right to take it.

But Ballinger, age sixty-two, was an old military man with a soldier's sense of duty. He'd served in the Air National Guard and Air Force Reserve, been a loadmaster on a C-119 cargo plane, and worked paratrooper school at Fort Benning. He knew he "owed" the airline a day from a previous scheduling period.

"So on my day off," he said, "I went in to repay the company the day I owed them."

It was just before 8:00 a.m. Eastern Daylight Time on September 11 when Ballinger checked in at United's headquarters near Chicago's O'Hare Airport. He'd been assigned sixteen cross-country flights originating in the New York area, Boston, and Philadelphia, all heading for the West Coast. Included on that list was Flight 93 out of Newark. A flight dispatcher monitors the progress of each flight; provides information to each pilot regarding weather, wind speed, congestion, turbulence, and other factors that may affect the safety of the flight; and must understand navigation and various airport operations and procedures. One of the first things he checks is the weather. "Everything was clear," Ballinger said. "It was a beautiful, clear day the whole way across."

7

The first sign of trouble he encountered wasn't really "trouble" at all. There was the typical congestion in the New York area, and some flights from its three airports (JFK, LaGuardia, and Newark) were going to be delayed. Ballinger dutifully notified his flights on the ground that their departure times might be pushed back. Each message was typed on a keyboard and sent to the cockpits using ACARS (Aircraft Communications Addressing and Reporting System). Once it was delivered, a chime would ring in the cockpit, and the message would appear on a screen on the console between the pilot and first officer.

As the first hour of Ballinger's shift progressed and planes began to take off amid the heavy traffic, the dispatcher exchanged routine messages with his pilots. Nothing seemed out of the ordinary until shortly before 9:00 a.m., when the dispatch manager advised him that one of his sixteen flights, United 175 out of Boston, was acting erratically. "My dispatch manager came over to me and says, 'Ed, one of your flights appears to be not operating correctly,'" he recalled. "'It might be hijacked.'"

Hijacked?

Not knowing who was in command of the aircraft, Ballinger, at 9:03 a.m., decided to send a discreet message: "HOW IS THE RIDE? ANYTHING DISPATCH CAN DO FOR YOU?"

There was no reply.

At 8:46 a.m., American Airlines Flight 11 plowed into the North Tower of the World Trade Center at nearly five hundred mph. It exploded and left a gaping hole with a haunting outline of its wings from the 93rd to the 99th floor. Fire crews rushed to the scene, and initial media speculation was that the building had been struck by a small plane. But it was not until United 175 smashed into the South Tower at 9:03 a.m. that bewildered aviation officials began to realize that New York City—and America itself—was under attack. One plane hitting one tower could have been an aberration, a horrible case of pilot error. Two planes hitting two towers in less than twenty minutes was a coordinated assault on the US homeland.

In retrospect, it is mystifying that Ballinger and other flight dispatchers did not receive immediate orders from the airlines to notify other aircraft of the danger at hand. The only possibly explanation is that no one in the history of American air travel ever had imagined multiple hijackings of large commercial airliners on the same day at the same time, and there was no specific procedure on how to respond. The raw confusion that resulted from these unprecedented attacks created temporary paralysis across the system. Al-Qaeda, as intended, had caught America completely off-guard.

Three years later, the 9/11 Commission reported, "We found no evidence . . . that American Airlines sent any cockpit warnings to its aircraft on 9/11. United's first decisive action did not come until 9:19, when a United flight dispatcher, Ed Ballinger, took the initiative to begin transmitting warnings to his 16 transcontinental flights."

Ballinger had become one of the first citizen-soldiers of September 11 and had acted heroically in an attempt to save lives. A supervisor later commended him for performing "expertly" under the circumstances. At 9:19 a.m., he began sending an alarming message to each of the flights under his jurisdiction: "BEWARE ANY COCKPIT INTROUSION [sic] . . . TWO AIRCRAFT IN NY, HIT TRADE CENTER BUILDS."

The veteran of four-plus decades with United Airlines did not believe he could send a message simultaneously to all sixteen aircraft, so he began transmitting a few at a time. Because there was no way of knowing which of the planes might be most vulnerable to attack, he did it chronologically according to departure time and en-route progress. The ACARS text about being on alert for cockpit intrusions was sent to Flight 93 at 9:23 a.m. Records show it was received in the cockpit at 9:24 a.m.

At 9:26 a.m., Captain Dahl sent a reply to Ballinger on ACARS: "ED, CONFIRM LATEST MSSG PLX—JASON."

Two minutes later, at 9:28 a.m., there was a commotion at the cockpit door.

CHAPTER TWO

Mastermind

The idea to hijack US commercial airliners and crash them into landmark buildings didn't originate with Osama bin Laden. It was a freelance terrorist named Khalid Sheikh Mohammed who first made the wildly ambitious proposal to the al-Qaeda leader during a meeting at Tora Bora in the mountains of eastern Afghanistan. This was in 1996.

The man American authorities would come to know as "KSM" already had impressive credentials. The common Western stereotype of a terrorist at the time may have been of a zealous, uneducated drifter, but KSM represented a new breed: educated, worldly, and fiercely resourceful. He'd lived for parts of four years in the United States and earned a degree at North Carolina A&T before committing himself to the Afghan resistance against the invading Soviets—and fighting alongside bin Laden in the Battle of Jaji in 1987. A convenient family connection also helped to fuel his rise in the jihadi world. It was KSM's nephew, Ramzi Yousef, who first tried to bring down the World Trade Center with a bomb in 1993.

Yousef's bold expedition into the heart of US economic power did not achieve his intended goal of destroying both towers, crumbling one onto the other, but, unbeknownst to the average American, it had enormous influence on a budding generation of young terrorists. Above all else, it gave them a sense that attacking the United States on its own soil wasn't as far-fetched as some of their elders believed. Using connections and knowledge gained at the training camps in Afghanistan, Yousef slipped into the country on a phony passport and built a bomb for three thousand dollars. He recruited a team of accomplices, drove a rental van into a garage under the North Tower of the World Trade Center, lit the fuse, and jumped into a getaway car. Six people died and many more were injured in the explosion. The physical damage wasn't anything close to what Yousef envisioned, but he'd struck a bloody blow on the streets of America's largest city, confounded US authorities, and effectively ushered in a new era of international terrorism. Then he bolted the country on a flight to Pakistan.

KSM played a seemingly minor role in the plot, serving as an advisor and wiring $660 on at least one occasion to help with funding, but the ease with which his nephew had entered and operated in the United States made a deep and lasting impression. Yousef even scored an impressive PR coup on his way back home, sending letters to several US newspapers to take credit for the attack in the name of the fictitious "fifth battalion in the Liberation Army." He demanded that the Americans stop supporting Israel and stay out of Middle East internal affairs. "If our demands are not met," he brazenly declared in a letter received by the *New York Times*, "all of our functional groups in the army will continue to execute our missions against the military and civilian targets in and out of the United States."

Yousef, of course, did not command any group called the fifth battalion and had no way of backing up his ambitious threats, but he'd helped lay the groundwork for the next phase of international terror. As Lawrence Wright noted in his book, *The Looming Tower: Al-Qaeda and the Road to 9/11*, Yousef was "the first Islamic terrorist to attack the American homeland." Many others of his ilk took notice, including Khalid Sheikh Mohammed.

It is reasonable to conclude that the journey leading KSM to bin Laden and Tora Bora in 1996—and eventually to the 9/11 attacks—began when Yousef parked his van under the Twin Towers and simply walked away.

———

Khalid Sheikh Mohammed was born in Kuwait on April 14, 1965. His father, a local imam, was a native of Pakistan, although he drew his ancestral lineage from the independent region of Baluchistan, which overlaps Iran, Pakistan, and Afghanistan. The family lived in Fahaheel, south of Kuwait City, and traveled on Pakistani passports. As US authorities who trailed him for years were soon to find out, KSM was a man from both everywhere and nowhere.

He and Yousef grew up together and displayed a penchant for bold missions even at an early age. Terry McDermott and Josh Meyer, in their book *The Hunt for KSM*, tell of an act of youthful defiance in elementary school where the two boys climbed a flagpole and ripped down the Kuwaiti flag. KSM, three years older than Yousef, joined a prominent Islamist group, the Muslim Brotherhood, at the age of sixteen, attended Brotherhood youth camps, and began to advocate for violent jihad. Terrorism was in his blood.

But there was another interest vying for KSM's attention, and this is where his story takes a unique twist. After completing his secondary schooling in Kuwait in 1983, KSM promptly left the country to further his education in the United States. He was the only September 11 plotter to do so.

KSM first enrolled at tiny Chowan College in the remote outpost of Murfreesboro, North Carolina. The selection of a little-known, two-year Baptist school in the rural South might seem bizarre for the son of an imam from the Middle East, but Chowan was an effective collegiate stepping-stone for foreign students because of one important factor: The school didn't require an English proficiency test. Many such students spent a semester or two at Chowan to improve their language skills and then moved on to another university. To these men, the tiny school was almost a secret pathway to the United States.

KSM's next stop was North Carolina Agricultural and Technical State University, a historically African-American school located in the larger city of Greensboro. Established in 1891 when Congress mandated "a separate college for the colored race," North Carolina A&T had developed a strong educational legacy. Its list of distinguished graduates included the Rev. Jesse Jackson, NASA astronaut Ronald McNair, Brigadier General Clara Adams Ender, and Pro Football Hall of Famer Elvin Bethea. In one of the historic and memorable snapshots of the Civil Rights era, a group of North Carolina A&T students staged a sit-in at a lunch counter at Woolworth's—sparking an iconic moment, photograph, and conflict of the 1960s.

By the time Khalid Sheikh Mohammed arrived at the school in the spring of 1984, there also was a small but growing contingent of Middle

Eastern students enrolled in classes. KSM was part of a religiously oriented group nicknamed the "mullahs." He applied himself to his studies, worked on improving his broken English, did his best to avoid the cultural temptations inherent in a US college campus, and earned a mechanical engineering degree in less than three years. He graduated in December 1986.

The extent to which KSM's exposure to life in America in the mid-1980s influenced his views about future terrorist activities cannot be known for certain. He is our only source on the matter, and he has told conflicting stories. *The 9/11 Commission Report* says, "By his own account, KSM's animus toward the United States stemmed not from his experiences there as a student, but rather from his violent disagreement with US foreign policy favoring Israel." However, a 2004 report by the CIA's inspector general that was released by the Justice Department says, "KSM's limited and negative experience in the United States—which included a brief jail stay because of unpaid bills—almost certainly helped propel him on his path to become a terrorist. He stated that his contact with Americans, while minimal, confirmed his views that the United States was a debauched and racist country."

KSM returned to the Middle East after graduation and in 1987 made his way to Peshawar, Pakistan, close to the Afghanistan border. That is where his brother, Zahid, already a committed jihadi, introduced him to the Afghan warlord Abdul Rasaf Sayyaf. The holy war against the Soviets was reaching its apex, and the powerful Sayyaf became an influential figure in KSM's life, sending him at first to the Sada camp in eastern Afghanistan for military training and then helping him land several jobs that supported the resistance. He worked in a media office, taught engineering at Sayyaf's university, and later joined the mujahideen in Bosnia. During this time, KSM also worked under Abdullah Azzam, the mentor of Osama bin Laden. He was making important connections that would serve him well in future terrorist endeavors.

It was sometime in 1991 or 1992 that KSM learned of Ramzi Yousef's plan to attack inside the United States. Yousef had received instruction in explosives at the terrorist camps in Afghanistan and developed such an aptitude that fellow trainees nicknamed him "The Chemist." He was determined to put that knowledge to work and send a message exploding across the Western world. Arriving in New York in September 1992, Yousef tempted fate by presenting a bogus passport and no entry visa. Questioned by authorities, he requested political asylum and was released on his own recognizance, pending a hearing. Then he vanished into a land of 250 million people. Investigators would learn that Yousef soon sought out and came under the influence of a radical Egyptian cleric named Omar Abdel Rahman, aka the "Blind Sheikh," who introduced him to some of the men who became his accomplices (and who later was arrested in connection with foiled plots to bomb other New York landmarks, including the Holland and Lincoln tunnels).

Yousef telephoned KSM often in late 1992 to consult on evolving plans for the attack. Devoted to the cause of Palestine and enraged by US support of Israel, he chose the World Trade Center as his target, convinced that thousands of Jews worked in the Twin Towers. There was just one major flaw in his scheme: a lack of funding. KSM wired $660 at one point and may have tried to tap other sources, but in the end Yousef had to abandon plans for a more elaborate explosive device and resigned himself to building a large but basic fertilizer bomb.

The resulting explosion ripped through the garage under the North Tower shortly after noon on February 26, 1993. Yousef was disappointed in the results, but his makeshift attack with a rental van still killed six people, injured more than one thousand, and, according to the FBI, "carved out a nearly 100-foot crater several stories deep." Smoke and flames filled the building, and the bomb caused property damage of three hundred million dollars. On the television news that night—and for weeks and months and years afterwards—the images of thousands of innocent workers scurrying from the building in chaos were seared into the American consciousness. Beyond the deaths and the damage was the statement Yousef had made with his brash incursion. The United States can be attacked. Not overseas. Not at an embassy. But right here at home.

The 9/11 Commission drew yet another conclusion from Yousef's attack on the World Trade Center in 1993. It determined that "Yousef's instant notoriety as the mastermind of the 1993 World Trade Center bombing inspired KSM to become involved in planning attacks against the United States." Up to that point, KSM had built a strong resume of his own—earning a college degree in America, devoting himself to jihad in Pakistan and Afghanistan, and providing valuable support in the WTC assault—but now he wanted to create a more prominent role for himself as a purveyor of international terrorism. He wanted to at least share center stage. Together, he and his nephew could be a potent tandem—Yousef's skills, cunning, and growing reputation combined with KSM's worldly view, ceaseless ambition, and creativity. The idea of forming a sort of "Terrorist, Inc." among the two family members had genuine and reciprocal appeal.

And so it was that in 1994, Khalid Sheik Mohammed and Ramzi Yousef traveled to the Philippines to set up shop. The list of potential plots they developed was truly dizzying. They discussed various methods to assassinate both President Bill Clinton and Pope John Paul II on their upcoming trips to Manila. They considered ways to bomb US-bound cargo ships by smuggling explosives on board. Those plans eventually were discarded as impractical because Philippine authorities had heightened their defenses at a time of major international visits. Eventually, they settled on another idea, known as "Bojinka."

The Bojinka plot called for the virtually simultaneous bombing of twelve US commercial jets over the Pacific, using operatives to plant the explosives. Had the two men succeeded, they would have created unmitigated horror in the international skies and likely crippled the American airline industry for years to come. No doubt the extreme nature of the explosions would have prevented millions of Americans from trusting air travel for a very long time. The economic ramifications could have been staggering.

KSM helped Yousef acquire materials to build the bombs and timers, and they began to study airline schedules and case specific flights. But the project itself came crashing down on January 6, 1995, when a fire broke out in the kitchen sink of a Manila apartment where Yousef "The Chemist" was building his bombs; it was just days before Pope John Paul's expected arrival in the country for World Youth Day. The men fled, but Philippine authorities showed up and found the bomb-making materials as well as a laptop full of names, addresses, and operational details of the assorted deadly plans they conceived. It was a huge discovery.

International investigators were astonished by the size and scope of the Bojinka plot, the sheer potential for damage. *Who thought up such a plan? Who had the ability to pull it off?* Fortunately, the laptop provided important clues. KSM evaded authorities and blended safely back into life in the Middle East, but Yousef was tracked to Islamabad, Pakistan, where an associate's tip led to his arrest by US officials and Pakistan's Inter-Services Intelligence (ISI) in February 1995.

The Feds eagerly brought Yousef back to the United States the same day, on a flight from Pakistan to an airfield north of New York City and then into a waiting helicopter for the final few miles to Manhattan. As the chopper approached the Twin Towers at night, with the bright lights of the big city shining all around, an FBI man removed a blindfold Yousef had been wearing and said, "Look, they're still standing."

KSM's nephew resisted the taunt. "They wouldn't be," he said, "if I had more money."

The next step for KSM in his quest for worldwide notoriety was to shore up the weaknesses in the WTC bombing and Bojinka plots—funding and organization. Yousef's near success in the New York City adventure gave him confidence that the United States could indeed be attacked on its homeland. The audacity of a plan using aircraft as weapons of mass destruction offered a way to strike in such an unconventional manner that the US military would be powerless to stop him. It could be thwarted only by an unprecedented resistance from alert and fearless civilians. What's more, an accomplice who was arrested in the Philippines, Abdul Murad, had developed his own idea to load an airplane full of explosives and crash it into CIA headquarters. Out-of-the-box thinking wasn't the problem.

Enter Osama bin Laden, who had money, a leadership structure, and an expanding group of disciples in al-Qaeda. Bin Laden and KSM had known each other from their days as jihadis in Pakistan and Afghanistan, but they were not close and reportedly had not even seen each other since 1989. To arrange a meeting, KSM went through Mohammed Atef, al-Qaeda's military commander. The get-together was scheduled for Tora Bora late in 1996.

Granted access at last to this unique stage and audience, KSM provided bin Laden with details about Yousef's 1993 bombing raid and an overview of their daring plans in the Philippines. He also offered several new proposals. One of them was so spectacular in scale that even bin Laden himself was initially skeptical.

KSM had weaved together elements of the Bojinka plot with Murad's idea to fly a plane into CIA headquarters and come up with a plan to hijack ten US domestic aircraft on the same day. Nine of them would be crashed into buildings on the East and West Coasts, including the World Trade Center, the Pentagon, and the Capitol, creating widespread panic. The tenth plane would then land safely at an unspecified US airport, and the pilot—KSM himself—would deliver a speech denouncing US policies in the Middle East.

Bin Laden listened. He thought the original version of the plan was unworkable because of its grand scope, and he was receiving a multitude of other proposals for attacks from other jihadi sources that deserved consideration. He sent KSM on his way without making any final determination.

But he did not say no.

A little more than two years later, in early 1999, bin Laden summoned KSM for another meeting. Al-Qaeda had rattled the US government and intelligence community with nearly simultaneous bombings of the American embassies in Kenya and Tanzania on August 7, 1998; now it was looking for an even more devastating blow. Bin Laden told KSM he liked the fundamental concept of his proposal, to use airplanes as missiles against US landmarks, but that the original idea of ten planes and multiple targets on both coasts was too complex. He agreed to adopt the plan but suggested they work together to determine the number of aircraft and select the specific targets. Bin Laden would provide the manpower.

From now on, it would be known as the "Planes Operation."

CHAPTER THREE

Forming a Cell

The stylish twenty-year-old from Lebanon blended easily into the student population at the ancient university in Greifswald, Germany, in the spring of 1996. Cosmopolitan and fluent in three languages, he wore American jeans, mingled with the ladies, drank alcohol, frequented discos, and knew his way around a dance floor. Ziad Jarrah seemed anything but a terrorist.

And he wasn't—at least not yet.

Jarrah had grown up in affluence in Beirut and the Bekaa Valley, the only son and middle child of a prominent and industrious family. His father, Samir, was a well-to-do civil servant; his mother, Nafisa, taught school. The Jarrahs owned a six-room apartment on Hamad Street in Beirut but often spent weekends at a second home in the valley, about thirty miles away in the town of al Marj—in part to escape the civil war that ravaged the city during Ziad's childhood in the 1980s. They drove Mercedes automobiles and treated themselves to many of life's luxuries.

As a little boy, Ziad was fascinated with airplanes. He was five years old when he built his first plane out of Legos and declared that he wanted to be a pilot. After he learned to read, he would show up at the local library and repeatedly check out books on planes and aviation—alarming his father, who preferred a safer vocation. Samir Jarrah quickly put an end to any such talk of a career with the airlines. "I have only one son," he said, "and I was afraid that he would crash."

The Jarrah family was Sunni Muslim but not especially observant. In fact, Ziad was sent by his parents to the best private Christian schools. He did not always capitalize on the educational opportunities there, expending much more energy on extracurricular activities—chasing girls and drinking—than on math and science. But he was outgoing and charismatic, playing sports and making friends easily. "He was good looking, flattered the girls," remembered one of his teachers, "so he was always popular."

In 1996 the Jarrahs decided that Ziad should travel outside of Lebanon to begin his pursuit of a college degree. He was given the choice of two locations where the family had relatives: Toronto, Canada, or Greifswald. Canada was an intriguing option, but it seemed too far away from home to be practical, and the deal would have involved marrying a cousin, so Ziad's choice was simple. That April, he and another cousin, Salim, who was the same age, headed off to the former East German city on the Baltic Sea.

As foreign students, the two Jarrahs were required to enroll in German language classes before advancing to a regular course of study. As young men on their own for the first time, they also became fixtures on the university party circuit. "Once," Salim said, "we drank so much beer we couldn't ride straight on a bike." They mocked the sorry state of discos in old-school Greifswald and often longed for the bright lights and lively nightclubs in their homeland. But Ziad quickly found another, more pleasant distraction. He fell in love.

Within his first weeks on campus, he was smitten by a striking dental student named Aysel Senguen, the daughter of Turkish immigrants. The inconvenient fact that she already had a boyfriend was no deterrent to the sophisticated newcomer from Beirut. Ziad quickly wooed her away; they began to date and spend much of their time together, seemingly a great match—two secular Muslims with potential, ambition, and curiosity.

Looking back at it years later, Aysel admitted, "We had problems since the beginning." But they were not evident to anyone who saw them during those early courtship days in Greifswald. Terry McDermott, in his book on the 9/11 hijackers, *Perfect Soldiers*, wrote, "They cooked meals together. She helped him learn German. Bleary-eyed photographs from the time, including one of Jarrah lighting a water pipe, indicated that they did their share of partying." In time, they would talk of getting married and having a family.

But something changed—dramatically—when Ziad returned from a winter holiday trip to Beirut late in 1996. He was decidedly more serious and almost preoccupied with religion for the first time in his life. Salim observed that he was reading an extremist Islamic publication called *al Jihad*. The former party boy started to criticize Aysel for the clothes she wore and the friends she chose. He wanted her to wear a veil. He grew a beard and began to live his life following the strict teachings of the Koran. A friend of Aysel's told investigators that, by early 1997, Ziad was talking about being "dissatisfied with his life up till now." Making it sound as though he already had considered martyrdom as a career option, the friend said he "didn't want to leave the Earth in a natural way."

What had caused the change? Not even those close to Jarrah know for sure. While it is possible that he was radicalized on his visit home to Lebanon, multiple sources have reported that he fell under the influence of a religious leader named Abdul Rahman al Makhadi during his time in Greifswald. Makhadi chided Jarrah as a "weak Muslim" and disapproved of his relationship with Aysel. He also harangued students into attending prayers at a local mosque. After prayers, Makhadi would preach there for hours. Journalist Mary Anne Weaver of the *London Review of Books* described the fiery cleric not only as a spokesman for radical Islam but also "an 'enforcer' of Islamic morality." It likely rubbed off on the impressionable Jarrah.

In the spring of 1997, after completing his mandatory courses in the German language, a noticeably different Jarrah began to apply at other universities around the country. Although he had talked about studying dentistry with Aysel and even applied to the biochemistry program at Greifswald, he announced, quite abruptly, a shocking change of plans before classes began that September. The young man who long ago had dreamed of a career in aviation now told friends and family that he would pursue a degree in aeronautical engineering at the University of Applied Sciences—in Hamburg. For the second time in a year, he was on the move.

Hamburg, on the surface, seemed an odd destination for a foreign student with no apparent links to the city. But *The 9/11 Commission Report* speculated that Jarrah "appears already to have had Hamburg contacts by this time, some of whom may have played a role in steering him toward Islamic extremism." Indeed, Makhadi, the imam from Greifswald, was a person who had such connections. He knew men who worshipped at the radical *al Quds* mosque in Hamburg. Conveniently, he also had landed an internship in Hamburg at the time Jarrah was contemplating the move. Makhadi would live there during the week and head back to Greifswald on weekends; they would be able to travel together when Jarrah returned periodically to visit Aysel. Another friend had become acquainted with several students at a summer job in Hamburg in 1996. A small support system was starting to form around the new aeronautical engineering student. He would not be alone.

Between 1992 and 1998, three other students from three different Middle Eastern countries also had made their way to Hamburg. They did not know one another at first. They did not have an agenda. But they would come together at the *al Quds* mosque and at a nearby apartment at 54 Marienstrasse—and they would form the core of a terror cell that would, in a few short years, shock and irrevocably change the world.

—◆—

Mohamed Atta arrived first, traveling from Egypt in 1992. He was the oldest of the group, and he would eventually become its leader. Born in 1968 in Egypt's Nile Delta, Atta had grown up in Cairo and earned a degree in architectural engineering at Cairo University before heading to Germany for graduate school. After initially applying to Hamburg's University of Applied Sciences (where Jarrah eventually would study), Atta enrolled at the Technical University of Hamburg–Harburg, in the Hamburg suburbs, with an emphasis on urban planning. Maybe it was his way of trying to change the world from the ground up.

Atta made a quick impression on those around him. He was meticulous, abrasive, dour, and relentlessly intense. "He was a perfectionist," Professor Dittmar Machule told the *Al Jazeera* TV network. "He wanted to do everything the perfect way. He would sit there quietly listening and observing, looking as if he was not there, and suddenly would come up with a sharp, intelligent question or remark. He was very special . . . unusual."

Religion already was a big part of Atta's life before he came to Germany. It became even more so after he made a *hajj* (pilgrimage) to the holy site of Mecca in 1995. The trip is required at least once in the lifetime of every able-bodied and financially capable Muslim. When he returned to the university, classmates said, Atta had grown a beard and become even more detached. He no longer seemed interested in his studies. It was at about the same time that he began to teach informal religious classes at several mosques in and around Hamburg, including *al Quds,* the one favored by a group of young radicals.

Late in 1995 a charismatic and resourceful newcomer from Yemen named Ramzi Binalshibh arrived in Germany and began frequenting the same Hamburg mosques. Sometime that winter the twenty-three-year-old Binalshibh was introduced to Atta. They were an odd couple of sorts. Whereas Atta was often sullen and guarded, Binalshibh was cheerful and extroverted. The Yemeni even told jokes. When it came to Islam, however, Binalshibh shared Atta's religious zeal. The two men clicked.

According to his brother, Binalshibh had dreamed of furthering his education in either the United States or Europe before settling on Germany as his destination. The journey to get there from Yemen was an adventure. Using an alias, Binalshibh concocted a tale about being a Sudanese student and asked German authorities for political asylum. While his request was pending, he lived in Hamburg and made acquaintances at the religious centers. Eventually sent home to Yemen, he returned to Germany under his own name and registered as a student in Hamburg. But something had changed along the way. Maybe it was during all the time he spent at the mosques. Binalshibh suddenly had little time for schoolwork and rarely attended classes. He couldn't hold a job. His faith had taken precedence over other matters, and he began to speak openly of jihad—holy war.

A third student, Marwan al Shehhi, was only eighteen years old when he traveled to Germany from the United Arab Emirates (UAE) in April 1996. Reared in a deeply religious home, the son of a man who called worshippers to prayers at the local mosque, he could recite verses from the Koran by heart and was considered by friends to be an authority on the scriptures. But he also wanted to see the world. Shehhi signed up for the UAE armed forces shortly after graduating from high school in 1995 and quickly took advantage of the military's generous scholarship program that would fund his undergraduate studies. The only requirement was that he undergo several months of basic training. The next year he packed his bags for the German city of Bonn.

Shehhi took an introductory course in German and signed up for preparatory classes at the University of Bonn. Described by friends as a "regular guy," he was known as happy and affable—and maybe a bit spoiled. But his demeanor started to change after his father passed away in the spring of 1997. Returning to Bonn after a visit home to the UAE, he seemed more extreme in his religious beliefs. He would not, for instance, patronize restaurants that cooked with or served alcohol. That winter, he abruptly asked the Emirati embassy if he could transfer to a school in Hamburg.

It is possible, and maybe even likely, that he had already met either Atta or Binalshibh by that time. The older men were known to travel to various mosques throughout Germany. The 9/11 Commission strongly speculates that such a connection existed. Shehhi's sudden transfer request "was apparently motivated by his desire to join Atta and Binalshibh," the commission wrote in its final report. "They seemed to know each other already when Shehhi relocated to Hamburg in early 1998."

Within a few months, Atta, Binalshibh, and Shehhi were living together in an apartment at 54 Marienstrasse that would become a hotbed of activity for the young Islamic extremists from *al Quds*. They dubbed the apartment *Dar al Ansar*, or House of the Followers.

Jarrah had not yet become a central figure in the Hamburg group, but he was residing in the same city, attending prayers and other events at the mosque and the apartment—and stoking his own growing radical beliefs.

It was only a matter of time before their paths would intersect.

Jarrah met Binalshibh at *al Quds* sometime late in 1997. It was Binalshibh who facilitated his entrance into the House of the Followers, but the integration took time. Jarrah often seemed on the fringe of the group's activities. Headstrong and independent, he lived on his own and attended classes in a different part of the city. He also had a special love interest that set him apart, especially in a group of young zealots talking jihad.

When he first arrived in Hamburg, Jarrah traveled back to Greifswald on weekends to visit Aysel. Their romance had been complicated by Jarrah's turn toward radical Islam, but they kept working at it through many quarrels and reconciliations. Aysel at one point became pregnant. She had an abortion because she was uncertain about their future—then apologized for it repeatedly. "I had to think about our baby today," she wrote to him in an e-mail. But she also confided to a friend, "I don't want to be left behind with the children, because my husband moved into a fanatic war."

Aysel made her own life change in 1998, transferring to a university in Bochum, near Dusseldorf. It made the trip about fifty miles longer than the journey between Hamburg and Greifswald, but Jarrah kept at it—still enamored of the future dentist he'd met during his first few weeks in Germany. "Despite the distance," Aysel later told investigators, "we tried to meet on a regular basis every two weeks." She said it was Jarrah who mostly did the traveling, taking public transportation and staying from Friday to Sunday. During the next two years, she visited him in Hamburg "three or four times only."

It is likely that Jarrah wanted to keep her shielded from his new acquaintances in Hamburg; the less time she spent there, the better. He was living an astonishing double life. None of the other young radicals had a girlfriend. None of the others even stayed in regular contact with their families back home. Through it all, though, Jarrah's commitment to the cause of jihad remained firm, and he started to become more involved with his future coconspirators and their activities at *al Quds*.

By this time, in 1998, the group meeting at the mosque and at 54 Marienstrasse had grown to become quite large. The unofficial roster numbered at least several dozen participants. Many of them were regulars. Among the most prominent were a German citizen of Moroccan descent named Said Bahaji and three other Morrocans—Zakariya Essabar, Mounir el Motassadeq, and Abdelghani Mzoudi. Members of the group were becoming so intertwined that they even worked the same part-time jobs. That summer, Jarrah, Essabar, and Motassadeq were employed in the paint shop of a Volkswagen plant. Atta, Binalshibh, and Shehhi worked in a nearby warehouse.

Some of the most passionate and incendiary speeches at the House of the Followers were now being delivered by a veteran of the Afghan jihad named Mohammed Haydar Zammar. Zammar was a huge man, standing six-foot, four-inches tall and weighing three hundred pounds, and his size and battlefield experience gave him a commanding presence among the young jihadis. Loud and flamboyant, he never missed an opportunity to encourage them to take part in holy war. Intelligence sources later described him as an active recruiter for al-Qaeda. There can be little doubt as to his influence on the impressionable members of the Hamburg cell.

By early 1999, Jarrah was heading inexorably down a path that would lead him to September 11. Wearing a full beard as a sign of his dedication to the cause, he told Aysel he was planning to wage jihad because there was no greater honor than to die for Allah. She was terrified. Asking her to wear a veil was one thing; this was something else entirely.

"Someone explained to me that jihad in the softer form means to write books, tell people about Islam," she said. "But Ziad's own jihad was more aggressive, the fighting kind."

And yet he couldn't let her go. In late March 1999, Jarrah showed up at Aysel's door in Bochum and asked her to marry him; despite his disturbing new focus, she agreed. The relationship had taken another curious turn. The unexpected ceremony was held the next month in Hamburg. As it turns out, however, the purpose may have been merely to appease Jarrah's jihadi friends (or, Terry McDermott theorizes, "his conscience"). The couple never registered the marriage with the state, and Aysel told friends she didn't consider it legitimate. They never lived together as husband and wife.

Within a few weeks, they broke up again.

—◦—

Aysel believed Jarrah's move toward extremism reached its peak in the summer of 1999. Though they had again reconciled by this point, their interactions became more infrequent as he burrowed deeper into his secret jihadi network. At 54 Marienstrasse, the pace of activity reached a fever pitch as summer turned to fall. The men sang martyrdom songs and watched inspiring battlefield videos from Chechnya, Bosnia, and Afghanistan—places where Islamists were at war with considerable larger forces—and Atta ranted about what he described as a global Jewish movement centered in New York City. But they also began to transfer control of bank accounts, apartment leases, and other personal records to trusted friends. Some downloaded generic forms for jihadi wills on computers.

They talked openly now of holy war, of committing themselves to becoming martyrs. One would shout, "Our Way!" and the others would chant, "Jihad!" Binalshibh declared that the mujahideen "die with a smile on their lips." Atta seethed with contempt for the United States and the West, and when one member of the group suggested that Muslims were too weak to do anything against the mighty United States, Atta snapped, "No, something can be done. There are ways. The USA is not omnipotent."

In October many of the key figures in the Hamburg cell attended the wedding of Said Bahaji at the *al Quds* mosque. A tape of the event, obtained by investigators late in 2001 but not released to the public until 2003, showed Jarrah, Shehhi, Binalshibh, Zammar, Essabar, and Mzoudi in attendance. It provided a rare peek behind the curtain of their shadowy world. Binalshibh took the microphone, congratulated Bahaji, and then delivered what the Associated Press later described as a "fiery speech" to the celebrants. He asserted that "Every Muslim must have the aim to free Islamic soil of any tyrant."

A later discovery of handwritten notes from October 1999 offered a glimpse into Jarrah's mind-set. German investigators found them after the September 11 attacks among his collection of university papers and textbooks. They were evidence of how a once easygoing, affluent, and secular young student had changed so dramatically during his three-plus years in Germany.

"The morning will come," Jarrah wrote. "The victors will come, will come. We swear to beat you. The earth will shake beneath your feet."

Later that same year, the four young men who had traveled independently to Hamburg between 1992 and 1998, who had worshipped together at *al Quds* and railed against the West at 54 Marienstrasse, made a joint decision to chart their destiny to paradise. Atta, Binalshibh, Shehhi, and Jarrah quietly gathered their belongings and tidied up the loose ends of their lives in Germany. Then they left for Afghanistan.

⸺

Since early 1999, when Osama bin Laden agreed to support the Planes Operation, the al-Qaeda leader had been working with his military chief, Mohammed Atef, and Khalid Sheikh Mohammed on planning and logistics. The three men met in Kandahar, in southeast Afghanistan, that spring to select a preliminary list of targets for the attack. They were unanimous in their belief that the US Capitol should be included. Bin Laden specifically wanted the White House and the Pentagon. KSM favored the World Trade Center. He would later say that the purpose of the attack on the Twin Towers was to "wake the American people up" and focus them on "the atrocities that America is committing by supporting Israel against the Palestinian people and America's self-serving foreign policy that corrupts Arab governments and leads to further exploitation of the Arab/Muslim peoples." He also wanted to finish what his nephew Ramzi Yousef had started in 1993.

Bin Laden personally assigned the first four suicide operatives who would carry out the attacks. These were seasoned al-Qaeda veterans, battle-tested jihadis. Nawaf al Hazmi and Khalid al Mihdhar were from Saudi Arabia. Walid bin Attash and Abu Bara al Yemeni were from Yemen. But despite bin Laden's confidence and personal endorsement, there were problems almost from the start.

The two Saudis already had proper documentation to travel to the United States; the two Yemenis did not. Their applications for US visas had been turned down. The rejections had nothing to do with the threat of terrorism—they were based on the potential for Yemenis to become economic migrants—but the unexpected roadblock became an important teaching moment for the al-Qaeda leaders. They learned very quickly that the ability to obtain a US visa was an essential requirement in the selection of the men who would fill out the hijacking crews. Possessing a Saudi passport made the process much easier, because the two countries were such strong allies. (In the end, fifteen of the nineteen hijackers were Saudis.)

At this point, however, in the first half of 1999, KSM still wanted the two Yemenis to be part of the attack. He decided to divide the Planes Operation into two separate missions. One would be conducted as originally envisioned, hijacking US domestic aircraft and crashing them into symbols of American power, utilizing Hazmi and Mihdhar. The other would be a replica of part of KSM's old Bojinka plot, having suicide operatives—led by the Yemenis—hijack US planes taking off from East Asia and blow them up in midair.

Hazmi, Mihdhar, bin Attash, and Abu Bara were sent to the elite Mes Aynak camp in Afghanistan in the fall for a basic training regimen that included instruction in physical fitness, firearms, and night operations. Afterward, they met with KSM in Karachi, Pakistan, for a crash course in Western culture. He taught them a few basic English words and phrases and then showed them how to accomplish such simple tasks as reading a phone book, making travel reservations, deciphering airline schedules, and using the Internet. They also tinkered with flight simulator computer games.

The four men were instructed to travel to Kuala Lumpur, Malaysia, in early January for a meeting on the progress of the plot. According to KSM, all they knew at this point was that they had volunteered for a martyrdom mission—and that Hazmi and Mihdhar would soon be heading to the United States. Additional operational details were discussed in Kuala Lumpur, and one of the Yemenis was tasked with taking flights on US carriers in East Asia to observe their security measures. Then they went their separate ways. On January 15, 2000, one week after leaving Malaysia, Hazmi and Mihdhar flew from Bangkok to Los Angeles and became the first 9/11 operatives to enter the United States.

It was a big day for al-Qaeda, even historic; two members of the advance guard had slipped behind enemy lines. But major changes in the plot would soon be under way. Sometime in the spring of 2000, bin Laden abruptly cancelled the East Asia portion of the operation. He determined that attempting to coordinate two different attacks on two continents in different time zones on the same day would be impractical if not impossible. He wanted simplicity in planning for efficiency and maximum effect. It would limit the chance for error in producing the "wow" factor al-Qaeda so desperately sought. The focus then returned to attacking the US homeland, hijacking domestic commercial airliners and crashing them into landmark buildings—the final, workable structure of KSM's initial proposal.

Shortly after their arrival in California, however, Hazmi and Mihdhar encountered problems of their own. Many of them were self-inflicted. As Richard Miniter wrote in the KSM biography *Mastermind*, "They had fought in Bosnia, Afghanistan, and Chechnya but couldn't figure out how to get an apartment in Los Angeles ... the pair could barely find their way out of LAX." Hazmi and Mihdhar found difficulty trying to function in a Western society. The two men moved to San Diego and began to check out flight schools so they could learn to be pilots, but the process proved awkward and almost comical—in part because they barely spoke English. A flight instructor at a small airfield remembers them showing up as complete novices and immediately wanting to learn how to fly large Boeing aircraft. Another instructor said, "They just didn't have the aptitude ... they were like Dumb and Dumber."

It was another moment of revelation for the al-Qaeda hierarchy. Hazmi and Mihdhar were veteran jihadis who had faithfully pledged themselves to martyrdom against the United States—they would eventually be two of the muscle hijackers on Flight 77, which slammed into the Pentagon—but the Planes Operation required a more sophisticated brand of operative to occupy leadership roles. The ideal candidates would be educated, reasonably fluent in English, and capable of operating smoothly and without suspicion in a Western society. As fate would have it, several of them had just arrived at a training camp in Afghanistan.

Ziad Jarrah left Germany on November 25, 1999. He flew to Karachi, Pakistan, before making his way to the border city of Chaman and entering Afghanistan over the Toba Kakar mountain range. The four members of the Hamburg cell traveled separately to avoid raising suspicion, but Jarrah, Mohamed Atta, and Marwan al Shehhi all were in Afghanistan by early December. Ramzi Binalshibh followed two weeks later.

The daily routine for recruits at the Afghan camps featured running, weight lifting, and the kind of agility drills often seen later in the al-Qaeda promotional videos obtained by US news agencies and shown on loop in the weeks after 9/11. There also were classes in weapons and explosives, with special time set aside for prayer and religious instruction. Occasionally, bin Laden himself would make a personal appearance. It gave him a chance to inspire the young jihadis—and to identify and observe candidates who exhibited certain qualities that would prove valuable for secret missions he and other al-Qaeda leaders were planning.

The Hamburg men quickly stood out among their peers. It is possible that al-Qaeda's leadership group was tipped off in advance about their unique qualifications for an operation in the United States—perhaps from its contacts in Germany. Not long after their arrival in Afghanistan, Atta, Jarrah, and Shehhi were summoned by bin Laden to a meeting at the House of Ghamdi in Kandahar. Each was asked to pledge a *bayat* (oath) to bin Laden and agree to take part in a martyrdom mission. They did. When Binalshibh rejoined them in mid-December, he met with bin Laden and also signed on. All the zeal and anger that had coalesced in their apartment at 54 Marienstresse could now be channeled into violence against the West.

Mohammed Atef, al-Qaeda's military leader, met with Atta, Jarrah, and Binalshibh to give them a basic outline of the Planes Operation. (Shehhi had left early, heading home to the United Arab Emirates for medical treatment, but he began his preparations in earnest, applying for a new passport and a US visa.) Bin Laden selected Atta as the leader of the group and conducted several additional meetings with him to discuss preliminary targets, including the World Trade Center, the Pentagon, and the US Capitol. The men were then advised that once they had finished their training in Afghanistan, they should return to Germany and enroll in flight training to become pilots.

One of their remaining tasks before leaving the Afghan camps was to shoot martyrdom videos that could be released to the public and media after the mission had been completed. Atta and Jarrah took part in a video session on the same day—January 18, 2000—at bin Laden's headquarters at Tarnak Farm. A video showing outtakes of the two men sitting together, with a date stamp, was discovered by US authorities in 2002 and released to the public in 2006. It became a significant piece of the 9/11 narrative because it is the only photo or video evidence ever uncovered showing fellow pilots Atta and Jarrah in the same setting. The two men talk and laugh, and at one point Jarrah smiles broadly. In a separate video, apparently shot the same day—and aired by NBC News in 2008—Jarrah appears to struggle while recording his martyrdom statement and has to be "coached" by individuals shouting instructions off camera.

On their return trip to Hamburg, Atta, Jarrah, and Binalshibh were sent to Karachi to meet with Khalid Sheikh Mohammed and receive additional details about the mission. He gave them pointers on living and operating in the United States and briefed them on general security measures. They also learned specific tasks related to the plot, such as how to read airline schedules and rent apartments. KSM then sent the three men on their way.

Jarrah had a far more harrowing travel experience back to Germany than the others. Connecting through Dubai in the United Arab Emirates, he was pulled aside for questioning by UAE authorities on January 30. A page of the Koran had been found in his passport, and his baggage was full of religious materials, including audio tapes and books. Six months earlier, according to *Vanity Fair* magazine, the CIA had asked border agents in the region to question anyone who might have traveled to the training camps in Afghanistan. Jarrah was interrogated for four hours before he was allowed to continue his trip to Germany. UAE officials say they informed the Americans of the situation, but a CIA spokesman denied to CNN in 2002 that the agency had any knowledge of Jarrah before September 11, 2001.

The next day, January 31, Jarrah was back in Hamburg. One of the first things he did was apply for a new passport. It was an old al-Qaeda trick for expunging any record of travel to undesirable places. He also shaved his beard and began to dress again in the Western-style clothing he had favored when he first arrived in Germany. He no longer answered to the nom de guerre he'd been assigned at the camps in Afghanistan—*Abu Tareq al Lubnani* (literally "father of the one who knocks on the door, the Lebanese"). The men clearly had been instructed to begin their mission by eliminating any signs of religious extremism and blending into the mainstream as well-adjusted Westerners. A few days later, Jarrah decided to travel to Bochum to surprise Aysel.

She was startled by the changes in his look and persona. This was the same Ziad she had met in 1996, the one who had stolen her heart. When she asked where he had been for the past two months, Jarrah told her, "Don't ask me, it's better for you." The nonanswer was disconcerting, but he brought her gifts and talked excitedly of their new life together, which temporarily appeased her. He also explained that he'd made an important decision while he was away. He was going to finally realize his dream of becoming an airline pilot.

Indeed.

Inspired by visions of martyrdom beyond anything a young jihadi could imagine, the four men decided not to remain in Hamburg for long. Jarrah inspected German flight schools, found them inadequate, and determined that better opportunities were available in the United States. Binalshibh independently checked out prospective flight schools in Germany and elsewhere in Europe but was advised that the United States offered better and cheaper options with shorter training periods. It was the eventual destination anyway.

On March 26, 2000, Jarrah faxed an application to the Florida Flight Training Center (FFTC) in Venice. He wasn't wasting any time.

Five days later, Atta sent e-mails to more than sixty US flight schools:

We are a small group of young men from different Arab countries. We would like to start training for the career of airline professional pilots.

CHAPTER FOUR

Infiltrators

Martyrdom mission or not, even Marwan al Shehhi might have marveled briefly at the skyline of New York City as his flight from Brussels completed its descent into Newark International Airport on May 29, 2000. The Statue of Liberty, the Empire State Building, and the gleaming towers of the World Trade Center would have been distinctively visible on the final approach. For millions of first-time visitors to the United States, this moment is cemented in their memories—the very first glimpse of the uniquely American symbols of freedom, economic power, and engineering ingenuity. But Shehhi wasn't here to see the sites.

By the time he gathered his carry-on luggage, proceeded down the Jetway with the other passengers, and set foot for the first time on the concourse at Newark International—US soil—the Planes Operation had moved into a new, more operational phase.

Mohamed Atta arrived five days later, flying to Newark from Prague in the Czech Republic. It was no coincidence that each man traveled alone and from different destination points. Even at this early stage, the soldiers of al-Qaeda were taking precautions to avoid any chance of detection. Atta and Shehhi used New York City as their base for June 2000, paying for short-term leases at several apartments and checking out flight schools in the region. Not much is known of their daily activities. Records show that Atta bought a cell phone and Shehhi enrolled in a one-month English language class at Accent on Language on the east side of Manhattan. Perhaps they wandered past the Twin Towers, getting a ground-level glimpse of their eventual targets. But despite all of Atta's preparation, including his barrage of e-mails to flight schools all across the country, they had not yet determined where they would train to become pilots.

Ziad Jarrah, by contrast, was decisive in his choice. Independent as ever, he had done his own research back in March and settled on the Florida Flight Training Center in Venice, twenty miles south of Sarasota. A copy of his faxed application form (using Aysel's address in Bochum) shows that he inquired about obtaining both a private pilot's license and a commercial license. Jarrah arrived in the United States on June 27, flying from Munich to Atlanta and then making his way to Florida's Gulf Coast. He reported to the flight school in Venice on June 28.

The proprietor of the Florida Flight Training Center, Arne Kruithof, made quick assessments of his new students during their first few days on the small campus at the Venice airport. "I want to know," Kruithof said, "if I have an airline pilot in my school or not." He trusted his instincts but also went down a checklist of qualities he deemed necessary for success—loyalty, dedication, attention to detail, and good social manners. Within about forty-five minutes, Kruithof labeled Jarrah "airline material."

The FFTC already had a large number of foreign nationals training to be pilots that summer, including many students from Middle Eastern countries; Kruithof estimated the school's enrollment at the time to be about 30 percent "Arab/Muslim." But the newcomer from Lebanon possessed another attribute that made him stand out from the others. He spoke multiple languages and had the ability to transition from, say, English to German in the same conversation. "Perfect English, perfect German, and perfect French," Kruithof said. "And I speak those languages, so I got interested in him *personally* because I always find it interesting when somebody can switch from language to language and keep a good conversation going. That's rather special."

Jarrah took his first lesson on June 28. FFTC records show he was back at it on June 29, June 30, and July 1. Ramzi Binalshibh, who was supposed to be his training partner, had yet to obtain a US visa and was still stranded back in Germany, but Jarrah forged ahead on his own. By the end of his first week in the United States, he already was making progress toward earning his private pilot's license.

At the same time, Atta and Shehhi were reaching the end of their monthlong search for a training site. In early July they traveled halfway across the country to Norman, Oklahoma, to check out the Airman Flight School, where one of bin Laden's personal pilots had once been a student. When that location also failed to meet their expectations, however, the two men caught a flight to Florida. Perhaps it was a phone call from Jarrah extolling the virtues of the Gulf Coast, where foreigners could blend in easily among the thousands of tourists from around the world. Perhaps it was scheduled as the next stop on their list. It couldn't have been coincidence. Whatever the reason, Atta and Shehhi soon strolled through the doorway of Huffman Aviation, another flight school located at the Venice airport, just a few hundred feet from where Jarrah was training. They started classes on July 7.

Barely six months after returning from Afghanistan, the three men tasked with flying airplanes into US buildings had migrated and switched their base of operations from Hamburg to a small town in Florida that fancies itself the Shark Tooth Capital of the World.

———

Ramzi Binalshibh was frustrated. Fuming.

Like the others in the Hamburg group who denounced the United States and dreamed of jihad, he'd sworn allegiance to Osama bin Laden and volunteered for martyrdom as a pilot in the Planes Operation. Now he couldn't get the documentation to even make the trip to the United States.

Twice, on May 17 and June 15, Binalshibh had applied for the same kind of tourist visa that enabled Atta, Shehhi, and Jarrah to enter the United States. Twice, he had been turned down—not because of any threat of terrorism, but because, as a native of Yemen, he was viewed as a potential economic migrant. United States border policy at the time was far more focused on potential immigrants from impoverished nations such as Yemen who might overstay their visas. Al-Qaeda apparently had not learned its lesson from the experience of the first two Yemenis selected by bin Laden. Perhaps there was a belief that Binalshibh could slip through the cracks because of his brief history as a university student in Germany.

It didn't work. On July 18, with pilot training in Venice already moving forward at a rapid pace, an anxious Binalshibh met with a consular officer in Berlin for an interview about his multiple visa applications. According to investigators who examined the records later, however, he failed to prove he was not an "intending immigrant."

But Binalshibh was nothing if not relentless. With the assistance of Jarrah, he contacted the Florida Flight Training Center about enrolling as a student pilot and on August 17 received a fax from FFTC requesting copies of his passport, a bank statement, and a completed application form. That month he also wired $2,200 to the school as a deposit. Binalshibh likely was trying to establish credentials for a new application—this time for a student visa—that would clear him for entrance to the United States. But immigration officials rejected him on two more attempts. One was in September from his native Yemen. The other was in October from Berlin.

He had run out of chances. After the fourth application, an official at the American embassy in Berlin told Binalshibh in the bluntest terms possible: "Please acknowledge that we cannot give you a visa."

There were immediate effects on the ground in coastal Florida. The intention was to have the four hijacker pilots train in two-man teams: Atta with Shehhi and Jarrah with Binalshibh. They were to live and work together as tandems in a foreign culture, one man supporting the other. Now, Jarrah was going to have to prepare for the brazen mission on his own.

Though Atta and Shehhi were training at a flight school just down the road, the al-Qaeda game plan called for secrecy and deception behind enemy lines; there is no record of the men interacting with Jarrah during their time in Venice. Atta and Shehhi stayed for a few days at the home of the bookkeeper at Huffman Aviation but soon rented their own apartment in the nearby town of Nokomis. They kept to themselves and did everything together. Jarrah, on the other hand, roomed with four European students who were training to be pilots—two from the Netherlands and two from Germany. "He was pretty social with them," Krutihof recalled. They shared chores and drank a few beers. The experience must have given him a starkly different view of life in America. As the one member of the Hamburg group who had a love interest back home, and whose mind occasionally wandered, Jarrah likely would have benefitted from a devoted jihadi partner to keep him focused on the mission. But that was no longer an option, at least in the short term. It was a risk.

Rebuked in his efforts to become a pilot but well-acquainted with the other candidates and the overall plan, Binalshibh was assigned a new role in the operation as the key liaison between Atta's men and al-Qaeda headquarters in Afghanistan. In the months to come, he would prove to be an invaluable resource, conducting meetings that would refine the specifics of the attack and facilitating the travel of additional operatives to the United States to fill out the hijacking teams. He became KSM's right-hand man.

But al-Qaeda had learned the hard way—again—that it wasn't enough merely to have volunteers willing to commit suicide in an attack from inside the United States. They had to be able to get there first.

And bin Laden now faced a new challenge. He had to find a fourth pilot—in a hurry.

Atta and Shehhi were diligent students and trained together constantly. They earned their private pilot certificates for single-engine aircraft on the same day in mid-August and added their commercial licenses for multiengine planes on the same day that December. By that time, each had accumulated approximately 250 flight hours. Before the end of the year, both men advanced to training on flight simulators for larger Boeing aircraft, starting with 727s and working their way up to 767s. They never would have a chance to fly the big airliners before the actual mission, of course, but working on the simulators allowed them to become familiar with the cockpit controls and gain what an aviation expert described as "the operational efficiency, 'feel,' and confidence to fly the aircraft into the intended target."

Jarrah passed the test for his private pilot certification in September and continued training through the end of 2000, but he never took the test for his commercial license—although Kruithof thinks it would have taken just a few more weeks of lessons. "He got his private license, then an instrument rating, and then he flew all the hours out of the commercial syllabus toward his commercial license," Kruithof said. The school's lone multiengine aircraft was undergoing maintenance when Jarrah advanced to that level and was temporarily unavailable. "He told us that he was going to go home," Kruithof said, "and come back later to finish it."

And yet records later obtained by the 9/11 Commission show that Jarrah had compiled just one hundred flight hours by mid-November—far fewer than Atta and Shehhi at roughly the same point in time. Even with his apparent dedication and announced intentions, he was falling behind. Some of the reason for the disparity almost certainly was because he was forced to operate in a strange country on his own, without the support and prodding of a training partner like Binalshibh. Some of it also was his continued interest in a dual life with Aysel Senguen.

On October 7, Jarrah took an unexpected break from his training, traveling from Atlanta to Frankfurt, Germany, and then on to Bochum—where Aysel was living and studying. He took Aysel on a side trip to Paris and spent a total of twenty-three days abroad. This would be the first of five overseas trips Jarrah took during a ten-month span between October 2000 and August 2001. All five trips were to Germany, and two included connections to Lebanon to see his family. In January he even brought Aysel to Florida with him for a ten-day visit. She never knew about the other Hamburg operatives living nearby and continued to believe his story about becoming a professional pilot.

Counting a two-day pleasure trip to the Bahamas that he took with fellow flight school students in November, Jarrah spent a total of more than ninety days outside the United States between October 2000 and August 2001, the equivalent of three full months. It interrupted his training and no doubt blurred his focus. It also put the mission at considerable risk: He had to pass through US immigration checks six times after his seamless initial entry into the country.

Atta took two European trips of his own during his time in America, but both were scheduled meetings with Binalshibh—one in January 2001 and one that July—to discuss the progress of the operation. Shehhi also made two trips, and while the purpose of his extracurricular travel is not known, these excursions certainly were approved in advance by Atta, his roommate and training partner. Jarrah was acting impulsively, on his own—and clearly testing the limits of Atta's patience.

Is it possible that Jarrah was wavering? Word reached him in January 2001 that his father, Samir, had suffered a heart attack. Jarrah rushed from Jacksonville to Dusseldorf on January 26 and on to Beirut the next day. He spent three weeks with his family in Lebanon, helping to see his father through bypass surgery before traveling to visit Aysel in Bochum. She later told investigators, "He was really moved, and said, he, Ziad, wants to have children soon, so his father could see them before he dies." On that trip alone, the seemingly conflicted jihadist spent thirty days outside the United States. He returned on February 25.

And yet he kept training, preparing for his mission in America. Like Atta and Shehhi, he began to take periodic lessons on flight simulators to replicate the experience of flying large commercial airliners. For four straight days in December 2000, he trained on Boeing 727 and 737 simulators at the Aeroservice Aviation Center in Miami. Immediately following one of his overseas trips, he returned to Aeroservice on January 8 and completed another simulator session. And he traveled domestically for additional flight training in small planes—in March, at an aviation center in Georgia (where Atta and Shehhi trained briefly), and in June, at Hortman Aviation in Philadelphia.

Jarrah also added physical fitness training to his regimen, taking a particular interest in martial arts and one-on-one combat. In the spring of 2001, he enrolled at the US1 Fitness Center in Dania, Florida, where the instructor, Bert Rodriquez, trained him for four months in classes ranging from kickboxing to knife-fighting. "He was learning to be in control," Rodriquez said.

Whatever his shortcomings, whatever his distractions, Ziad Jarrah still wanted to be a pilot for al-Qaeda.

Meanwhile, in the summer of 2000, a recruit at the al-Faruq training camp in Afghanistan gave the Planes Operation a sudden and unexpected boost. He revealed in background documents that he'd earned a commercial pilot certificate in the United States. The news spread quickly through al-Qaeda's leadership ranks. The new candidate, a Saudi named Hani Hanjour, was whisked up several levels of the chain of command until one of bin Laden's senior lieutenants, Mohammed Atef, told him to report to KSM. It was a fortuitous moment for the men behind the plot.

Hanjour, twenty-seven years old at the time, had traveled periodically to the United States since 1991, entering the country at least three times and taking English as a Second Language courses in both Arizona and California. He started his pilot training as early as 1996. He struggled with it—one instructor indicated he was "not serious" and another criticized his poor English—but he persevered. After attending at least four flight schools, Hanjour earned his private pilot license in April 1998 and added his commercial, multiengine certificate in April 1999.

He returned home to Saudi Arabia with his new aviation credentials but was unable to find a job as a pilot. Like many disaffected, impressionable young men from the region, he found his way to Afghanistan. KSM immediately recruited him for the mission and told him to head back to Saudi Arabia, where citizens of the kingdom, an important US ally, could readily obtain proper documentation for travel to the United States. Hanjour received his US visa on September 25, 2000. He was then introduced to a man in the United Arab Emirates named Ali Abdul Aziz Ali—KSM's nephew—who was helping to facilitate the financial aspects of the Planes Operation. Ali already had wired more than $100,000 in several installments to the joint account of Atta and Shehhi at SunTrust Bank in Florida between July and September. He now made all of the new pilot's arrangements.

Hanjour entered the United States on December 8, 2000, and traveled to San Diego, where he was met by Nawaf al Hazmi, one of the original operatives assigned to the plot, who had been living by himself in San Diego for six months. Hazmi was part of the two-man advance guard that came to Los Angeles in January 2000, but his coconspirator, Khalid al Mihdhar, had grown disenchanted with life in America and had abruptly returned to the Middle East in June.

Mihdhar vowed to return to the United States in time to take part in the attacks, but his departure had left Hazmi stranded in southern

California. The arrival of Hanjour was a welcome occurrence—for both Hazmi *and* al-Qaeda.

Within a matter of days, Hazmi and Hanjour moved to Arizona and rented an apartment in Mesa. Hanjour signed up to refine his flight training at Arizona Aviation and began taking lessons on a Boeing 737 flight simulator at Pan American International Jet Tech in Phoenix. It had been a perilous time for al-Qaeda—Binalshibh's failure to get travel clearance to the United States left a gaping hole in the roster—but the leadership group in Afghanistan had responded quickly to the challenge, identifying and recruiting another trained pilot who was eager to give his life for the cause. In addition, Hazmi now had a jihadi partner on the West Coast. With four pilots finally in place, and on US soil, the Planes Operation was on track.

CHAPTER FIVE

Final Preparations

Since the summer of 2000, bin Laden and his senior associates in Afghanistan had been keeping a close eye on the training camps to identify additional young zealots who would fill out the hijack rosters. These would be the hit teams, the men who would attack the cockpits and control the passengers. To make the cut, the bare-minimum requirement was a willingness to give your life for the cause.

The selection process began in earnest in early September 2000 when the initial candidates, approved by bin Laden himself, were instructed to apply for US visas. Many of these young men had taken hard turns toward extremism in the past year and were searching for outlets for their newfound rage. One such example was Ahmed al Nami, the youngest of six children of a middle-class family from Abha in Saudi Arabia. Within a year, he would be assigned to the hijack team for Flight 93.

Nami once had a fondness for singing, playing music, and smoking—activities that did not indicate a strict Islamic background. But his outlook changed dramatically after he attended a religious camp in the summer of 1999. He grew a beard, frequented a fundamentalist mosque, and began to study Islamic law. His family said he never returned home following a pilgrimage to Mecca in the late spring of 2000.

The twenty-three-year-old Nami and most of the men selected as muscle hijackers applied for their US visas between September and November of 2000. The term *muscle hijackers* was developed by investigators following the September 11 attacks as a convenient and widely accepted description for the nonpilot operatives, but it was far from accurate. These were not large, muscular men chosen to overpower the passengers and crew with their physical might. Nami, for instance, was only five-foot, seven-inches tall. According to the 9/11 Commission, most of the muscle hijackers were "between 5'5" and 5'7" in height and slender in build." What they brought to the mission was a fierce devotion to martyrdom in the name of jihad. The utter willingness to die would be their most important weapon. Al-Qaeda also knew it would have the element of surprise on its side.

Members of the hit teams received the same introductory training as other raw al-Qaeda recruits at the camps: physical fitness, firearms, explosives. As their skills improved, they underwent more specific sessions in wielding knives, conducting hijackings, and even dealing with the possibility of air marshals. KSM insisted that these men were not informed of the precise details of the Planes Operation until after they had arrived in the United States. They only knew they had volunteered for a martyrdom mission in the American homeland. Along the way, they also got instruction in other terror disciplines, such as truck bombing, in order to camouflage the true intent of what their leaders had in mind.

By the spring of 2001, thirteen specially selected muscle hijackers had completed their training and obtained their travel documents to enter the United States. One of the men was from the United Arab Emirates, but the other twelve were from Saudi Arabia. Bin Laden and KSM were taking no chances. In addition to their ability to gain entry to the United States, the future hijackers had strikingly similar pedigrees. They ranged in age from twenty to twenty-eight. None had a college degree. Most were unemployed and unmarried.

In anticipation of the new arrivals, the five al-Qaeda operatives who already were living in the United States shifted their headquarters to the East Coast. By now, Nawaf al Hazmi had been designated second in command of the mission. Mohamed Atta, Marwan al Shehhi, and Ziad Jarrah moved to the southeast coast of Florida. Hazmi and Hani Hanjour drove east from Arizona and set up a new base in Paterson, New Jersey. Had anyone been tracking them—and no one was, even though Hazmi's name was listed in the information systems of the intelligence community—they would have been alarmed by the mass movement. It was significant. The next segment of the Planes Operation unfolded, and no one in authority was paying any attention.

The muscle hijackers traveled to the United States in small groups between April 23 and June 29, 2001. Nine of them arrived in Florida, where Atta helped them get acclimated and find living accommodations. Four flew to northern airports and made their way to New Jersey, where Hazmi was in charge. By this point, the date for the attacks still had not been set. Nor had the specific hijack teams been selected or assigned. The men did their best to bide their time by easing quietly into modern American society, eating at fast-food restaurants and shopping at Wal-Mart. They joined gyms to lift weights as the final step in their operational training.

No one was more obsessive about his new gym membership than Saeed al Ghamdi—another future member of the Flight 93 hijack team. It is believed that the twenty-one-year-old Saudi already was a veteran of the battlefields in Chechnya. Before breaking off communication with his family in the al Bahah province one year earlier, Ghamdi announced that Chechnya was his destination. The 9/11 Commission would later find documentation "suggesting travel to a Russian republic." Now, he was committed to a martyrdom mission in the United States.

On July 9 Ghamdi purchased a two-month membership at Y 2 Fitness in Boca Raton. Records show that he worked out at the gym for twenty-eight of the next thirty-one days, including twenty days in a row from July 20 through August 8. Following a brief break, he returned each day from August 16 to August 25. He was taking advantage of every opportunity to add bulk to his five-foot, nine-inch frame.

Among the final duties assigned to the muscle hijackers before leaving Afghanistan had been to record martyrdom videos to be used as propaganda in future jihadi recruiting efforts. The existence of these videos was not revealed until well after the attacks, but the language and the tone—and the confidence—also provided insight into al-Qaeda's pre-September 11 mind-set. In anticipation of their success, many of the jihadis taunted the United States.

One such man was Ahmed al Haznawi, the fourth and youngest member of the Flight 93 hijacking team. Haznawi, age twenty, came from the same region as Nami and shared a tribal affiliation with Ghamdi. Devoutly religious, he already had memorized the Koran. In 1999 he asked his father for permission to leave for jihad in Chechnya and was turned down. He left anyway—and returned later to recruit other members of the clan.

One report said that Haznawi was the only Saudi hijacker known to have maintained even limited contact with his family after coming to America. He called his aunt to ask about his mother, who was ill at the time—something Atta would have frowned upon. But closeness with his family didn't deter him. His martyrdom statement, released only seven months after the attacks, left no doubt about his commitment to the cause.

"We left our families to send a message that has the color of blood," Haznawi thundered. "The message says, 'The time of humiliation and subjugation are over.' It is time to kill Americans in their homeland, among their sons, and near their forces and intelligence. . . . The United States is nothing but propaganda and a huge mass of false statements and exaggeration. However, the truth is what you saw. We killed them outside their land, praised be Allah. Today, we kill them in the middle of their home."

***

The late spring and summer months of 2001 were times of apprehension, decision making, and strategic travel. At least six of the hijackers, including all four pilots, took cross-country surveillance flights between May and August, searching for weaknesses in airline security systems and observing the routines of the crew. Jarrah, for instance, flew from Baltimore-Washington International Airport to Los Angeles on June 7, taking the same kind of aircraft—a Boeing 757—that he would pilot on his final mission. He sat in first class, with an easy view of the cockpit. On their return trips, the hijackers all stopped in Las Vegas for between one and three days.

Atta made another longer, more significant journey in the middle of the summer. Leaving Miami, he flew to Zurich, Switzerland, on July 8 and continued on to Madrid, Spain. He picked up Binalshibh, who was serving as the middleman between Atta and al-Qaeda's leadership, and they drove to Tarragona on the Spanish coast. With the Mediterranean

Sea as a backdrop, the mission leader and the plot's key facilitator held their final face-to-face planning sessions for the Planes Operation.

Bin Laden was pushing for the attacks to happen soon, Binalshibh said. But Atta had yet to select a date. He said he needed five or six more weeks to organize the newly arrived operatives and coordinate logistics for boarding transcontinental flights that would take off almost simultaneously. Atta already had determined that he and Shehhi would attack the towers of the World Trade Center, Hanjour would strike the Pentagon, and Jarrah would hit the Capitol. He knew bin Laden wanted the list of targets to include the White House. But while Atta understood the psychological impact of an attack against the home of the US president, he told Binalshibh that he thought the building would be too difficult to identify from above, during the pilot's harrowing final approach to Washington, DC. In an earlier reconnaissance of the area, al-Qaeda operatives described the White House as a structure "not easily spotted from the air." The Capitol, with its high and prominent dome, seemed a more achievable target.

Nonetheless, the debate about Jarrah's target continued beyond the July meeting. At one point Atta even agreed to put the White House on the list of targets to appease bin Laden, while keeping the Capitol as an alternative. But Atta also told Binalshibh the attacks would not occur until after the first week of September, which is when the US Congress was back in session. Surely it was a sign that he was zeroing in on the Capitol. In an interview conducted seven months after September 11, Binalshibh told *Al Jazeera* reporter Yosri Fouda that Jarrah's target was "Capitol Hill," meaning the Capitol. KSM also told investigators the target was indeed the Capitol.

When talk at the July meeting got around to tactics, Atta said that he, Shehhi, and Jarrah had been able to carry small box cutters onto their surveillance flights without being stopped by security. The men decided that the best time to launch the assaults would be ten to fifteen minutes after the planes had taken off, when the cockpit doors were usually opened for the first time. They also had selected code names for the targets, to be used in their internal communications. The World Trade Center was the "Faculty of Town Planning." The Pentagon was the "Faculty of Fine Arts." The Capitol was the "Faculty of Law."

Then the subject turned to Jarrah. It was perhaps the most crucial part of the weeklong strategy session in Spain. Both KSM and Binalshibh knew that Jarrah and Atta were having problems—that Jarrah "chafed" under Atta's authority. His repeated overseas trips to see Aysel and his family were points of contention. KSM was worried that Jarrah actually might back out of the Planes Operation with only weeks left in the planning process. It would have been a crippling blow to lose a pilot at this late date. Adding to the tension, Jarrah was planning to leave on another trip to visit Aysel in Germany on July 25—and she had bought him a one-way ticket.

KSM expressed his growing angst over Jarrah's status in a coded conversation with Binalshibh on July 20. He referred to Jarrah and Atta as an unhappy couple and said that if Jarrah "asks for a divorce, it is going to cost a lot of money." KSM also instructed Binalshibh to "send the skirts to Sally." It was his way of approving additional funding for another al-Qaeda operative who was training to be a pilot in the United States—a French national of Moroccan descent named Zacarias Moussaoui.

It is possible, and maybe even likely, that Moussaoui was being groomed as a backup pilot for the plot in case Jarrah withdrew. KSM later insisted that he never was intended for the 9/11 operation, that he was merely an early arrival for a "second wave" of attacks on the US mainland. But Moussaoui's potential role confounded authorities for years. Early on, some even described him as the "twentieth hijacker," believing he'd been targeted to fill out the muscle team on Flight 93. He had not. Eventually, the evidence showed that he was focused on becoming a pilot.

Moussaoui first came to the United States in Feburary 2001, enrolling for flight training at the Airman Flight School in Norman, Oklahoma—the same place that Atta and Shehhi had visited briefly in July 2000. In early August, after receiving $14,000 from Binalshibh ("send the skirts to Sally"), he traveled to Minnesota and registered for instruction at the Pan American Flight School in Minneapolis. He paid $6,800 in cash and said he wanted to train on Boeing 747 flight simulators.

His arrival struck the school's instructors as suspicious. The new student didn't even have a private pilot's license, and he suddenly wanted to learn to fly large commercial airliners. They reported the situation to the FBI, and it was quickly determined that Moussaoui had overstayed his visa. On August 17 he was detained by the Immigration and Naturalization Service (INS) and arrested on immigration charges. Local FBI agents were unable to get permission from headquarters to search his laptop before September 11, and the Bureau's handling of the case received criticism in the coming months and years. But the short-term effect was that Moussaoui—whatever his purpose—was no longer available for the operation.

It became a moot point because Jarrah never dropped out. Maybe it was because of the pressure applied by his fellow jihadis at both ends of his late-July trip to Germany. Atta drove Jarrah to the airport in Miami and Binalshibh was waiting for him when he landed in Dusseldorf. Although Jarrah spent most of the next two weeks alone with Aysel, he still found time to meet with Binalshibh—who, during an "emotional" conversation, implored him to finish the mission. We never will know how close Jarrah came to actually backing out, but, in the end, he chose martyrdom. The ticket for his return flight was purchased on August 3, and he touched down at Miami International Airport on August 5.

The man who once had written, *"The morning will come . . . the earth will shake beneath your feet,"* was now back in the country, wholly invested in the cause.

In a matter of weeks, twenty-six-year-old Ziad Jarrah would help make the unthinkable happen on US soil.

—◦—

Sometime around the third week of August, Atta sent a cryptic e-mail to Binalshibh to update him on their progress. He posed as a young man sending a note to his girlfriend in Germany.

The e-mail—translated from its original German—read:

The first semester commences in three weeks. There are no changes. All is well. There are good signs and encouraging ideas. Two high schools and two universities. Everything is going according to plan. This summer will surely be hot. I want to talk to you about some details. Nineteen certificates for private education and four exams. Regards to the Professor. Goodbye.

Months after the attacks, in an interview with reporter Yosri Fouda of *Al Jazeera*, Binalshibh gave a line-by-line explanation of the message sent from Atta:

> *The zero hour is going to be in three weeks' time. There are no changes. All is well. The brothers have been seeing encouraging visions and dreams. The Twin Towers, the Pentagon, and Capitol Hill. Everything is going according to plan. This summer will surely be hot. I want to talk to you about some details. Nineteen hijackers and four targets. Regards to Khalid/Osama. I will call you nearer the time.*

Jarrah clearly was re-energized during those final few weeks in South Florida; he prepared for the mission with a focus that bordered on the fanatical.

On August 17 he paid for 1.3 hours of flight time at Airborne Systems, Inc., in Fort Lauderdale. In the next two and a half weeks, he rented a plane eleven times for solo practice flights.

On August 22 he visited the Oshkosh Pilot Shop in Miami and attempted to purchase four Global Positioning System (GPS) devices; the store had only one in stock. Jarrah returned on August 27 to pick up the single GPS device and also bought a GPS antenna and posters of a 757 cockpit. He then visited Banyan Air Service in Fort Lauderdale, purchasing three aeronautical charts.

Later on the same day, August 27, Jarrah flew to Baltimore and checked into a motel in Laurel, Maryland. The eventual members of the Flight 77 hijack team were concentrated in that area, and Jarrah likely made the trip to meet with Nawaf al Hazmi and Hani Hanjour, comparing notes and coordinating strategy. He returned to Fort Lauderdale two days later.

The date for the attacks was selected by Atta by the third week of August. He alerted Binalshibh during a phone call on August 29 when he asked his friend to solve a riddle: "Two sticks, a dash, and a cake with a stick down—what is it?" After some thought, Binalshibh realized that two sticks were the number eleven, and cake with a stick down was the number nine. 11-9. In the Arabic style of writing dates, it represented September 11.

The four flights were scheduled to take off within a tight time frame of twenty-five minutes. That would make it virtually impossible for the US military to respond once the assault was under way. All would be transcontinental trips with full fuel loads for maximum explosions on impact. All would be either 757s or 767s, which had almost identical cockpits—they had been a focus of the pilots' simulator training. All would leave from East Coast cities.

The assignments and pilots:

- American Airlines Flight 11, Boston to Los Angeles, 7:45 a.m.—Atta
- United Airlines Flight 175, Boston to Los Angeles, 8:00 a.m.—Shehhi
- United Airlines Flight 93, Newark to San Francisco, 8:00 am.—Jarrah
- American Airlines Flight 77, Washington, DC, to Los Angeles, 8:10 am.—Hanjour

Atta also had determined the makeup of the specific hijack teams. Originally, KSM wanted to use twenty-five or twenty-six hijackers, creating a force with enough strength and depth to confidently take over the planes, control the passengers, and ensure that the planes could be crashed into their targets without a struggle. But even with the return of Khalid al Mihdhar to the United States on the Fourth of July, they still had only nineteen.

At the very least, al-Qaeda was trying to build that number to twenty—one pilot and four muscle hijackers assigned to each flight. The 9/11 Commission identifies no fewer than nine men who, over the course of the final year, were nominated to fill the position of the "twentieth hijacker." Some of them couldn't get the proper travel documents. Some were deemed unreliable. Some simply decided they didn't want to be martyrs. The best chance came on August 4 when a Saudi named Mohammed al Kahtani flew from Dubai through London to Orlando with a valid US visa in hand. Atta was waiting for him at the airport.

Kahtani never made it past the immigration check. He was detained by immigration authorities and denied entry into the United States. This was unusual for a citizen of Saudi Arabia, but Kahtani had been evasive and hostile while being questioned—and a sharp immigration official named Jose Melendez-Perez grew suspicious of his intent. Kahtani's Emirates Airlines flight had landed in Orlando at 4:40 p.m. Less than five hours later, he was back on a flight to London. Records show that Atta's car entered the parking garage at the Orlando airport at 4:18 p.m. and left at 9:04 p.m.

KSM still made one final, frantic effort to fill out the roster. Ali Abdul Aziz Ali, his nephew, who had assisted him in providing finances and travel arrangements for some of the muscle hijackers, was assigned to make a last-minute application for a US visa. Ali, a native of Pakistan, applied in Dubai on August 27—stating that he hoped to enter the United States on September 4 and planned to stay for "one week." Like Binalshibh before him, however, he was declined as an intending immigrant.

In 2006 al-Qaeda identified a Saudi named Fawaz al Nashmi as the man selected to be the twentieth hijacker. In a video and statement, al-Qaeda said Nashmi was killed in a gun battle with Saudi security forces in 2004. Despite the unusual claim, the organization gave no explanation as to why he did not take part in the September 11 attacks.

***

The tickets for the September 11 flights were reserved between August 25 and August 31. By this time, the hijack teams had begun to form in their final groups—five men for Flight 11, five for Flight 175, five for Flight 77, and four for Flight 93. It is odd, given Jarrah's vacillation during his time in America, that the Flight 93 team would be the smallest and therefore the most vulnerable to a passenger uprising. No explanation ever was given. Perhaps Jarrah had convinced them that he was up to the challenge.

On August 27 Saeed al Ghamdi called the United Airlines reservation office to purchase two one-way tickets in first class on Flight 93—one for him, and one for his roommate, Ahmed al Nami. The only glitch was that Ghamdi hung up before learning his credit was turned down, and United was unable to reach him at any time during the week to inform him of the problem. He probably had given the airline a bogus telephone number. It was not until September 5 that a curious Nami called United Airlines reservations to check on the status of their tickets and was told of the rejection. He alerted Ghamdi, who immediately supplied a new credit card number, and the transaction was approved—two one-way tickets for $3,539.50.

They selected two seats next to each other, 3C for Nami and 3D for Ghamdi.

On August 29 Ahmed al Haznawi avoided any similar drama, walking into a Kinko's store, logging on to travelocity.com, and buying a one-way ticket in first class for $1,722. He chose seat 6B.

On August 30 Ziad Jarrah completed the arrangements by going to the United Airlines website and purchasing a one-way ticket in the first row of first class for $1,621.50. He reserved seat 1B, where he would have easy access to the cockpit once the moment was right to seize control of the plane.

Along with the plane tickets, one of the few remaining acts for the nineteen hijackers in late August was to purchase knives to be used in the attacks. Four of them bought Leatherman Wave multitools from stores such as Lowe's Home Improvement and Target. One purchased a Stanley two-piece snap knife set at Wal-Mart. Another picked up two four-inch black pocketknives at Sports Authority. Atta himself bought two Victorinox Swiss Army Knives at the Zurich airport on his July trip to Spain. Certainly there were more transactions that did not leave a paper trail of credit card receipts. FAA regulations at the time allowed knives with blades smaller than four inches to be carried onto flights. They had done their homework and would not cause any suspicion.

Ziad Jarrah and the three other members of the Flight 93 hijack team flew north from Fort Lauderdale to Newark on September 7. They took two rooms at the Newark Airport Marriott, registering for two nights.

On September 8 Jarrah then made a side trip on his own, driving a rental car to Maryland—apparently for a strategy session with Hazmi and Hanjour of the Flight 77 team. Mohamed Atta also was in the area at the time, having flown from Miami to Baltimore. It would have been their final major meeting before the attacks.

In one last potential mishap, Jarrah was pulled over for speeding in Maryland on his way back to Newark. It was very early on the morning of September 9, a few minutes after midnight, when his red Mitsubishi Galant was clocked at ninety mph in a sixty-five-mph zone in a rural area north of Baltimore. A Maryland state trooper wrote him a ticket for $270 and sent him on his way. Jarrah's name was not on any federal watch list, he was not in the country illegally, and he did nothing during the routine traffic stop to raise any suspicions. The trooper described him as "extremely calm and cooperative."

Once back at his base of operations in Newark, a nonplussed Jarrah checked out of the Marriott on the afternoon of September 9 and herded the others into two rooms at the nearby Days Inn, where they would quietly spend the last two nights of their lives.

Jarrah placed two significant phone calls on September 9, still trying to tie up loose ends before the mission. The first was to his family in Lebanon, and it was deceptive. He told them that he would be home for a cousin's wedding in mid-September. "He said he had even bought a new suit for the occasion," said his uncle Jamal. The next was to Atta. The two men had not been close in Germany, and Atta's heavy-handed leadership style often rankled the independent Jarrah during their time in Florida. But there was an important message to deliver as the date for the attacks approached. Insubordination would not be an issue. In a cell-phone voice message later retrieved by investigators, Jarrah was heard addressing Atta as "boss."

Then, sometime on September 10, as the clock ticked toward the Zero Hour, Jarrah composed an emotional letter to Aysel Senguen in Germany. It was the closest thing to a suicide note from any of the hijackers. She never received it. We know of its existence only because Jarrah made a mistake in the address and it found its way into the hands of the FBI after September 11.

It said in part:

I do not want you to be sad. I am still alive somewhere, where you cannot see and hear me, but I will see you and know how you are doing. I will wait for you until you come to me. There comes a time for everyone to make a move. It is my fault that I gave you so many hopes about marriage, wedding, children, family and many other things.

I am what you wish for, but unfortunately you must wait a little bit until we will be together again. I did not flee from you, but did what I was supposed to do. You ought to be very proud, because it is an honor, and you will see the result, and everybody will be happy.

CHAPTER SIX

Just Living Their Lives

The thirty-three regular passengers and seven crew members who would board United Flight 93 on the morning of September 11, 2001, did not have the benefit of years of planning and instruction for the mission that would steal their futures in the skies over western Pennsylvania. They did not have leaders designated in advance or an international organization providing advice and financial support from overseas. They did not sign up to be martyrs. They were forty people traveling on a Tuesday morning, just living their lives.

What we know now, though, is that they were special lives, *remarkable* lives, a tapestry of achievements and struggles, celebrations and heart-aches, challenges and dreams that defined the American spirit.

Many were on their own personal, special missions that day. Hilda Marcin, a seventy-nine-year-old grandmother, was moving to California to start a new life with her daughter. Mark "Mickey" Rothenberg, owner of an importing business, was touching down briefly in San Francisco on his way to Taiwan. Old buddies William Cashman and Patrick "Joe" Driscoll were making their annual trip west to go hiking at Yosemite National Park. In *Among the Heroes*, his account of the Flight 93 passengers, crew, and the uprising that day, author Jere Longman wrote that the streetwise Driscoll would begin their hikes by yelling, "Hey, bear, here we come." Joe DeLuca and Linda Gronlund, longtime friends who had just started dating, planned to celebrate Linda's forty-seventh birthday on September 13. After a business meeting, they would tour the California vineyards.

Some were on the back end of their trips and heading home to the West Coast. Richard Guadagno, manager of a wildlife reserve in

California, had come east to celebrate his grandmother's hundredth birthday. Lauren Grandcolas, an advertising sales consultant and budding author, had come for her grandmother's funeral. She was three months pregnant with her first child. Deora Bodley, a twenty-year-old psychology major—the youngest person on board—was returning from a final summer sojourn to visit friends in New Jersey and Connecticut. One of three college students on the flight, she was looking forward to starting her junior year at Santa Clara University.

Two businessmen making the trip, Todd Beamer and Mark Bingham, briefly had attended the same high school in northern California in the late 1980s. Todd was one year ahead of Mark at Los Gatos High. It never has been established whether the two men knew each other at Los Gatos, but Mark's mother, Alice Hoglan, said, "I wouldn't have been surprised if they'd seen each other in school, maybe even talked." Perhaps there was a hint of recognition as they settled into their seats. Mark's PR firm had offices in New York and California. Todd, a sales account manager for Oracle in New Jersey, was heading west to a meeting and planned to return on a red-eye flight that night.

Work commitments brought several other passengers together by pure chance in the coach cabin of Flight 93. Ed Felt, a software engineer for BEA Systems, and a man who'd already earned two patents for encryption technology, was traveling to a business meeting in San Francisco. Marion Britton and Waleska Martinez, coworkers at the US Census Bureau in New York City, were heading to a computer operations conference. Elizabeth Wainio, a regional manager for Discovery Channel Stores in the New York/New Jersey area, was on her way to a company-wide business meeting after a much-anticipated European vacation. Lizz had attended a friend's wedding in Italy and then spent a week in Paris. She flew back to the United States on September 9.

Captain Jason Dahl and First Officer LeRoy Homer never had flown together before that morning, but in many ways they were kindred spirits. Both had been fascinated with aviation from the time they were little boys.

In fact, Jason learned to fly before he learned to drive. He joined the Civil Air Patrol at age thirteen and was flying solo before he was sixteen. His father would have to drive him to the San Jose airport and drop him off for his lessons. After studying aeronautic operations at San Jose State University, he worked as a flight instructor and then as a pilot for a private jet company, delivering newly constructed aircraft around the West Coast. He was hired by United Airlines in 1985.

A skilled aviator who worked his way up from flight engineer to copilot to pilot—and from 727s to 757s and 767s—Dahl also was valued for his talent as an instructor. He became a "standards captain," spending about half of each year flying and the other half training and testing other pilots. In May 2001, however, he decided he wanted to start flying more often. He re-entered the "scheduled pilots" program at United; the slight adjustment in his career path led him to the cockpit of Flight 93 that morning.

LeRoy Homer had the passion of an Air Force man long before he ever became one. He started taking flying lessons at age fifteen and flew solo for the first time at sixteen. A 1987 graduate of the Air Force Academy, he was decorated for his service in Desert Shield and Desert Storm in Iraq and also supported US operations in Somalia. In 1993 he was named the 21st Air Force Aircrew Instructor of the Year.

LeRoy joined United as a pilot in 1995 after being honorably discharged from active duty, but he continued his connection to the military as a member of the Air Force Reserves, working as an instructor pilot and later recruiting candidates for the Air Force Academy and the Reserve Officer Training Corps. He began his civilian career as a Second Officer on 737s and was quickly promoted to First Officer on 757s and 767s. Like Dahl, he was born to fly.

Most of the flight attendants assigned to the Newark-to–San Francisco route that day were veterans of the business. Lorraine Bay had spent a lifetime in the air and was working her thirty-seventh year with United. She ranked fourth in seniority out of the seven hundred attendants based in Newark and doted on other crew members as well as her passengers. But one member of the crew was a relative newcomer to the profession. CeeCee Lyles, a former police officer in Fort Pierce, Florida, had enrolled in training in December 2000 and was still in her first year on the job.

Debbie Welsh was the "purser"—the lead attendant on the flight—issuing assignments and serving as a liaison with the pilots. Friends called her the "Little Apostle of the Airlines" because she carried unused meals from Newark Airport and distributed them to the homeless on the way back to her Hell's Kitchen neighborhood in New York City. Debbie would be paired in first class with Wanda Green, who was in her twenty-ninth year with the airline. Wanda also was dabbling in real estate and planned to leave United in a year or two to start her own agency.

Flight attendant Sandy Bradshaw loved to travel but had cut back her work schedule to two trips a month after giving birth to a daughter in 1998 and a son in 2000. Sandy's plan for September was to get those two flights behind her as early as possible, because she wanted to focus her attention on son Nathan's first birthday party. It was coming up in ten days.

Especially for a flight with only thirty-three passengers, there was an astounding amount of athletic prowess on board—and not just weekend warriors who played some high school ball. The manifest included a black belt in judo, a brown belt in karate, a national rugby champion, two wrestlers, a weight lifter, an all-county field hockey player, a swimmer, a sprinter, and a skydiver. These were driven, competitive people.

Jeremy Glick won a national collegiate judo championship for the University of Rochester in 1993. He had been an all-state wrestler and captain of the soccer team at Saddle River Day School in New Jersey, but at six-foot-one with a muscular physique, he'd grown into a dominant force in the world of judo, earning a black belt to go with his national title. Now, at age thirty-one, he was working as a sales manager for an Internet services provider and traveling to California on business. If a fight broke out, Jeremy Glick was the right guy to have on your side.

Tom Burnett had been a standout high school quarterback in Bloomington, Minnesota, leading the Jefferson High Jaguars to the state finals in 1980. He earned a scholarship to St. John's University in Minnesota before an injury cut short his football career; the leadership skills he honed as a quarterback were evident as he rose through graduate school and the business world. Still an imposing presence at 6'2", 205 pounds, Tom was thirty-eight and working as chief operating officer of Thoratec Corporation, a manufacturer of medical devices. He was heading home to his wife, Deena, and three children in California.

Mark Bingham was an adventurer. He'd once jumped off a fifty-foot cliff into the Pacific Ocean. He'd run with the bulls at Pamplona. He'd wrestled a gun out of the hands of a would-be mugger. And he played rugby—using his 6'4", 220-pound frame to help propel the University of California, Berkeley, to two national championships. "He was like a guided missile, head down, going," a friend once said of his playing style. "He wasn't that fast, but he was everywhere." Mark also happened to be gay. The thirty-one-year-old had turned his elite Cal education into a career in public relations, founding The Bingham Group, and shuttling between his offices in New York and San Francisco.

Todd Beamer grew up a sports junkie, excelling at baseball, basketball, and soccer at Wheaton Christian Academy near Chicago—and then, after his family moved to California, as a senior at Los Gatos High. He tried out for the Division I baseball team at Fresno State before transferring closer to his roots at smaller Wheaton College, where he was a shortstop and also played basketball. In the final at-bat of his collegiate baseball career, he hit a game-winning home run. Todd was a rising star in the sales department at Oracle and was married with two sons—and a third child on the way. At age thirty-two, he still had the look of an athlete but was a few pounds over his "playing weight" at 6', 200 pounds.

Don Greene wrestled in high school and at Brown University; now in his early fifties, he stayed active by sailing, scuba diving, and skiing. He was executive vice president of Safe Flight Instrument Corporation, which manufactured products used by thousands of aircraft worldwide. He also was licensed to fly small planes. Andrew "Sonny" Garcia had been a sprinter and wrestler at San Jose State and kept himself in excellent shape with regular workouts at age sixty-two. The owner of Cinco Group, Inc., an industrial products supply business, he still ran three miles a day. Louis "Joey" Nacke, a distribution manager for a toy company in New Jersey, was a weight lifter who packed two hundred pounds onto his five-foot, nine-inch frame. As a boy, Joey once dressed up as Superman and ran through a glass door, opening a gash that required 140 stitches. It explained the Superman tattoo on his shoulder. Ironworker Bill Cashman had been an army paratrooper in the 101st Airborne Division and took lessons in martial arts. He'd helped construct the World Trade Center. Joe Driscoll, a retired executive director of software development for Bell Communications, once had been scouted by the New York Giants baseball team and served four years aboard a US Navy destroyer in the Korean War.

But the athleticism and fierce competitiveness weren't restricted to the men. The profoundly energetic Nicole Miller was a swimmer and softball player in high school. Now, as a student at West Valley College in Saratoga, California, she was teaching corporate exercise and weight-training classes at a local gym. Linda Gronlund, an attorney and engineer for BMW North America, held a brown belt in karate—and once reset her own dislocated kneecap before an ambulance arrived. Deora Bodley had been captain of the basketball team at La Jolla Country Day School in San Diego. Elizabeth Wainio was a county all-star in field hockey at Catonsville High in Maryland. Lauren Grandcolas, daughter of a college football coach, loved roller blades and mountain bikes and celebrated her thirtieth birthday by jumping out of a plane. Officer CeeCee Lyles was trained in self-defense and close-quarter combat and once tackled a male suspect when he tried to flee.

These were people who played hard, took on challenges, and often pushed the limits of their endurance. Little did they know how well their lives had prepared them for the unimaginable task about to confront them.

***

The melting-pot nature of the United States was reflected in the roster of individuals who bought tickets for that cross-country flight out of Newark. Although twenty-seven of the thirty-three regular passengers were born and raised in the United States, two others were natives of Germany, one was a citizen of Japan, one was born in Italy, one was a transplanted New Zealander, and one hailed from Puerto Rico. The cross-section of passengers was fitting; their diversity was representative of the very America that was under attack that morning.

Twenty-year-old Toshiya Kuge was a student at Waseda University in Tokyo, but he dreamed of coming to the United States to earn his master's degree. Toshiya had taken an English language course at the University of Utah earlier in 2001. He was wrapping up a vacation where he'd seen the sights—including both sides of Niagara Falls—and visited several colleges for future reference. He grew up playing soccer but tried his hand at "American football" at Waseda, where he was a linebacker and rooted for the Pittsburgh Steelers. "He *loved* the United States," said his older brother, Naoya. "He wanted to live there. That's how big a dream he had."

Alan Beaven, an environmental lawyer based in Oakland, California, was a man of the world—licensed to practice law in England and his native New Zealand as well as in California and New York. He'd taught at King's College in London and worked as a prosecutor at Scotland Yard but found his niche in environmental litigation in the United States, helping to enforce the Clean Water Act. Alan and his wife, Kimi, were preparing for a year's sabbatical to India, where he would do environmental work related to pollution and deforestation. They would leave from New York. But Alan had to make one final trip back to the West Coast to wrap up a pending case.

Waleska Martinez graduated first in her class at the University of Puerto Rico in 1986 and taught computer science on her native island before moving to New York City, where she became a supervisory computer specialist for the regional office of the US Census Bureau. "She was a manager's dream, responsible and great at resolving problems," her boss at the bureau told the *Pittsburgh Post-Gazette*. She also played softball and tennis, rooted for the New York Yankees, and danced the night away at concerts by Madonna and Tina Turner. "Oh my god," said a friend, "could she let herself loose."

Christian Adams was deputy director of the prestigious German Wine Institute and director of its export department, but the connoisseur from Biebelsheim, Germany, knew the United States well. Christian studied at the University of California, Davis, earning a marketing degree that helped him succeed in the competitive world of international wine production and promotion. And his brother lived in the Bay

Area. Christian attended an elite wine-testing event in New York and was traveling to another in San Francisco on September 12. He spent the night of September 10 at the Newark Airport Marriott, the same hotel where the four men who would hijack Flight 93 had stayed just two nights earlier.

John Talignani was born in Italy but grew up in Brooklyn and served in the US Army in World War II. At age seventy-four, retired from his job as a bartender at the Palm restaurants in Manhattan (and an earlier stint as owner of a pizzeria), he enjoyed following the New York Mets and cooking pizza for family get-togethers. But John was traveling with a heavy heart. He was headed west to attend a memorial service for his stepson, who had just died in a car crash while on his honeymoon in California.

At age seventy-nine, Hilda Marcin was the oldest person on board and had a decidedly unique background. Born in Germany as Hildegarde Zill, she was seven years old and spoke no English when her family arrived in the United States in 1928. Hilda married welder Edward Marcin in 1943, and they raised two daughters—passing on a strong work ethic and a thriftiness borne of the Depression. A bookkeeper and teacher's aide who worked until her late seventies, she also had spunk. Once, when a man tried to steal her purse at a bus stop, Hilda said, "I know your game," and thumped him over the head with an umbrella. Her daughter, Betty Kemmerer, put it best: "Oh, she was *feisty*."

The narrative that developed in the days and weeks after September 11 was that these were ordinary people who did extraordinary things in the face of unthinkable terror. But that piece of mythology, understandable as it is, doesn't give them their due. By no means were these people ordinary. They were energetic, ambitious, curious, dedicated, compassionate, and courageous. Exactly the kind of people it would take to quickly process the chaos unfolding in the final frantic minutes of a hijacked flight, to launch a desperate counterattack aimed at overcoming the assailants—and to boldly try to seize control of the plane.

The men of al-Qaeda planned, and planned well, for many contingencies in the years leading up to the attacks, but one important variable with the potential to disrupt the entire operation was completely beyond their control: They couldn't predict the character and mettle of the forty people who would arrive at Gate 17 at Newark International Airport that morning and step through the doorway onto United Flight 93.

CHAPTER SEVEN

Zero Hour

At 5:01 a.m. on the morning of September 11, Ziad Jarrah placed a cell phone call from Newark to Marwan al Shehhi in Boston. They spoke for less than a minute—probably nothing more than a final confirmation that everyone was awake and things were moving forward in both cities. The pilots of Flight 93 and Flight 175, respectively, were leaving nothing to chance.

Jarrah couldn't resist making one last long-distance call to Germany to speak with Aysel, who was recuperating in the hospital after having her tonsils removed. She told German authorities two days later that the conversation was "held in a normal atmosphere and at no time appeared conspicuous." Jarrah was straddling the starkly different worlds of his dual life until the very end. He told her that he loved her. Then he said he had to go.

In various cities on the East Coast, the al-Qaeda terrorists packed their belongings, checked out of their hotels, and traveled in pairs to their designated airports: Logan in Boston, Dulles in Washington, DC, and Newark International. In one final mysterious twist to the plot, Mohamed Atta and fellow Flight 11 hijacker Abdul Aziz al Omari had driven more than one hundred miles to Portland, Maine, on the evening of September 10, then caught a 6:00 a.m. flight to Boston on the morning of the attacks. Although the reason for the trip has never been determined, Ramzi Binalshibh told *Al Jazeera* in 2002 that it was a key part of Atta's tactical planning. Two teams of ten hijackers would be leaving from Boston that morning, and Atta was concerned that one or more men might be detained by security. If too many were stopped, it would put the operation in peril. According to Binalshibh, Atta "knew that transit passengers from another airport [Portland] would not be subjected to such serious security checks, and that, therefore, at least one group had a chance of getting through." Still, the leader of the plot did risk missing the connection to Boston.

There were moments of extraordinary tension for the nineteen men as they passed through airport security, especially when Flight 77 hijackers Nawaf al Hazmi and Majed Moqed each set off two alarms and were subjected to a metal-detection hand wand. Hazmi had his shoulder-strap bag swiped by an explosive trace detector. Others were stopped for secondary inspections. But in September 2001, US aviation security was astonishingly unprepared for the careful planning and deceptions of the Planes Operation. Al-Qaeda knew of and exploited its many weaknesses that morning. Atta and Omari made their connection to Boston, and all nineteen terrorists were cleared for boarding without significant incident.

As the 9/11 Commission described it later, in the coldest terms possible: "By 8 a.m. on the morning of Tuesday, September 11, 2001, they had defeated all the security layers that America's civil aviation system then had in place to prevent a hijacking."

~ ⌣ ~

Mohamed Atta had carefully selected cross-country flights with heavy fuel loads for maximum destructive power. The strategic seating arrangements were determined in advance according to the type of aircraft. The Boeing 757s (Flights 77 and 93) had only a single aisle down the middle, which offered limited mobility. The 767s (Flights 11 and 175) featured two aisles and allowed more room to maneuver. On all four flights, however, there was one constant: A two-man team was assigned to sit side by side near the front of first class, ready to storm the cockpit and kill or disable the pilots when the signal was given.

We now have a unique window into Atta's battle plan because of an interview that Ramzi Binalshibh and KSM arranged with reporter Yosri Fouda of the *Al Jazeera* television network in 2002. It formed the basis of an *Al Jazeera* documentary on the one-year anniversary of the attacks and later a book that Fouda cowrote with Nick Fielding, *Masterminds of*

65

Terror. A boastful Binalshibh did most of the talking and explained the preparation and strategy. "It was crucial to consider the first fifteen minutes as the golden opportunity to take control of the [airplane] and steer it to its target," he said.

> *Each brother knew exactly what he was supposed to do. The break-in team would seize the earliest opportunity to rush into the cockpit and get rid of everyone inside, whereas the protection team would deal with passengers and security men—slaughtering them if necessary, and moving all passengers to the back. Meanwhile, the pilot would be taking his place inside the cockpit, steering the (airplane). At worst, all this should be done within a maximum of six minutes—the sooner the better.*

In Boston, Newark, and Washington, the unsuspecting passengers began the routine process of boarding the four planes—many of them searching for pillows or checking in-flight movie schedules to help fill the time on the six-hour trip to the West Coast. The pilots and crew members went through their customary checklists of preflight operations. They had been through this routine countless times before. But for the nineteen men from the Middle East, well aware of their impending deaths and seated among their victims, the scene on board the planes must have been surreal. They were a long way from the training camps of Afghanistan, a long way from Huffman Aviation and the Florida Flight Training Center and Pan American International Jet Tech.

"These were very apprehensive moments," Binalshibh said. "You are going into battle, a very large military battle, an unconventional battle against the most powerful force on Earth. You are facing them on their own soil, among their forces and soldiers with a small group of nineteen."

The hijackers prayed.

American Airlines Flight 11 took off from Boston's Logan Airport at 7:59 a.m. with ninety-two people on board: seventy-six regular passengers, eleven crew members, and five al-Qaeda suicide operatives. Fifteen minutes into the flight, at 8:14 a.m., the Boston Air Route Traffic Control Center instructed the pilots to "turn twenty degrees right," and the cockpit answered in the affirmative.

It was the last routine communication from Flight 11. Zero Hour had arrived.

Someone, probably Atta, gave the signal. Brothers Wail and Waleed al Shehri, seated in 2A and 2B, within easy striking distance of the cockpit, bolted from their seats and began the assault. In a matter of seconds, they ushered in a new and unthinkable era of twenty-first-century terror. Members of the flight crew in the rear of the plane used AT&T airphones to report that two flight attendants in first class had been stabbed and that "the guys doing the stabbing" had "jammed" their way into the cockpit.

A few rows back in business class, the mayhem continued. Muscle hijacker Satam al Suqami, seated in 10B, stabbed and probably slashed the throat of passenger Daniel Lewin, seated directly in front of him in 9B. One assumption is that Suqami's sudden and vicious attack was part of a premeditated plan to terrify the rest of the passengers and make it easier to keep them under control. But there may have been another explanation: Lewin had served four years as an officer in the Israeli military; he may have been the first person on any of the 9/11 flights to fight back against the hijackers.

At 8:19 a.m., flight attendant Betty Ong placed a call to the American Airlines reservations office in Cary, North Carolina, to report an emergency; it was far beyond anything she'd ever experienced in her aviation career. "The cockpit's not answering, somebody's been stabbed in business class, and . . . I think there's mace . . . we can't breathe," Ong said. "I don't know, I think we're getting hijacked."

Amid all the chaos, Atta slipped into the cockpit to take the controls—possibly joined by Omari, who'd been seated next to him in row eight of business class. In retrospect, it is not surprising that Atta's unit was the only one of the four al-Qaeda groups that precisely followed preflight instructions to attack within fifteen minutes of takeoff. Attention to detail was Atta's greatest operational asset. Less than twenty minutes after Flight 11 had left Boston, the mission leader was in control and flying the plane.

The only error Atta committed during his time in the cockpit was a relatively minor one, but it confirmed his intentions to the rest of the world in a way he could not have envisioned. When he tried to make an announcement to the passengers shortly before 8:25 a.m., he hit the wrong button and communicated instead to air traffic control. That meant the audio message was broadcast to people on the ground and other pilots in the air, and—maybe most important—it was recorded for posterity. "We have some planes," Atta declared in heavily accented English. "Just stay quiet and you'll be ok. We're returning to the airport."

Seconds later Atta attempted another transmission over the same frequency, still thinking he was warning the passengers: "Nobody move. Everything will be ok. If you try to make any moves, you'll endanger yourself and the airplane. Just stay quiet."

If anyone on the ground had doubted that this was an actual hijacking, the raw reality of the situation was now clear. Mohamed Atta had announced it himself. By using the plural—"planes"—he also served notice, intentionally or not, that other attacks were coming. Atta's next move was to turn off Flight 11's transponder, which sends out a signal identifying an aircraft in flight, making it more difficult for authorities to monitor the flight path. Repeated inquiries from air traffic control to the cockpit were met by stubborn silence. It was anyone's guess where Atta was headed.

At 8:32 a.m., another flight attendant on Flight 11, Amy Sweeney, called the American Flight Services Office in Boston—the plane's origin—and reached flight service manager Michael Woodward, who happened to be a longtime friend. Sweeney provided some of the same information as Betty Ong: They had been hijacked; two flight attendants had been stabbed; a man in first class had his throat slashed; they couldn't contact the cockpit. Sweeney said the hijackers were Middle Eastern and that one spoke "excellent English." She also mentioned something about a bomb.

"How do you know it's a bomb?" Woodward asked.

"Because the hijackers showed me a bomb," said Sweeney, describing its red and yellow wires.

If there was hysteria among the passengers, neither flight attendant reported it. Sweeney said people in coach were under the impression that there was a routine medical emergency in first class. Other flight attendants were searching feverishly for medical supplies. She seemed remarkably calm and composed.

At 8:44 a.m., however, her tone became more desperate; Sweeney said the plane was in rapid descent and exclaimed, "Something is wrong . . . we are all over the place."

Woodward asked her to look out the window, to see if she could determine their location. She could, and what she saw stunned her.

"We are flying low," Sweeney said. "We are flying very, very low. We are flying way too low. Oh my God, we are way too low."

At 8:46 a.m., American Airlines Flight 11 rammed into the North Tower of the World Trade Center at almost five hundred mph.

—~—

The national TV networks soon switched to live images of smoke and flames spewing from the upper floors of one the country's most iconic buildings. There was no available footage of the impact, so early speculation was that a small plane had somehow veered off course and inadvertently struck the tower. Perhaps it was just a bad case of pilot error. First responders and news camera crews rushed to the scene, while dazed and curious onlookers milled around and kept looking up. They couldn't have imagined what else they were about to witness.

—~—

Before September 11, 2001, the prevailing sentiment in the aviation industry was that domestic hijackings were largely a thing of the past. No US-flagged airliner had been bombed or hijacked in more than a decade. According to one public opinion poll conducted in the late 1990s, 78 percent of respondents cited poor aircraft maintenance as "a greater threat to airline safety" than terrorism. Al-Qaeda had targeted the soft underbelly of US aviation security.

The Air Carrier Standard Security Program in effect at the time instructed aircrews to exercise extreme caution in the unlikely event of a hijacking. Pilots and flight attendants were told to refrain from confronting or negotiating with the assailants and to accommodate them whenever possible. The approach outlined by the program, known as the Common Strategy, was to "optimize actions taken by a flight crew to resolve hijackings peacefully." The overarching goal was to get the plane landed safely so that authorities could deal promptly with the hijackers' demands.

Many of the safeguards in place at the time of the attacks focused on the danger of explosives smuggled onto civilian aircraft. The last major terrorist attack on a US-flagged airliner had been thirteen years earlier, in 1988, when Pan Am 103 was destroyed by planted explosives while flying over Lockerbie, Scotland, killing more than 250 people on board. Starting in 1998, the Federal Aviation Administration instructed airlines to institute the Computer-Assisted Passenger Prescreening Program (CAPPS), which would identify passengers in need of additional scrutiny. The only requirement was that each selectee's checked baggage would be screened for explosives. Selectees were not required to undergo additional screening of themselves or their carry-on baggage.

Nine of the nineteen hijackers were singled out by CAPPS for additional screening on the morning of September 11. Four of them faced no consequences because they did not check bags. Five others, including Ahmed al Haznawi of Flight 93, had their checked bags screened before they were loaded on to the planes. But Haznawi and the others weren't worried about their luggage—there *were* no explosives. The system was completely unprepared for a plan involving terrorists who were willing to die. Nothing was in place to stop suicidal hijackers from commandeering civilian aircraft to fly them into buildings.

At least six of the al-Qaeda operatives had taken surveillance flights that summer to monitor US aviation security systems and probe for flaws. They knew that knives of less than four inches could pass legally through airport checkpoints. They learned enough about the history of hijacking to understand the psychological impact of bomb threats in controlling the passengers. They saw that cockpit doors weren't fortified, and that flight attendants often had easy access to the captain and first officer. They planned similar tactics on all four flights—gaining access to the cockpit in violent assaults on the pilots and then sealing off the front of each aircraft from the startled passengers and crew.

In the spring and summer of 2001, there had been a steady buildup of warnings from intelligence sources that Osama bin Laden and al-Qaeda were preparing for a major attack. Reports presented to top officials included "Bin Laden Network's Plans Advancing," "Bin Laden Planning High-Profile Attacks," and "Bin Laden Threats Are Real." On August 6, a now-famous Presidential Daily Brief prepared for President Bush by the CIA was headlined "Bin Laden Determined to Strike in US." It mentioned information that indicated "patterns of suspicious activity in this country consistent with preparations for hijackings or other types of attacks, including recent surveillance of federal buildings in New York."

But despite the repeated threats and warnings from intelligence reports, there was no substantial increase in security at airports to antici- pate the possibility of terrorist hijackings in early September. Compound- ing matters, Mohamed Atta and his men had identified weak points in the system and developed clever ways to exploit them. American authori- ties were outmaneuvered and overmatched.

Several years later, in a staff statement prepared during its investiga- tion of the attacks, the 9/11 Commission concluded quite plainly:

> *Plotters who were determined, highly motivated individuals, who escaped notice on no-fly lists, who studied publicly available vulner- abilities of the aviation security system, who used items with a metal content less than a handgun and most likely permissible, and who knew to exploit training received by aircraft personnel to be noncon- frontational were likely to be successful in hijacking a US domestic aircraft.*

United Airlines Flight 175 rumbled down Boston's Logan Airport runway that morning at 8:14 a.m., departing for Los Angeles at the same minute that Flight 11 was being hijacked. There were sixty-five people on board: fifty-one regular passengers, nine crew members, and five hijackers.

The strategy called for the hijackers to strike within fifteen minutes of takeoff, but only Atta's team on Flight 11 followed that plan to the letter.

Flight 175 proceeded normally for almost a half hour; flight attendants had begun cabin service before Marwan al Shehhi's unit finally sprang into action. The first sign of trouble did not come until 8:42 a.m., when United Airlines pilots in Flight 175's cockpit contacted air traffic control to report hearing "a suspicious transmission" just after they departed from Boston. Eerily, they had heard Atta's inadvertent message from Flight 11. The pilots' warning to air traffic control would be the last time they would communicate with officials on the ground.

The hijackers attacked at about 8:42 a.m. The muscle team of Fayez Banihammad and Mohand al Shehri, seated in 2A and 2B, respectively, likely crashed the cockpit. Calls placed minutes later from the back of the plane reported that a flight attendant had been stabbed and both pilots had been killed in a bloody assault. The hijackers also used mace and the threat of a bomb.

By no later than 8:46 a.m., Shehhi had taken his assigned position in the cockpit. That is when the transponder code was changed to a frequency not recognized by air traffic control. A few minutes later, flight attendant Robert Fangman contacted the United Airlines office in San Francisco to report the chaotic scene and inform airline officials that hijackers were in the cockpit and likely flying the plane.

At 8:52 a.m., passenger Peter Hanson called his father in Easton, Connecticut, using a seat-back airphone located in row thirty. He said the plane had been hijacked and was making "strange moves." A flight attendant had been stabbed. "Call United Airlines," Hanson said. "Tell them it's Flight 175, Boston to L.A."

At 9:00 a.m., shortly after leaving a message for his wife on their home answering machine, passenger Brian Sweeney called his mother from row thirty-one. He told her the plane had been hijacked and that passengers were thinking about storming the cockpit to try to take it back.

If Sweeney, a former Navy lieutenant and former football player at Boston University, was looking for others to mount a counterattack, he would not have had to look far. There were two former professional athletes nearby. One, Garnet "Ace" Bailey, was attempting to place calls to his home from a phone just across the aisle in row thirty-two. Bailey, age fifty-three, had played ten seasons in the National Hockey League with Boston, Detroit, St. Louis, and Washington, accumulating 633 penalty minutes in 568 games. Another, Mark Bavis, age thirty-one, had spent three seasons in hockey's unforgiving minor leagues and compiled 101 penalty minutes in just 44 games in 1995–1996. These were not men to be trifled with. Bailey and Bavis were now scouts for the Los Angeles Kings of the NHL and heading to the West Coast for the start of training camp.

Surely there were other willing and able combatants on board. But they didn't have the information that was later available to those on Flight 93—and they simply didn't have enough time. Just after 9:00 a.m., as the plane approached New York City, Shehhi would have seen the fire and smoke pouring from the North Tower in the distance. The sight must have thrilled him. Atta had struck; we can only guess that it was a final motivation for him to do the same.

Peter Hanson placed a second call to his father in Connecticut at 9:00 a.m. Phone records later obtained by the 9/11 Commission show that the call lasted 192 seconds—just more than three minutes.

"It's getting bad, Dad," Hanson said. "A stewardess was stabbed. They seem to have knives and mace. They said they have a bomb. It's getting very bad on the plane. Passengers are throwing up and getting sick. The plane is making jerky movements. I don't think the pilot is flying the plane. I think we are going down. I think they intend to go to Chicago or someplace and fly into a building. Don't worry, Dad. If it happens, it'll be very fast. My God, my God."

At 9:03 a.m., United Airlines Flight 175 screamed low toward the tip of Manhattan and—on live television—ripped into the South Tower of the World Trade Center, exploding glass, steel, and fuselage out the other side. Shehhi's approach was lower and faster than Atta's, and he noticeably banked the plane to the left upon impact. The fireball was enormous. Many viewers thought they were watching a video replay of the first crash—which had not been captured by news cameras—until stunned commentators explained that they were indeed broadcasting live. This was no replay, no accident, and certainly no happenstance of pilot error. It was a second plane deliberately hitting a second tower.

Across the country, the speculation came to a horrifying stop. America was clearly under attack.

❧

American Airlines Flight 77 took off from Washington's Dulles Airport at 8:20 a.m. with sixty-four people aboard: fifty-three regular passengers, six crew members, and five hijackers.

The flight proceeded without incident for the first half hour, and crew members prepared to offer their normal cabin service. No one had received any word of chaos erupting in the skies above Manhattan. Flight 77 reached its normal cruising altitude of 35,000 feet at 8:46 a.m., the same time that Flight 11 struck the North Tower. At 8:51 a.m., the pilots acknowledged receiving a navigational message from air traffic control and settled in for the long trek to Los Angeles.

It was the last anyone heard from them. The hijackers gained control of the plane by at least 8:54 a.m., when Flight 77 slightly altered its course, turning south. Nawaf al Hazmi and his brother, Salem, seated in 5E and 5F, respectively, were the likely break-in team that breeched the cockpit and disabled the pilots, allowing Hani Hanjour to take the controls. At 8:56 a.m., Hanjour turned off the transponder. Atta's plan had worked a third time.

Only two people aboard Flight 77 placed phone calls to loved ones—flight attendant Renee May and passenger Barbara Olson—but they still provided important details about the hijackers' method of operation. They reported that the assailants used knives and ordered the passengers to the rear of the plane, similar to the procedures on the first two flights. However, neither mentioned an actual stabbing, nor mace, nor the threat of a bomb. One said the "pilot" had made an announcement that the plane was hijacked—meaning that Hanjour had not repeated the same mistake as Atta on Flight 11, when Atta tried to address the passengers and unwittingly reached air traffic control.

Olson was a lawyer and conservative TV commentator who appeared frequently on CNN and Fox News. She reached her husband, Ted, who was no ordinary citizen himself. Ted Olson was solicitor general of the

United States. During the 2000 presidential election controversy, he had argued the case for George W. Bush before the US Supreme Court. But that day, under those circumstances, not even a high-ranking government official with the ear of the president could offer any assistance to the terrified people in the air.

Ted Olson told Barbara the news of the two previous hijackings, and both quickly realized that her flight likely was headed for the same fate.

At 9:29 a.m., the Boeing 757 was about thirty-eight miles west of the nation's capital, flying at seven thousand feet, closing in. The automatic pilot was turned off.

At 9:34 a.m., Hanjour began a severe 330-degree turn that pointed the plane straight at the Pentagon. He pitched the nose down. He increased the power to its maximum speed.

It had been almost an hour since Flight 11 hit the North Tower and more than a half hour since Flight 175 smashed the South Tower, but the country still was shell-shocked and defenseless. There would be no challenge to Hanjour's approach. At 9:37 a.m., American Airlines Flight 77, traveling at an estimated 530 mph, entered the most secure air space in America and plowed into the headquarters of the most powerful military force the world had ever known.

Americans watching television that morning in office buildings and living rooms were riveted by images of unthinkable destruction in New York City. Not since the Japanese bombed Pearl Harbor in 1941 had foreign invaders mounted such a brazen attack on US soil. And this one was on the mainland.

But if the nation's sense of invincibility had been strained by the dual assaults on the World Trade Center, it was summarily shattered by news of fire and smoke belching from the Pentagon, of all places. In cities across the northeastern United States, bewildered workers evacuated tall buildings—fearful that there were other planes, other targets, other crashes to come—and scurried for their cars, heading for home.

The fears weren't unfounded. Just before 10:00 a.m. in Pittsburgh, Pennsylvania, thousands of commuters streamed past the sixty-four-story

USX Tower toward parking lots in the city's Hill District and Uptown sections—completely unaware of the danger lurking just a few thousand feet above their heads.

Al-Qaeda had one more plane, and it was still hurtling toward its target.

CHAPTER EIGHT

Mayday

Lauren Grandcolas was excited. The expectant mother had a ticket to fly home that morning on United Flight 91, departing Newark Airport for San Francisco at 9:20 a.m., but her car service arrived early—so early, in fact, that there was time to catch a different flight. Unable to reach her husband, Jack, she left a message for him on their home answering machine: "Hey, I just want to let you know I'm on the eight o'clock instead of the nine-twenty." By a quirk of fate—and traffic—she got a seat on Flight 93.

Jeremy Glick already was a day late, and now he was agitated. The new father had expected to head to San Francisco for a business meeting on September 10, but a fire at the Newark Airport disrupted service and cancelled flights. Given the option to take a later flight that would have arrived in California at 2:00 a.m., Jeremy declined. "Screw it," he told his wife, Lyz, who was visiting her parents with their three-month-old daughter, Emmy. "I'm going to go home, get a good night's sleep, and I'll just get up early tomorrow." A travel snag put him on Flight 93.

As it turned out, more than ten of the passengers who boarded Flight 93 that morning had been booked on other flights or made last-minute calls to reserve their seats. Tom Burnett and Donald and Jean Peterson all had tickets for later departures. For many of them, the opportunity to leave early was a welcome surprise. Georgine Corrigan, an antiques dealer from Hawaii, was scheduled to make two stops just to get to San Francisco on her way home to Honolulu. When she arrived at check-in, she realized she could transfer to a nonstop flight and reduce her travel time.

Christine Snyder changed her itinerary three times before settling on Flight 93. Sisters-in-law Patricia Cushing and Jane Folger decided several days earlier to make the switch. Mark Bingham considered flying to the coast on September 10 but woke up with a hangover following a friend's birthday celebration. Nicole Miller missed her connection a day earlier because of weather and chose to wait until the next morning for the trip home. Deora Bodley was scheduled for a later flight but opted to try standby and easily got a seat.

Joey Nacke, manager of a Kay-Bee Toys distribution center in Clinton, New Jersey, had just learned the night before of a work issue in California that required his attention. Ed Felt, a software engineer who usually flew Continental Airlines, booked a seat with United at the last moment to get to a business meeting on the West Coast. Todd Beamer thought of flying a night earlier but wanted to spend more time with his two boys.

Among the crew, flight attendant Wanda Green had been scheduled for duty on September 13 but changed flights for business reasons. She also worked as a real estate broker and wanted to be back in New Jersey for a closing. Debbie Welsh was filling in for another flight attendant who had asked for a day off. Captain Jason Dahl switched to Flight 93 in exchange for time off later in the month. He was planning on taking time to visit his mom in California and then prepare to celebrate his wedding anniversary.

They were forty people from all walks of life, strangers for the most part, traveling to different destinations for different reasons, brought together by sheer happenstance on September 11, 2001.

The four al-Qaeda operatives arrived at the Newark Airport well ahead of their scheduled 8:00 a.m. departure. Haznawi and Ghamdi boarded together at 7:39 a.m. and Nami followed at 7:40 a.m. Jarrah waited a bit longer, perhaps to make a final phone call, entering the Jetway at 7:48 a.m. No doubt, tensions were high. According to the handwritten document distributed to each hijacking team before the mission, they were instructed to recite multiple prayers, review their assignments, and quietly gird themselves for the battle in the sky. But even in those harrowing minutes of impending martyrdom, it would have been impossible for them *not* to notice the size and strength of some of the passengers filing past them.

Jeremy Glick, the 6'1", 220-pound judo champ, would have stood out as a formidable opponent. So, too, would Joey Nacke, the 5'9", 200-pound barrel-chested weight lifter; Todd Beamer, the 6-foot, 200-pound multisport collegiate athlete; and Alan Beaven, the 6'3", 205-pound former Scotland Yard prosecutor.

Taking seats in first class one row behind Ghamdi and Nami were Mark Bingham, the 6'4", 220-pound rugby player, and Tom Burnett, the 6'2", 205-pound former high school quarterback.

In a fair fight, this would have been a mismatch.

But the hijackers knew it wouldn't be. They came armed with a coordinated plan of attack that had been years in the making. They carried knives and a fake bomb to keep passengers at bay. They also had the crucial and overwhelming element of surprise. It had been years since anyone had hijacked a commercial airliner in the United States—and even then the prevailing image was of a hostage situation or a redirection of the plane. No passenger stepped onto a commercial airliner thinking of self-defense, much less a life-and-death fight. And the four hijackers had something that would make them virtually unstoppable: a willingness—a preference, in fact—to die.

> *You should feel complete tranquility, because the time between you and your marriage (in heaven) is very short. Afterwards begins the happy life, where God is satisfied with you . . .*
>
> *Remember the words of Almighty God: "You were looking to the battle before you engaged it, and now you see it with your own two eyes." Remember: "How many small groups beat big groups by the will of God."*

United Flight 93 pulled back from the gate at 8:01 a.m. Then it sat on the tarmac for almost three-quarters of an hour, waiting for its turn to take off.

Any observant passenger, and certainly all of the hijackers, would have noticed that the plane was virtually empty—only 33 regular passengers on an aircraft that could hold 182. It was the lightest load by far of the four targeted flights. Flight 11 had seventy-six passengers, Flight 175 had fifty-one, and Flight 77 had fifty-three. The flight with the smallest hijacking crew also had the least number of potential resisters.

Flight 93 finally took off at 8:42 a.m. The extent of the delay is crucial in the September 11 timeline. Had they departed Newark just a few minutes later, passengers and crew may have spotted a small image off in the distance streaking erratically south toward the New York City skyline. Such a realization might have altered the way that day's events unfolded. As it was, Captain Jason Dahl banked sharply to the left shortly after takeoff and pointed Flight 93 west on its customary flight path to San Francisco. It was 8:44 a.m.

Two minutes later, behind them and out of sight, Flight 11 tore through the sky and smashed into the North Tower of the World Trade Center.

———

Flight 93 soared over Pennsylvania toward the Ohio border, reaching its cruising altitude of 35,000 feet at 9:02 a.m.—just one minute before Flight 175 struck the second tower. Unaware of the terror unfolding in the skies above New York City, first-class flight attendants Debbie Welsh and Wanda Green began their cabin service, offering breakfast to all ten of the passengers in their seating area: Bingham, Burnett, Ed Felt, Joe DeLuca, Linda Gronlund, and Mickey Rothenberg as well as Jarrah, Ghamdi, Haznawi, and Nami, who were offered what they knew would be their last meal.

The extent to which the flight was proceeding normally in the eyes of the crew is reflected in a text message that Dahl sent to United flight dispatcher Ed Ballinger at 9:21 a.m.:

GOOD MORNIN' . . . NICE CLIMB OUTTA EWR [Newark] AFTER A NICE TOUR OF THE APT [apartment] COURTS Y [and] GRND CNTRL . . . AT 350 OCCL LT [occasional light] CHOP. WIND 290/50 AIN'T HELPING. J.

It was a beautiful morning, the kind that pilots describe as "severe clear." The first indication to Dahl and First Officer LeRoy Homer that something was amiss might have come at 9:22 a.m., when Homer's wife, Melodie—having seen media reports from the World Trade Center—asked United to relay a text message to her husband to check on his safety. The text was sent; we don't know if he ever received it.

At 9:24 a.m., Ballinger's own alarming text message arrived in the Flight 93 cockpit: "BEWARE ANY COCKPIT INTROUSION [*sic*] ... TWO AIRCRAFT IN NY, HIT TRADE CENTER BUILDS." After the second plane hit the South Tower at 9:03 a.m., the veteran dispatcher had begun sending warnings to each of his sixteen cross-country flights at 9:19 a.m. But he had done it chronologically, starting with the planes that had been in the air the longest. From his base near Chicago—and on the most bewildering morning of his career—he had no idea which one might be the next hijack. Dahl responded quizzically at 9:26 a.m.: "ED, CONFIRM LATEST MSSG PLZ—JASON." On face value, and with no context or outside information at all, Ballinger's note must have seemed beyond the realm of possibility to Dahl.

By this time, as it was crossing into Ohio airspace, Flight 93 had moved into the area regulated by Cleveland's air traffic control center. At 9:27:25 a.m., Cleveland controller John Werth made a routine transmission to the cockpit, and at 9:27:30 a.m. the pilots responded. It would be the last regular communication from Dahl and Homer.

Within a matter of seconds, the hijackers tied red bandanas around their heads and sprang from their seats. The evidence is that they attacked the pilots by at least 9:28:05 a.m., because the flight plummeted dramatically at that point—a drastic 680 feet in 30 seconds. At 9:28:16 a.m., Cleveland air traffic control heard the first chilling sounds of the battle in the cockpit. "Mayday! ... hey, get out of here!"

Thirty-two seconds later came an even more desperate and garbled refrain. "Get out of here! ... get out of here! ... get out of here!"

John Werth remembered hearing screaming and "just some guttural, guttural sounds."

It is likely that either Dahl or Homer purposely keyed the microphone so sounds of the struggle would be heard by officials on the ground.

"The crew tried to give us some kind of warning," Werth said. The pilots were fighting back in any way they could.

During the next ninety seconds, Werth made seven attempts to contact Flight 93, to no avail. And soon he learned why. At 9:31:57 a.m., an unfamiliar person, speaking thickly accented English and breathing heavily after an apparent struggle, made a transmission that was intended for the passengers but went instead to air traffic control. Mohamed Atta had made the same error on Flight 11. The speaker said: "Ladies and gentlemen: Here the captain. Please sit down keep remaining sitting. We have a bomb on board. So, sit."

Ziad Jarrah was now in control of the plane.

———

Using Ramzi Binalshibh's explanation of the general battle plan on 9/11 and all the clues from calls and transmissions from the flights, we can piece together how the terrorists gained access to the cockpits and seized control of the planes. Binalshibh described a system in which the four muscle hijackers on each flight would be divided into a "break-in team" to storm the cockpit and a "protection team" to deal with the passengers and crew. Once the cockpit was cleared and secured, the trained al-Qaeda pilot would then take command and fly the aircraft into its target.

Seating arrangements alone offer reasonable evidence as to the roles of the muscle hijackers on the first three flights. The pair seated side by side closest to the cockpit would be the break-in team, and two others scattered a few rows back would be the protection team. But Flight 93 is more difficult to analyze. The hijacking team had only four members, not five. That meant there were only three muscle hijackers. Jarrah, Ghamdi, Haznawi, and Nami had to improvise.

Similar to the other flights, two hijackers were seated side by side near the front of first class. It is likely that Nami in 3C and Ghamdi in 3D were designated as the break-in team. But, if so, did that mean that Haznawi in 6B was expected to control the remaining thirty-plus passengers and crew by himself? Or would Jarrah in 1B assist him before taking the controls?

The 9/11 Commission, for its part, does not believe that Jarrah participated in the attacks to take over the plane. The commission members reached this conclusion while investigating yet another puzzle of the flight—specifically, why multiple passengers making phone calls to their loved ones described seeing *three* hijackers, not four. Among the random scenarios proposed was that one of the hijackers had been given access to a cockpit jump seat from the outset of the flight and therefore already was in the cockpit when the attack commenced. The commission says it found no evidence to support this claim, certain that "Jarrah, the crucial pilot-trained member of their team, remained seated and inconspicuous until after the cockpit was seized; and once inside, he would not have been visible to the passengers."

Indeed, it is unlikely that the hijackers would have taken the risk of exposing Jarrah to injury in their bloody knife assault on Dahl and Homer. Jarrah was irreplaceable, the only one among them who was trained to fly a plane. Another possibility is that Jarrah remained seated during the attack but then helped drag the dead or wounded pilots out of the cockpit. Certainly some type of strenuous physical activity must explain why he was panting during that first audio message. Almost thirteen years later, the precise method of takeover remains one of the enduring and unsolvable mysteries of Flight 93.

***

Ziad Jarrah's time in the pilot's seat began with a steady ascent over Ohio, still facing west. Though the plane had dropped dramatically when the cockpit was attacked, it still was at 34,315 feet when it stabilized, not far from its cruising altitude of 35,000 feet. It soon headed back up.

At 9:35 a.m., Jarrah began to turn to the southeast, just three minutes after making his first audio transmission. He still was climbing. Information obtained from the "black boxes" recovered at the crash site—the flight data recorder and the cockpit voice recorder—offer a certified record of the location, altitude, and direction of the aircraft and voices and other sounds from the cockpit. As Jarrah maneuvered Flight 93 in the general direction of Washington, DC, he took the plane up to 40,700 feet at 9:39 a.m.

before beginning an uneven and uncommonly rapid descent that had to be terrifying to everyone in the cabin.

Aside from the fact that he was flying a Boeing 757 for the first time of his life, Jarrah may have had another reason to be distracted.

Starting at 9:32:09 a.m., the voice recorder revealed a flurry of unusual directives from the cockpit:

"Don't move! Shut up. Come on, Come. Shut up!

"Don't move! Stop! Sit, sit, sit down!

"Stop!"

One of the muscle hijackers, probably Saeed al Ghamdi, was seated next to Jarrah to provide protection and support in the unlikely event of a passenger uprising, but confrontational commands such as these clearly weren't directed at fellow al-Qaeda members. At 9:33:43 a.m., the harangue continued:

"Finish, no more. NO MORE! . . .

"Down! Go ahead, lie down. Lie down!

"Down, down DOWN!"

Someone else was still alive in the cockpit—and apparently not following orders.

About a minute later, a voice identified in the transcript as a "Female native English-speaking person" is heard for the first time:

"Please, please, please . . . Please, please, don't hurt me . . . Oh, God!"

Investigators believe this was one of the first-class flight attendants, either Debbie Welsh or Wanda Green. One of the most common theories of how the hijackers began their attacks on all the September 11 flights was by stabbing or physically threatening the flight attendants. Reports from aboard American Flight 11 indicate that two of the flight attendants were stabbed. At least one of the callers from Flight 93 also said a flight attendant was stabbed.

At 9:35:03 a.m., as Flight 93 continued its turn toward the southeast and kept climbing, the hijacker commands continued:

"No more. Down, down, down!

"No, no, no, no, no, no.

"Sit down, sit down, sit down! DOWN!"

The attendant spoke again at 9:35:24 a.m., saying, "Are you talking to me?" and then—chillingly—"I don't want to die."

"No, no. Down, DOWN!"

"I don't want to die. I don't want to die . . . No, no please."

The transcript of the voice recorder describes the "sound of a snap." Over the next half minute, it identifies, "The sound of a female crying. And a struggle that lasted for a few seconds. . . . The sound of a struggle with a female."

By 9:37 a.m., the protests had ended. "Everything is fine. I finished," the hijacker (likely Ghamdi) coldly said. There were no more sounds from the female flight attendant. It is likely she was killed at this point.

Jarrah now had the plane turned around and heading east, whisking back across Ohio toward the Pennsylvania border. At 9:39 a.m., he made his second attempt at a transmission—this time in a much calmer and more measured voice. He supplied more information to continue the deception and discourage any resistance. It, too, went by accident to air traffic control: "Ah. Here's the captain. I would like you all to remain seated. We have a bomb aboard and we are going back to the airport and we have our demands. So, please remain quiet."

Passengers and crew who flew United Airlines in 2001 had the ability to make air-to-ground phone calls with a specific brand of air-telephone technology known as the Verizon Airfone. There were two Airfones located in seat-backs in each row in coach—one for seats A-B-C and another for seats D-E-F.

On any normal day, this system was intended as nothing more than a perk of modern aviation—an ability to stay connected even while cruising at 35,000 feet. But September 11 had long ceased to be a normal day.

In a period of about thirty minutes starting immediately after the hijacking of Flight 93, twelve people on board made a total of thirty-five phone calls from the Airfones located between rows twenty-three and thirty-four. Reception from the air was often spotty and unreliable, and twenty of those calls were disconnected so quickly that no conversation was possible. But fifteen got through. Those calls provide an enormous amount of insight into how events unfolded that morning.

The passengers and flight attendants reached family members to report what one called "a little problem," to express their love—and in some cases to say emotional good-byes. But an unintended consequence—one that benefitted them and the nation—was that the information ended up going the other way. The people on board actually *gathered* information from loved ones about events in New York and Washington that shaped their actions in the frenetic minutes that followed. Flight 93 had taken off minutes before the first plane plowed into the North Tower of the World Trade Center. Passengers and crew initially had no idea that their hijacking was part of a well-coordinated terrorist attack taking place that morning in America's skies. They must have thought they were the only one.

By the time they started making phone calls, however, a second plane had crashed in New York City, and a third was streaking in the wrong direction toward Washington, DC. America was at war—and their family members, like millions of other Americans, were glued to the network coverage. Just about the only people who didn't know about it were up in the air—and quickly becoming part of it.

Starting at about 9:30 a.m., Tom Burnett, moving between rows twenty-four and twenty-five, placed a series of brief phone calls to his wife, Deena, at their home in San Ramon, California. A former flight attendant, Deena had been keeping a nervous eye on television reports from New York while preparing breakfast for their three girls and getting the youngest, Anna Clare, ready for her first day of preschool.

"Tom, are you ok?" Deena asked.

"No, I'm not," he said. The reply must have stunned her. "I'm on an airplane that's been hijacked . . . the hijackers have already knifed a guy . . . they're telling us there's a bomb on board. Please call the authorities." He said he would call back.

Flight attendant Sandy Bradshaw was the first to report the hijacking directly to United Airlines. She called a Speed Dial Fix number from row thirty-three at 9:35 a.m. and got through to the United maintenance facility in San Francisco; she told a manager that assailants had taken over the cockpit and some were in the cabin behind the first-class curtain.

Everyone else had been moved to the back of the plane. Bradshaw reported the hijackers had pulled a knife, killed a flight attendant (likely the attendant heard on the voice recorder in the cockpit), and announced that they had a bomb. Sandy stayed on the line for almost six minutes. The manager described her voice and demeanor as "shockingly calm." It was a common refrain from authorities about the poise and professionalism of the crew members on all four flights that day.

In addition to Tom Burnett, two other passengers made contact with loved ones in the first ten minutes after the hijacking. Mark Bingham reached his mother, Alice Hoglan, at her brother's home in Saratoga, California. Jeremy Glick talked with his wife, Lyz, who was visiting her parents in Windham, New York.

Bingham, calling from row twenty-five, spoke first to his aunt. In a composed voice, he told her that his plane had been hijacked. He specifically identified the flight as "United Flight 93." It was not until Alice came to the phone that Mark began to show the tension that had been building among the passengers since the terrorists struck.

"Mom," he said, "this is Mark Bingham." The stress caused him to address his own mother using his full name.

"I want to let you know I love you. I love you all . . . I'm on a flight from Newark to San Francisco and there are three guys who have taken over the plane and they say they have a bomb. I'm calling you from the Airfone."

"Who are they, Mark?" Alice asked.

Bingham seemed distracted and didn't answer.

"You've got to believe me," he said. "It's true."

"I do believe you, Mark. Who are these guys?"

There was no reply. Alice heard murmurs in the background, but no screams. People were talking among themselves, sharing information. Perhaps they were in the early stages of planning their strategy. Then the connection was lost.

Jeremy Glick called his wife, Lyz, from row twenty-seven. Her father answered the phone and said, "Thank God it's you." The family was aware of the other plane hijackings and crashes. Hearing Jeremy's voice was good news—or so it seemed.

Lyz grabbed the phone. "Jer?"

"Hi. Listen, there are some bad men on the plane."

"What do you mean?"

"These three Iranian guys took over the plane. They put on these red headbands."

The hijackers had stood up and yelled and run into the cockpit, Jeremy said. "We didn't hear from the pilots after that." One of the hijackers said he had a bomb in a red box and another had a knife. They were threatening to blow up the plane.

Lyz began to cry. She described herself as "not completely irrational but on the cusp." Processing the information in a matter of seconds was impossible. There was no precedent for this—no instructions on how to speak to your husband during a hijacking that might end in a crash. "Physically" she said, "I was shaking and nauseous."

They both said they loved each other, over and over. "I don't think I'm going to make it out of here. I don't want to die," Jeremy said. Lyz tried to calm him. "Put a picture of me and Emmy in your head and only have really good thoughts," she said.

Jeremy was preparing for the worst, just in case. "You've got to promise me you're going to be happy," he said. "For Emmy to know how much I love her. And (that) whatever decisions you make in your life, no matter what, I'll support you."

Tom Burnett made another call to Deena, informing her that the passenger who had been knifed was now dead. He had tried to help him but it was too late; he couldn't get a pulse. This almost certainly was Mickey Rothenberg. There were six regular passengers seated in first class among the hijackers when the takeover began, and Mickey was the only one who didn't make a phone call later in the flight.

Mickey had been seated in 5B, directly in front of muscle hijacker Ahmed al Haznawi in 6B. It is possible that he was assaulted because he put up some resistance and had to be silenced. It also may have been part of a pre-arranged al-Qaeda tactic to draw immediate blood and frighten the other passengers. Barely an hour earlier on Flight 11, Satam al Suqami in seat 10B stabbed passenger Daniel Lewin, who was seated directly in front of him in 9B.

The flight had turned back toward the east by now, and even if the passengers and crew couldn't guess their direction or destination, they certainly knew they were no longer headed to San Francisco. They were starting to descend—rapidly at times. The lack of control must have been staggering. But it also was at about this time that they got the first clear indication of what the men in the red bandanas had been planning. They weren't going back to the airport, any airport. In fact, they weren't going to land at all.

"Tom," Deena said, "they are hijacking planes all up and down the East Coast. They are taking them and hitting designated targets. They've already hit both towers of the World Trade Center."

Her husband got quiet for a moment. She thought she might have lost the connection. "They're talking about crashing this plane," Tom said. "It's a suicide mission!" Burnett put it all together in that instant; the realization must have absolutely leveled him.

CHAPTER NINE

"We're Going to Do Something"

Scattered among twelve rows in the back of the plane, other passengers attempted to place calls to loved ones. Lauren Grandcolas dialed her husband, Jack, in San Rafael, California, and Linda Gronlund tried to reach her sister, Elsa Strong, in New Hampshire. Neither answered—but both passengers were able to leave voice messages.

"Honey, are you there? Jack, pick up sweetie," Lauren said. It was 9:39 a.m. when the call was made—just 6:39 a.m. at the Grandcolas home on the West Coast. She left a message:

> *OK, well I just wanted to tell you that I love you. We're having a little problem on the plane. I'm totally fine. I love you more than anything, just know that. I'm comfortable and I'm OK for now. I'll, I . . . just a little problem. I love you. Please tell my family I love them, too. Bye, honey.*

Lauren attempted seven more calls in the next four minutes, including one to her sister Vaughn, but none of them connected for more than seven seconds.

Several people on board said the hijackers never tried to stop them from using Airfones. Perhaps there just weren't enough men to prevent it; perhaps Atta and Binalshibh may not have considered the threat of passengers receiving information from loved ones on the ground and then planning a counterattack. Airfone technology allowed only eight calls to be placed from one airplane at the same time, but the outreach from the doomed flight to homes across America continued unabated. Joe

DeLuca, Linda Gronlund's traveling companion, called his father from row twenty-six at 9:43 a.m. and spoke for about two minutes, telling him the plane had been hijacked. When Joe was finished, Linda used the same Airfone to call her sister and leave a message:

It's Lynn. Um, I only have a minute. I'm on United 93 and it's been hijacked, uh, by terrorists who say they have a bomb. Apparently, they, flown [sic] a couple of planes into the World Trade Center already and it looks like they're going to take this one down as well. Mostly, I just wanted to say I love you . . . and . . . I'm going to miss you . . . and . . . and please give my love to Mom and Dad and . . . mostly, I just love you and I just wanted to tell you that. I don't know if I'm going to get the chance to tell you that again or not . . . Um . . . [unintelligible] All my stuff is in the safe. The, uh, the safe is in my closet in my bedroom. The combination is . . . you push C for clear and then 0-9-1-3 and then, uh, and then it should . . . and maybe pound and then it should unlock . . . I love you and I hope that I can talk to you soon. Bye.

Even in a moment of extreme distress, girding herself for a violent death, Linda had the presence of mind to provide her sister with the secret combination of her safe. At many points that day, passengers and crew were thinking of their families more than themselves. They didn't want their loved ones to worry. Flight attendant CeeCee Lyles, the former police officer from Fort Pierce, Florida, was a few rows back in row thirty-two, trying frantically to reach her husband, Lorne. She was sitting across the aisle from passenger Todd Beamer, who also was making calls. When Lorne Lyles didn't pick up the phone, CeeCee also left a message:

Hi, Baby. I'm . . . Baby, you have to listen to me carefully. I'm on a plane that's been hijacked. I'm on the plane. I'm calling from the plane. I want to tell you I love you. Please tell my children that I love them very much and I'm so sorry, babe. Umm. I don't know what to say. There's three guys. They've hijacked the plane. I'm trying to be calm. We've turned around and I've heard that there's planes that's been,

been flown into the World Trade Center. I hope to be able to see your
face again, baby. I love you. Good-bye.

—◆—

"We have a bomb aboard and we are going back to the airport."

The transmission made by Ziad Jarrah at 9:39 a.m. was likely never heard by the passengers of Flight 93. Such an announcement surely would have been mentioned in passengers' phone calls to loved ones—and it wasn't. But the ominous message came crackling into headquarters of air traffic control in Cleveland, stunning controllers who were already struggling to make sense of the terror in the sky. *A bomb?* Probably out of shock, and a little bit out of helplessness, they could do little but request a clarification from the cockpit:

"Ok, that's United ninety three calling?

"United ninety three, understand you have a bomb on board, go ahead.

"United ninety three, go ahead.

"United ninety three, go ahead.

"United ninety three, do you hear Cleveland Center?"

Unsurprisingly, there was no response from the cockpit. Jarrah had zero interest in communicating with FAA employees on the ground. At 9:41 a.m., he attempted to make their job more difficult by turning off the transponder, which sends out a signal identifying a plane in flight. Cleveland Center was still able to track the aircraft using radar, as John Werth and others scrambled to match readings and visual sightings from planes in the immediate area. But it was yet another sign that this was not a traditional hijacking.

An even bigger challenge for Werth and air traffic controllers across the country came at 9:42 a.m., when the FAA ordered all commercial and private aircraft in US airspace to land at the nearest airport. This move was unprecedented in the history of American aviation. Ben Sliney, national operations manager at the Air Traffic Control System Command Center in Herndon, Virginia, issued the directive shortly after Flight 77 struck the Pentagon: "Order everyone to land!" Sliney reportedly yelled. "Let's get them on the ground!"

That morning, the men and women in the nation's control towers became another set of unsung heroes, drawing on their vast reservoir of skill, poise, experience, and creativity—under unimaginable pressure—to do something that up to that point had never been even attempted: successfully guide an estimated 4,500 planes all over the country to new destinations during the next two hours.

But one rogue aircraft over Ohio refused to cooperate. It kept speeding along defiantly, locked in on its own freelance flight path toward Washington, DC.

"United ninety three, do you still hear the center?

"United ninety three, do you still hear Cleveland?

"United ninety three, United niner three, do you still hear Cleveland?

"United ninety three, United ninety three, Cleveland.

"United ninety three, United ninety three, do you hear Cleveland center?"

Shortly after hearing sounds of the initial assault, Werth had warned his supervisor, "We're not talking to the pilots anymore." Yet he kept sending probing messages to the cockpit out of raw desperation. "He was still on my frequency, so I kept trying to call him periodically just to see if [he would respond]," the veteran controller later said. "I really never expected a response. But it's the only thing you can do."

Todd Beamer, now relocated to row thirty-two in the back of the plane, desperately wanted to talk to *someone* on the ground, anyone. The business trip was supposed to be a quick one for him—he had planned to return to New Jersey on a red-eye flight that same night. Beamer had considered flying to San Francisco the day before but decided against it, opting to spend some time with his two young boys.

On the other side of row thirty-two, across the aisle from flight attendant CeeCee Lyles, Todd attempted four calls in rapid succession from the Airfone. The first three calls didn't connect. Two were to an AT&T 1-800 number. Another was to his home in Cranbury, New Jersey. Finally, just before 9:44 a.m., he successfully reached the GTE-Verizon call center in Chicago, where a company representative—overwhelmed by the information Todd provided—transferred the call to supervisor Lisa Jefferson. The ensuing conversation between Lisa and Todd became an integral part of the national narrative in the days and weeks following September 11.

"Can you explain to me in detail exactly what's taking place?" Lisa asked in a calming voice.

He could. Todd told her that three men had hijacked the plane and two were now in the cockpit. "They're flying the plane," he said. Two of the hijackers had knives and one had what looked like a bomb strapped to his waist with a red belt. They'd closed the curtain between first class and coach so that the passengers could no longer see into the first-class cabin.

"They've ordered everyone to sit down," Todd said. "The flight attendants were standing. The hijackers ordered them to sit, and one [CeeCee Lyles] just happened to sit next to me. That's how I'm getting my information."

One of the most valuable bits of news Todd provided was about the pilots. As with the three previous flights, it was assumed that the captain and first officer were killed or incapacitated when the knife-wielding hijackers attacked the cockpit. Jeremy Glick told his wife the pilots hadn't been heard from since the hijackers struck, but, curiously, no other caller mentioned them until Todd's call with Lisa Jefferson.

Relaying a description that most likely came from CeeCee Lyles, Todd said that two people were lying on the floor of first class, injured and possibly dead. It was probably Captain Dahl and First Officer Homer.

As the plane careened across Ohio toward the Pennsylvania line, the fact that Flight 93 was now being piloted by an amateur was readily apparent to those in the cabin. In swift descent for six minutes since turning around at 9:39 a.m., the plane began an especially heart-throbbing plunge about a minute and a half into Todd's call.

"Oh my God, we're going down! We're going down! Jesus help us!"

Lisa Jefferson heard screams and loud gasps in the background. She would later describe the sounds as "desperate, anguished cries for help from people clinging to a sheer thread of life."

"Oh my God, Jesus!" Todd shrieked. "Oh my God!"

Another man in a baritone voice, yelled, "Oh, no! No! God, no!"

And then—in an instant—the screaming stopped.

"No, wait. We're coming back up," Todd said. "I think we're okay now."

He asked Lisa to recite the Lord's Prayer with him. She did:

Our Father who art in Heaven,
Hallowed be thy name.
Thy kingdom come.
Thy will be done in earth,
As it is in heaven.
Give us this day our daily bread.
And forgive us our trespasses
As we forgive those who trespass against us.
And lead us not into temptation,
But deliver us from evil:
For thine is the kindgom, and the power,
And the glory, forever, Amen.

The explanation for the plane's sudden spasm during Beamer's call with Jefferson was provided later by the flight data recorder and the NTSB's animation of the flight path. Flight 93 had descended more than 20,000 feet from a peak of 40,700 feet between 9:39 and 9:45 a.m. Some dips were steeper than others. At that point, it leveled off briefly at an altitude of 19,100 feet. The pause was followed by a temporary climb to 20,500 feet in the next minute ("we're coming back up"), and then yet another descent.

Ziad Jarrah was having obvious trouble flying the plane. He was the only one of the four September 11 hijacker pilots who hadn't earned a commercial pilot's license, and he'd devoted less time to training than the others. As recently as July, his al-Qaeda handlers were worried that he might remove himself from the mission. He'd called Aysel Senguen the morning of the attacks to tell her that he loved her. In hindsight, it is not surprising that he had difficulty manning the controls that morning.

At 9:45 a.m., with the plane's altitude dropping quickly, Jarrah and Ghamdi discussed whether they should bring Nami and Haznawi into the cockpit. It was a curious exchange.

"How about we let them in?" Ghamdi asked in Arabic. "We let the guys in now . . . Should we let the guys in?"

"Inform them," Jarrah said, "and tell him to talk to the pilot. Bring the pilot back."

This sudden and unexpected reference to the "pilot" on the cockpit voice recorder is very revealing—on several fronts. It underscored the notion that Jarrah was overmatched by the Boeing 757. It also was apparent confirmation that at least one of the United pilots—either Captain Dahl or First Officer Homer—was still alive, and likely in the first-class cabin. Just a few minutes earlier, according to the transcript, someone described as a "low-pitch native English-speaking male" had said, "Oh, man!" Could that have been either Dahl or Homer? Was one of them lying near the cockpit door, wounded but still fighting for life?

The mystery, like many others in the saga of Flight 93, can never be untangled. No one ever was brought to the cockpit to assist with the aircraft's operation, and the hijackers never mentioned "the pilot" again.

Jarrah, overwhelmed but still alone at the controls, invoked religion rather than ask for assistance. The plane finally had been stabilized by 9:46 a.m. before beginning another more gradual descent. Speaking in Arabic, Jarrah said, "In the name of Allah. In the name of Allah. I bear witness that there is no other God but Allah."

Jeremy Glick and Todd Beamer both remained on the phone until the moment they charged the cockpit; Tom Burnett also made several more calls to his wife in California in the minutes before the assault.

But while the three men collected information from the ground that was essential to their planning, their conversations also became highly personal at times.

"Where are the kids?" Tom asked Deena at one point. He no doubt had an image in his mind of twin daughters Halley and Madison as well as little Anna Clare.

"They're fine. They're sitting at the table having breakfast. They're asking to talk to you."

"Tell them I'll talk to them later."

"I called your parents. They know your plane has been hijacked."

"Oh . . . you shouldn't have worried them." Burnett again echoed a common sentiment that day—at their moment of crisis, passengers were continually looking out for their loved ones.

Todd Beamer was in a different situation, connected to a total stranger through nothing but her voice, but it must have been calming to speak about his family. He informed Lisa Jefferson about his wife—he expressed surprise that the two shared the name Lisa—and their two young boys, David and Andrew. He told Jefferson that Lisa was pregnant with their third child, who was due in January. He passed on his home phone number, just in case.

"If I don't make it through this, will you do me a favor?" Todd asked. "Would you tell my wife and family how much I love them?" Jefferson said she would.

Other passengers and crew members also continued to place calls as the plane veered menacingly toward Pennsylvania. Among them were Waleska Martinez and Marion Britton, coworkers at the New York office of the Census Bureau and now contemplating their shared fate one row apart. Waleska dialed a friend's office in Manhattan but couldn't make a connection. Marion tried her friend Fred Fiumano at his auto repair shop in Queens—and got through.

Marion said her plane was hijacked and "they've slit two people's throats already. They killed two people on the plane." Fiumano tried to calm her down by saying the hijackers were taking them on a joyride, maybe to another country. Fiumano saw no need to compound what was obviously the tensest moment of his friend's life. ("What was I gonna say?" he later told *Vanity Fair* magazine.)

But Marion wasn't persuaded. "We're going to go down," she said, "and we're going to crash."

Marion, using the Airfone in row thirty-three A-B-C, spoke with Fiumano for almost four minutes. Then she handed the phone to a passenger seated in the same row, Elizabeth Wainio, urging her to call her family.

Elizabeth was twenty-seven years old and a rising star in the business world, the manager of Discovery Channel stores in the lucrative New York/New Jersey region. She reached her stepmother, Esther Heymann, in Catonsville, Maryland. Elizabeth relayed the horror of what was happening on her flight.

"Elizabeth, I've got my arms around you, and I'm holding you, and I love you," her stepmother said.

"I can feel your arms around me. And I love you, too."

Overwhelmed, they both stopped talking for a moment. Elizabeth worried about how her family would react to the inevitable news. "It just makes me so sad," she said, "knowing how much harder this is going to be on you than it is for me."

Flight attendant Sandy Bradshaw, seated across the aisle from Elizabeth and Marion in row thirty-three, dialed her husband, Phil, at home in North Carolina. It was Sandy who had called the United Airlines maintenance office in San Francisco earlier to alert them of the hijacking. Phil was a pilot for US Airways. He was aware that two planes had crashed into the World Trade Center. Now he was getting the shocking word that his wife's flight was under siege. Sandy described the hijackers as three men with dark skin wearing red bandanas and carrying knives. She told Phil she wasn't sure of the location of the plane but that they'd just passed over a river. She thought it might be the Mississippi, but Flight 93 never made it west of Cleveland. Sandy probably saw one of the three rivers that intersect at Pittsburgh—most likely the Ohio.

"We were talking about the kids, and I think she knew she was going to die," Phil said later, "but she was very calm and very relaxed. We were talking about each other and how much we loved each other, and she wanted me to raise the kids right."

Reports of a third plane crash, this one near Washington, DC, caused yet another spike in tension among the passengers and crew in the back of the aircraft. Flight 77 had slammed into the Pentagon at 9:37 a.m. and the news spread quickly, adding a new dimension to the panic. The carnage was no longer limited to the Manhattan skyline. The country's military nerve center had come under attack. No city, no building, no person seemed safe.

"They just hit the Pentagon," Deena Burnett told Tom.

"The Pentagon," Lyz Glick told Jeremy.

If there was a singular moment that galvanized the passengers and crew and gave them a clear sense of destiny as they crossed the Pennsylvania border, this was it. The hijackers had no intention of landing the plane and issuing a list of demands. The growing sense among the passengers was that the "bomb" being flaunted was likely a fake, meant only to frighten and subdue the captives on board. The Twin Towers had been hit; the Pentagon was in flames. A horrendous death beckoned. The only option left was to try to take back the plane.

Tom Burnett said they were putting together a plan. "We have to do something," he told Deena. She asked who was helping him. "Different people. Several people. There's a group of us."

Jeremy Glick knew they couldn't wait any longer. They'd placed calls, traded ideas, and mulled their fate. "I'm going to take a vote," he said. "There's three guys as big as me and we're thinking of attacking the guy with the bomb."

Lyz asked him if the hijackers had weapons, maybe guns. No, he said. Just knives. Jeremy paused. He considered what he might use for a weapon. "I still have my butter knife from breakfast," he mused. The Glicks shared a tense laugh together.

Five rows back, Todd Beamer told Lisa Jefferson about the surreal scene unfolding on the plane. "A few of us passengers are getting together. I think we're going to jump the guy with the bomb."

"Are you sure that's what you want to do?" she asked.

"Yes," Todd said. "I'm going to have to go out on faith. At this point, I don't have much of a choice."

But of course he did.

They all did.

It could not have been an easy decision to make. They were going to join a group of strangers for a frontal assault in a narrow airplane aisle against hijackers armed with knives and willing to martyr themselves. The men of al-Qaeda long ago chose death as their preferred option. The odds were stacked. But the passengers and crew of Flight 93 would not just sit there and accept their fate.

It was 9:53 a.m. In the cockpit, Ziad Jarrah and Saeed al Ghamdi began to sense the possibility of a passenger revolt.

Ahmed al Haznawi and Ahmed al Nami, still standing guard, would have told them by now about the multiple phone calls, the small-group meetings, the desperate glares. For reasons that never can be explained, the Flight 93 hijackers had waited forty-six minutes after takeoff before mounting their attack—fifteen minutes longer than any of the other flights. That, coupled with the delay in takeoff, gave the passengers and crew a crucial window to learn and digest the news of the day. Jarrah knew they were still about half an hour from their target. The jittery hijackers considered an amateurish plan to use the plane's fire ax, holding it against the peephole of the cockpit door—as though that alone might have terrified the passengers and blunted a counterattack. The cockpit recorder picked up Ghamdi saying, "The best thing: The guys will go in, [you] lift up the [unintelligible] and they put the ax into it. So, everyone will be scared."

It was sometime in the next four minutes that the passengers and crew plotted the final details of their uprising. We don't know the precise battle plan they developed. We don't even know how many took part. Burnett, Glick, and Beamer spoke directly of an attempt to retake the plane, so we can be virtually certain that they were key figures in the assault. Bingham didn't mention an attack in the lone conversation with his mom, but that call had taken place at 9:37 a.m., well before the plan for a counteroffensive had been developed. Bingham was an elite athlete with a willingness to take risks—the rugby star had jumped off cliffs and run with the bulls in Pamplona. He fit Jeremy Glick's description of "three guys as big as me" who were gearing up to charge the hijackers. The consensus is that Burnett, Glick, Beamer, and Bingham were all part of the attack.

Surely there were others beyond those four. Joey Nacke was a weight lifter who didn't take any guff. He once told his wife, "No one will ever take me down without a fight." Richard Guadagno was trained in hand-to-hand combat as a federal law-enforcement officer and could bench-press 350 pounds. Alan Beaven was 6' 3" and 205 pounds, described by a friend as a "sleeping volcano." Toshiya Kuge was a twenty-year-old athlete who played American football in Japan. These were men who would have fought for their lives. And likely did.

Although no one mentioned the presence of a licensed pilot on board in calls to loved ones on the ground, the passengers probably learned that Don Greene had a license to fly small planes—and, therefore, would have been an essential part of any plan to regain control of the cockpit and land Flight 93. Don could fly single-engine aircraft and twin-engine turboprops. In that sense, he had no more experience operating a Boeing 757 than Ziad Jarrah did. But Don understood aviation and was an executive for a company called Safe Flight Instrument Corp. On a clear day such as this, and with detailed instruction each step of the way from air traffic control, he *might* have been able to land the plane safely. Sonny Garcia, a former air traffic controller for the California Air National Guard, could have offered some assistance. Between the two of them, Flight 93 would have had at least a fighting chance to land.

The leaders of the passenger insurgency gathered in or around the center aisle. Flight attendant Sandy Bradshaw was at the back of the plane preparing hot water to throw on the hijackers. Some investigators believe they also commandeered a food cart to use as a battering ram against the cockpit door.

The United States' fight against terrorism would officially be launched four weeks later in Afghanistan, but, in actuality, it began right there in the coach cabin of United Flight 93.

"I'm going to put the phone down," Jeremy Glick told Lyz. "I'm going to leave it here, and I'm going to come right back to it."

"I'll be home for dinner," Tom Burnett told Deena. "I may be late, but I'll be home. . . . Don't worry. We're going to do something."

At her office in Chicago, operator Lisa Jefferson listened intently as Todd Beamer cut short their conversation and turned away from the phone.

"Are you ready?" Todd said. "OK. Let's roll."

～～

The counterattack began at 9:57 a.m. Never before in the history of commercial aviation had unarmed passengers been so bold as to assault armed hijackers in midflight. Elizabeth Wainio was still on the phone to her stepmother in Maryland. "They're getting ready to break into the cockpit," Elizabeth said. "I have to go. I love you. Good-bye."

"Phil!" Sandy Bradshaw said to her husband in North Carolina. "Everyone's running to first class. I've got to go. Bye."

And so they thundered down the narrow single aisle of the 757, a tidal wave of angry humanity—husbands, fathers, brothers, sisters, sons, and daughters—barreling toward the cockpit and their only hope for salvation. If Haznawi was indeed the hijacker wearing the fake bomb, he would have been the first to go down. Almost immediately, Jarrah and Ghamdi heard sounds of a struggle in the cabin. They were having enough problems just flying the plane. The ruckus outside the cockpit door must have been unnerving.

"Is there something?" Jarrah asked at 9:57:55 a.m. "A fight?"

The transcript of the voice recorder then notes "the sound of a male scream from a distance," and fighting in the background.

"Let's go guys!" Jarrah implored in Arabic. "Allah is the Greatest. Allah is the Greatest. Oh guys! Allah is the greatest."

The final two phone calls from Flight 93 were made at 9:58 a.m., when the plane was barely at 5,000 feet. Both were from cell phones. Ed Felt dialed 911 from a lavatory in the back of the plane and reached a dispatcher in nearby Westmoreland County. Felt provided the basic details of the hijacking, giving local authorities their first report of the events unfolding in the skies above Pennsylvania. CeeCee Lyles called her husband in Florida. She had left a message earlier. This time, Lorne Lyles answered the phone. CeeCee told him about the hijacking. Then she shouted, "I think they're going to do it! Babe, they're forcing their way into the cockpit . . ."

Up front, the cockpit voice recorder picked up more sounds of the frenzied struggle. Jarrah began jerking the yoke from right to left in an effort to throw the passengers off balance, causing the plane to rock its wings. Then one of the passengers up front—most likely Burnett—issued the battle cry: "In the cockpit! In the cockpit!"

Jarrah, flustered now, yelled in Arabic, "They want to get in there. Hold [the door] . . . hold from the inside. Hold from the inside. Hold."

The battle had reached the cockpit door. Jarrah kept rocking the wings as the plane dipped below 5,000 feet, determined to knock his assailants off balance and disrupt the attack. The passengers were still outmatched, weaponless, and at the mercy of a suicidal pilot; but they had strength in numbers and maybe even momentum on their side. Jarrah knew it. "There are some guys," he said to Ghamdi. "All those guys."

"Let's get them!" one of the male passengers shouted.

At 9:59:50 a.m., Jarrah changed tactics and began pitching the nose up and down. The plane started to climb again. There were thumps and snaps and crashes in the background. Three times in a period of five seconds there were shouts of pain or distress from one of the hijackers. This is when the passengers may have taken down the other muscle hijacker, Ahmed al Nami.

Just after 10:00 a.m., with the muscle hijackers under assault, the terrorists in the cockpit discussed crashing the plane on their own. However, this was not a sign of panic; in fact, it had been part of the al-Qaeda game plan were things to go awry.

Months before the mission, Mohamed Atta had instructed each pilot to intentionally bring down the aircraft if he could not reach his assigned target. To emphasize the point, Atta had told Ramzi Binalshibh that he would crash his plane into the streets of New York City if he could not hit the World Trade Center.

"Is that it? Shall we finish it off?" Jarrah asked.

"No. Not yet," Ghamdi said. "When they all come, we finish it off."

"Oh Allah!" Jarrah yelled. "Oh Allah! Oh gracious!"

Flight 93 dipped yet again; one of the male passengers could be heard screaming, "Ah! I'm injured." It may have been the first casualty the passengers had taken since the counterattack began three minutes earlier. They'd been unable to break through by this point, and the hijackers still had control of the plane. "In the cockpit!" a male passenger bellowed at 10:00:25 a.m., perhaps signaling a final push, perhaps entreating other passengers who hadn't been part of the first counterattack. "If we don't, we'll die!"

Jarrah, aware by now that the attackers were not being deterred, issued some frantic instructions of his own, addressing Ghamdi by name for the first time. "Up, down. Saeed, up down!"

Five seconds later, a passenger yelled "Roll it!"—possibly referring to the food cart. There were loud sounds of plates and glass crashing all around.

～

With Jarrah still alternately pitching and rocking, the plane began to rise once more at 10:01 a.m.

"Is that it?" Jarrah said. "I mean, shall we pull it down?"

"Yes," Ghamdi said, "put it in and pull it down."

There was even more clatter—crashes and grunts and shrieks and snaps. The hijackers must've known they were going to be overwhelmed if they allowed the fight to continue.

"Saeed!" Jarrah yelled in desperation. "Cut off the oxygen! Cut off the oxygen! Cut off the oxygen! Cut off the oxygen!"

Defiant, the passengers kept coming. "Go! Go!" one of them yelled. "Move, move."

Then, at 10:02:17 a.m., the voice recorder transcript describes a "very loud shout" by a male passenger: "Turn it up!"

Turn it up? Is this evidence that they had breached the cockpit and attempted to start gaining altitude? It is possible—maybe even likely. The "very loud shout" was picked up by a cockpit microphone, so, at the very least, the door must have been jarred open. And there seemed to be a struggle for control. Only one second after a passenger yelled, "Turn it up!" either Jarrah or Ghamdi yelled, in Arabic, "Down, down. Pull it down! Pull it down!"

Turn it up. Pull it down.

Seconds later, at 10:02:33 a.m., there was another desperate plea in Arabic, believed to be from Ghamdi: "Hey! Hey! Give it to me. Give it to me. Give it to me. Give it to me. Give it to me. Give it to me. Give it to me. Give it to me."

The passengers were probably in the cockpit by now, manhandling Jarrah. Maybe Ghamdi was somehow trying to grab the controls. But by this point, it was too late for all of them. Flight 93 was in a death plunge over rural Somerset County, Pennsylvania.

At 10:03:02 a.m., one of the hijackers said, "Allah is the Greatest! Allah is the Greatest! Allah is the Greatest! Allah is the Greatest! Allah is the Greatest!"

A sudden hard turn to the right caused the plane to spin out of control, turning upside-down in midair.

"No!" a male passenger shouted loudly.

At 10:03:09 a.m., one of the hijackers said in a whisper, "Allah is the Greatest! Allah is the Greatest! Allah is the Greatest! Allah is the Greatest!"

Two seconds later, the recording stopped.

CHAPTER TEN

Where Is the Plane?

Paula Pluta knew something was wrong when the walls started to shake.

She was watching television at her home along Lambertsville Road in Stonycreek Township, Pennsylvania, less than half a mile from the site of the old Diamond T strip mine. Paula had taken the day off from her job as a hairdresser, gotten her two kids off to school, prepared a quick breakfast, and remembered settling in for a morning rerun of *Little House on the Prairie*. She had no idea about the horrific scenes on the national news from the World Trade Center in New York City. Until she heard the roar in the skies above her, everything had been quiet and normal. The sudden noise was completely jarring.

It sounded like an airplane, coming low and fast.

"The house started to vibrate and things started rattling and shaking," Paula said. "The noise got louder and louder." Both frightened and curious, she ran to the living-room window. She saw nothing. Then she opened the front door and stepped onto the front porch. What she saw was nothing short of paralyzing.

Paula described a "silver streak" plummeting at an angle. Trees blocked her vision of the impact, but it was swift and loud and violent, causing an explosion "just over the tree tops from our house." That was followed by a "huge, huge fireball" and a smoke plume. "It hit so hard that it almost took my feet out from under me," she said. Looking around her home, she noticed that a garage door had buckled and a window had popped out.

Paula frantically dialed 9-1-1, making her the first of about twenty local residents to report the crash of Flight 93 to the authorities. "Oh my God!" she exclaimed. "There was an airplane crash here!" Her next two calls were to her husband, Andrew, and to the Shanksville-Stonycreek School, where her children, Steven, age eleven, and Marissa, age nine, were attending classes. "I still didn't know where it had crashed," Paula said, "and the school is not that far from us." The school building was only three miles from where Flight 93 went down. It might have been in the flight path had the plane been airborne a few seconds longer. The school official who answered the phone told her they'd heard and felt the impact—the building shook, windows rattled—but that everyone was fine.

After scrambling to pull on tennis shoes, Paula jumped in her car and sped in the direction of the chaos. A man pointed her toward a dead-end road—"I think it crashed down there," he said—and it led to an open field that was once the strip mine. The view was surreal. A large hole had been gouged near the edge of the woods and it was smoldering; some scattered small fires flickered among the trees. Paula was amazed to find a rescue unit already on the scene.

"I stood around and was looking and there just . . . there wasn't anything to see," she said. "Just a big crater that looked . . . like something had gone into it and it rolled the dirt up around and buried itself. . . . The trees were smoking where they had been blown off. And I'm standing at the crater wondering, 'OK, did I just see what I just saw?' And I'm looking around for plane wreckage and there's nothing. I just stood there in amazement. Where did this thing *go*?"

For many curious residents and desperate first responders rushing to the crash site, that was a common refrain: *Where is the plane? Where did it go?* Dave and Cathy Berkebile arrived not long after Paula from their home on Bluebird Lane about two miles away. Their experience had been strikingly similar: They'd heard the thunderous impact, felt their house shudder, saw the smoke billowing over the trees. Dave even videotaped the smoke from a distance. They raced to the scene, hoping to assist with survivors.

"I walked over to the crash site to see if there was anything we could possibly do," Dave said. "And whenever I had walked up to the big crater, I knew there wasn't *anything* that we could do." He couldn't see any large airplane parts among the charred and shattered wreckage. The biggest chunk of debris he identified was a cooling unit that was maybe eight inches by twelve inches. Citizens of Somerset County faced the stark reality before anyone, including the state police and the FBI: There weren't going to be any survivors.

Homer Barron and other employees of Stoystown Auto Wreckers on US Route 30 rushed several miles to the crash site only to find what Barron described to the *Pittsburgh Post-Gazette* as a "big pile of charcoal." Charles Sturtz, who lived just over the hill from the old strip mine, got there quickly and was aghast at what he saw. "The biggest pieces you could find were probably four feet [long]," he said. "Most of the pieces you could put into a shopping bag, and there were clothes hanging from the trees."

Others only heard the noises or felt the tremors, which added to the mystery. Rose Goodwin, a ninth-grader at the Shanksville-Stonycreek School, said students were watching television coverage from the World Trade Center when the plane hit. "Everybody sort of panicked," she told the *Post-Gazette*. "I went to the window and saw all this smoke coming up and I just pointed and screamed." Ten miles away in Berlin, Don Miller and his coworkers at a warehouse were watching the same coverage when they felt their building shake. Impossible as it seemed, the terror they had been watching on the television, from hundreds of miles away, was literally hitting home.

"The guys said, 'Now they're coming to get us,'" Miller said.

❧

It had been Rick King's day to do his banking. The proprietor of Ida's Store on Main Street in nearby Shanksville reported to work early that morning, opening the tiny convenience store that had been a local institution for fifty years. Ida's, he said, was a "busy little place for a small, little town," offering coffee, groceries, a full deli, and delicious lunch specials, including pizza. Rick arrived at 7:30 a.m., brewing the first pot of coffee for local patrons. By 9:00 a.m., when his wife and another employee took over, he'd headed home.

Rick had planned to pay bills from his home office that day but couldn't take his eyes off the disturbing scenes on the television news. An airplane had struck the World Trade Center in New York City and small fires were visible through the upper windows of one of the towers.

Rick's thoughts at the time were probably with the first responders of the New York Fire Department, men he considered brothers in arms. A lifetime member of the Shanksville Volunteer Fire Department, he was serving as assistant fire chief in September 2001. After a second plane hit the other tower, Rick brought a card table into the living room so he could work while still monitoring the live reports. "I started to really get concerned," he said. "It was pretty obvious that it was a planned attack . . . a terrorist attack."

Troubled, Rick had called his father, a Vietnam veteran living in Ohio. They were on the phone together when news broke of the crash at the Pentagon. Then he called his sister, Jody, who lived nearby in Lambertsville. She was watching TV with her kids—*Barney and Friends*—and wasn't aware the nation was under attack. He told her to turn on the news.

"Rick," she said, "I hear a plane!"

He didn't think much of it at first.

"Rick, it's loud. It sounds like a jet!"

He stepped onto his porch and looked to the northwest. "Oh my God!"

"I mean, I could hear the engine screaming and . . . and this, just loud noise," Rick said years later, recalling the scene. "I couldn't see it. It was behind the trees, behind the terrain. But I could hear the noise and seconds later it hit and this huge fireball just went up into the sky, into this clear blue sky. And my porch just rumbled, just shook."

"Jody!" he said.

"Oh my God, Rick! It crashed!"

"I know. I've got to go."

The assistant fire chief started running. He ran first to Ida's Store to tell his wife, and then he hoofed it one block up a slight rise to the Shanksville Fire Hall while the siren was going off. The little town (population: 245) was both frantic and shocked. Breathless now, Rick got on the radio with the Somerset County 9-1-1 dispatcher and was startled to hear that only three local fire companies had been ordered to the scene of the crash. The dispatcher must have assumed it was a small plane, but Rick knew better. "I came back on the radio and I said, 'County, I heard this plane crash. I heard it. It was a—I'm, I'm convinced it was a commercial airliner.

I want additional departments.'" He also asked for Somerset's Hazmat unit, fearing the worst.

Three other Shanksville volunteers answered the first fire whistle that morning: Keith Custer, Merle Flick, and Robert Kelly. Together with Rick, they hopped on Engine 627-1 and rumbled down North Street toward the spot where Flight 93 had crashed into the earth only minutes earlier. They'd faced horrific scenes before, gut-wrenching ones, but all four knew this would be different. One man told Rick his mouth was dry and he was having trouble swallowing. "Mine was too," the assistant chief said. "It just sucked everything out of me."

They weren't even sure where they were going, so they just followed the smoke. An access road for the old Diamond T strip mine brought them to the edge of a belt of woods and the lip of a smoldering hole in the ground. The hemlock trees beyond the crater were burned and smoking. The acrid stench of jet fuel filled the air.

"I (remember) stepping out of the engine and looking at the ground and there's pieces of metal and debris laying everywhere," Rick said. "I could see where there was a tire burning. The trees in front were just all singed, the leaves gone. I can remember smelling jet fuel and just seeing all this smoke coming off the trees, little whiffs of smoke."

Two men in an ambulance raced in and wanted to search for survivors—a noble thought, and one shared by many of the early responders. But as more people arrived on the scene, by foot and by car, the totality of the destruction began to sink in for all of them. Rick and the others could see tiny pieces of the wreckage scattered from the crater into the trees: small bits of metal, paper, wire, insulation, foam. The burning tire. A piece of the landing gear. But no people anywhere. No sign of people at all.

"The local police showed up . . . and we had some firemen gathered and we sent them in through the woods to do a search," Rick said. "And they kept coming back with . . . no signs of anybody. Nothing.

"So I'm thinking to myself, 'OK, was it a Lear jet? Was it just a pilot and a copilot?' I just wondered where all these people were that I thought were going to be on this plane. And the other thing is: Where's the plane? . . . Where's the fuselage? Where are the wings? Where's *anything*?"

It was still less than half an hour after the crash, and Pennsylvania State Police officers had arrived on the scene. Soon, Somerset County coroner Wally Miller pulled up in his truck, parking just beyond the woods. They all huddled, trying to make sense of the devastation. Wally wanted to know if anyone had seen human remains. He and Rick decided to walk down into the woods.

"This was my first time walking into the woods itself—into the hemlocks," Rick said. "And that's when I started seeing more insulation. I saw a window out of the plane. I saw a seat, a piece of a seat. I saw clothing hanging in the hemlocks. I saw tennis shoes lying on the ground.

"I had my fireman's helmet on and Wally didn't have [any protective gear]. And things are falling out of the trees, pieces of metal and stuff, and kind of hitting us a little bit here and there. Finally, Wally says, 'Rick, I've got to get out of here. I don't have a helmet on or anything. Let's get out of here. Stuff's falling out of these trees.'"

Where was the plane? They had their answer.

It was everywhere.

———— ~ ————

Flight 93 was traveling at 563 mph when it slammed into an open field in Stonycreek Township at 10:03:11 a.m. After flipping upside down in the final desperate seconds of the passenger revolt, the 155-foot-long plane impacted the ground "in a 40-degree nose-down, inverted attitude," according to the official report filed by Jim Ritter of the National Transportation Safety Board. The result was utter destruction.

The coroner ruled that everyone on board who was still alive at the time of the crash died instantly of blunt-force trauma. The front of the plane—including the cockpit—sheared off, broke apart, and sprayed into the hemlock trees. The rest of it plowed into dirt that had been transported there to fill in and "reclaim" the old strip mine in the 1990s. The fuselage and wings shattered as they burrowed deep into the soft, unconsolidated earth. More than 5,500 gallons of jet fuel exploded on impact, unleashing the frightening fireball described by Paula Pluta, Rick King, and others.

The crash gouged out a crater that early eyewitnesses estimated to be thirty feet wide by ten to fifteen feet deep and framed by indentations where the wings had clearly struck the ground. It was not unlike the haunting outline that Flight 175 had made when it crashed into the South Tower of the World Trade Center. But the size of the crater was deceptive. Pieces of the plane had plunged thirty-five feet beneath the surface. Whole compartments had splintered and been buried underground. Investigators would end up digging for days, sifting through soil and rock until there were no more remnants of the plane to retrieve. By the time they finished their excavation, the crater had grown to eighty-five feet wide by forty feet deep. One of the first responders described the scene as "freakish."

There were four stone cabins in the woods beyond the crash site, nestled peacefully among the hemlock trees. Three of them were used by their owners on a seasonal basis—perhaps for a getaway weekend or brief vacation. But the fourth was a permanent residence.

Barry Hoover, age thirty-four, lived in one of the cabins. The place was maybe a hundred yards from the spot where Flight 93 went down. Barry wasn't home at the time, but friends soon began calling him at his place of business—a lumberyard in Somerset, just more than ten miles away. They were fearful that a plane had crashed on or near his property.

Barry hustled home. He was joined by his father, the Rev. Larry Hoover, who owned another of the dwellings nearby. What they found was devastation. All the structures were damaged by the force of the crash. The windows and doors were blown out of Barry's cabin, and a garage door had been pried off its hinges and twisted inside out. In time, investigators would find small bits of airplane shrapnel and human remains scattered across his property.

"It looked like what you see after a tornado or hurricane goes through—a total ruin," Barry said. "I had no idea until I got home that it was this disaster."

Stunned as he was, Barry quickly realized the enormity of what had just taken place in this obscure little patch of Somerset County. It would never be obscure again.

"Our family owned a piece of paradise," he said. "The next time we owned a cemetery. . . . A lot of people lost their lives in my backyard."

———

In an era just before the dawn of social media and the ubiquity of smart phones with cameras and Internet access, news spread locally by word of mouth. In fact, 9/11 was probably the last historic event that the country shared this way. Coroner Wally Miller's phone rang at 10:20 that morning. The secretary from the coroner's office in nearby Cambria County was on the line, asking if he needed any help with the plane crash.

"What are you *talking* about?" Wally said.

"You know, the jet that just crashed in northern Somerset County."

"You shouldn't be kidding around," Wally said.

She wasn't. Her boss was out of town at a conference, but they'd received multiple reports that a plane had gone down. They assumed it might have been trying to land at the Cambria County airport and somehow lost its bearings. They were wrong, but they were sure it had crashed in Wally's jurisdiction.

Wally tried to call 9-1-1, but the lines were suddenly jammed and he couldn't get a dial tone. So he went to the low-band radio in his truck and reached the 9-1-1 emergency service center that way. The confirmation stunned him. Officials there said it might have been a 747, which was a wide-body commercial airliner. He recoiled in disbelief and repeated the words with emphasis. *"Seven forty seven?"*

It was mind-boggling. A large airliner meant multiple casualties, maybe hundreds of people. Wally had handled small plane crashes in his time as coroner—"twin engines or single-engine jobs" that went awry in the mountain fog—but nothing on the magnitude of a huge commercial jet. He always wore a tie to death scenes, out of respect. That wouldn't be possible this time. Dressed in "a summer shirt, khaki pants, and my old pair of gum boots," he jumped in his truck and headed toward the scene.

He knew the Diamond T area well. He'd fished in the Stonycreek River and gone cross-country skiing out there as a kid. He even visited the strip mine at the height of its operation. Workers stripping the coal had recognized the presence of an old cemetery with names of settlers carved on fieldstones. Wally and his dad were asked to assist local residents in moving it to another location. "There were no bodies anymore," he said, "just buttons and handles off caskets." The place already had been a burial site; now, within an instant, it became one again.

Cars lined both sides of the dirt road as the coroner pulled up. Firefighters and police officers and ambulance drivers were milling around. Everyone was in a daze. The first person Wally recognized was Officer Pat Stewart of the Pennsylvania State Police. Wally and Pat and Rick King stood in an old country lane trying to make sense of it all.

"Where did it hit?" Wally asked Rick.

"You're looking at it. This is it," Rick answered.

On the tree branches above them, melted plastic was sizzling.

"I kept thinking there should be pieces of the fuselage lying around but nothing like that was readily visible," Wally later recounted. "You actually had to look around to find something that looked like a window or a seat. It was just all debris.

"I walked over to the crater and there were about eighteen inches of jet fuel pooled up at the bottom. Not everything ignited in the fireball. They estimated the fireball to be about seventy-five-feet high. Tops of the trees were burned. The top of a telephone pole was charred. None of us had seen anything like this before." The coroner and funeral home director was used to dealing with death on a daily basis, but he said even he was "freaked out by the devastation of the whole scene."

He remembered what a pathologist had told him on the day he took the Somerset County oath of office. His job was to determine the cause and manner of death, collect the remains, notify the next of kin, collect the personal effects, and file the paperwork. Beyond that, he was a consultant to a police investigation. The task facing him in the days to come would be overwhelming. He buckled down and prepared himself for the worst.

Wally began to walk the site with Pat Stewart and Rick King, looking for human remains. None were immediately obvious. As he searched more closely, he came across small chunks of flesh, strewn indiscriminately from the crater into the woods. Experts later told him that most of the bodies were vaporized on impact. "Anything that wasn't connected to bone or sinew just got obliterated," he said. Over time, he would find a hand, a foot, a flap of skin—nothing larger. Most of the remains were miniscule, unrecognizable to the untrained eye.

The tempo of the work at the site changed by midday when agents from the Federal Bureau of Investigation took control. Arriving by car because all air traffic in the country had been suspended, they cordoned off the area and instructed Wally to set up a temporary morgue. The small town was now a federal crime scene. Cars that had lined the dirt road in the first hour after the crash suddenly vanished; no one without a badge or a credential could access the site. Only then did Wally recognize the connection between the smoking crater in front of him and the carnage at the Twin Towers in New York and the Pentagon in Washington. He soon saw how this crash was part of the puzzle, a piece of what was happening across the country and unfolding on millions of television screens.

"The rank-and-file Somerset County guys did not know until that point about the ties to New York City and the Pentagon," Wally said. "We were too busy trying to figure out what had happened right here. We didn't have time to put it all together. Remember, there was no social media back then. We didn't text. We had no idea. Hey, all of us hicks were amazed that all the FBI guys had cell phones."

The FBI was now the lead investigative agency in charge of the crime scene, but it was working in conjunction with the National Transportation Safety Board; the Federal Aviation Administration; the Bureau of Alcohol, Tobacco, and Firearms; the Somerset County Emergency Management Agency; the Red Cross; the Disaster Mortuary Operational Response Team (DMORT); the Pennsylvania State Police; and numerous other entities. Astoundingly, more than one thousand people representing seventy federal, state, and local agencies were credentialed to work the site. That was larger than the populations of many of the small towns in the region. But despite the dizzying influx of officers, investigators, and technical experts from around the country, the massive crisis-response operation could not rely solely on the efforts of out-of-town professionals. The regular citizens of Shanksville and Somerset County also played essential roles.

Twelve other members of the little Shanksville Fire Department, including Chief Terry Shaffer, arrived that first day to join Rick King and the original crew. They remained on the scene for ten hours and were on standby for the next thirteen days. Local residents gathered at the United Methodist Church on Main Street for prayer services and donated food and drinks for first responders at the Shanksville Fire Hall, where the makeshift relief effort was based. During a horrifying and confusing time, they opened their hearts and their homes in a time of civic need.

Wally Miller stayed on-site until well after dark that first night, assisting with the grim work. Then he got a hint of the dual life he would be living in the weeks and months ahead. Before he nodded off to sleep on the most stressful day of his life, Wally's phone rang. A friend of the family had died. The body had to be delivered to the funeral home.

"Of course, I had to go," Wally said. It was his job, even in a time of national crisis.

He worked into the wee hours, a small-town mortician doing his duty. He would be back at the crash site the next morning. Wally couldn't have imagined it then, but his own legacy would become intertwined with the families of the victims and inextricably linked to the most devastating terror attack in the history of the American mainland.

CHAPTER ELEVEN

One Big Family

The first news reports that a fourth airplane had gone down in a field in rural Pennsylvania sent shock waves around the country. It also raised more questions. *Was this part of the same attack that had targeted the Twin Towers and the Pentagon? Mechanical error? Pilot mishap?* No one knew for sure.

At 10:37 a.m., CNN was monitoring coverage at the World Trade Center when anchor Aaron Brown announced, "We are getting reports . . . and we want to be careful to tell you when we have confirmed them and not, but we have a report that a 747 is down in Pennsylvania, and that remains unconfirmed at this point."

Reporters worked their sources and got nothing. Details were scant. Like a lot of things that morning, confusion about the crash was rampant. But for Lorne Lyles and Lyz Glick and Phil Bradshaw and Esther Heymann— who'd been on the phone with loved ones when the final assault began— early and vague reports of a plane crash confirmed their deepest, most gut-wrenching fears.

They had a sense of what was happening before anyone else did. Lyz had passed the phone to her father when Jeremy and the others attacked the cockpit. Soon her dad was crying. Deena Burnett's knees buckled and she began to sob. Operator Lisa Jefferson, who barely knew Todd Beamer, developed such a bond in those frenzied fifteen minutes that she refused to hang up the phone even after screams turned to silence. "Release the phone line," one of her colleagues said. "Lisa . . . Flight 93 is down, please release the phone line." She later wrote, quite movingly, that she knew "that brave man on the other side of the phone had perished and a part of me went with him."

Family members who had not received calls or retrieved their voice mail messages could only hope and wonder. The flight that crashed was not even immediately identified as a United Airlines jet. Forgotten now in the twenty-twenty clarity of hindsight—and after so much has been written and investigated—is that very little was known about the attacks in the raw confusion of that morning, and very little solid information was relayed to the public in real time. "We have a report now that a large plane crashed this morning, north of the Somerset County Airport, which is in western Pennsylvania, not too terribly far from Pittsburgh," Brown told his CNN viewers at 10:49 a.m. "Don't know whose airline it was, whose airplane it was, and we don't have any details beyond that which I have just given you. We don't know—we don't know—if this is somehow connected to what has gone on in New York and Washington."

Lori Guadagno knew that her brother, Richard, was flying out of Newark. They'd been together for their grandmother's hundredth birthday party over the weekend. Lori was back at her high school job in Vermont that morning, working with special-needs students, when word arrived that a plane had hit the World Trade Center. She stiffened, worried that Richard was on the tarmac waiting for his flight to take off and that he'd seen the crash and the carnage.

Then there were reports of other crashes, more planes. Something unconfirmed about a flight out of Newark. She called her parents' house and reached her father. "Dad, what is going on?" she said. "Where's Richard?"

"Lori, it doesn't look good. It doesn't look good."

"What do you *mean* it doesn't look good?"

"I don't know, Lor. It just doesn't look good."

She left school and rushed home and turned on the television, started making calls. No one was answering. No one was home. Lines in and out of the New York City area were jammed. Suddenly she saw news footage of a crash site near Shanksville for the first time. Her heart sank.

"I'm watching . . . and there's no sign of anything or anyone. And I just see these trees beyond this hole, and all I could remember is one of our favorite movies that we watched together many times, *Fearless*. And in that film, people do walk away from a crash. Not all, but some. And I just said, 'Well, I know Richard. He's so strong. He's so resourceful. He's so fit. He knows so many survival skills. He made it out . . . He's going to be coming out any minute.'"

The phone rang. It was her cousin.

"Lori, sit down. I have to tell you that Richard was a passenger on that plane. It really was Richard. I'm sorry."

Sandy Dahl was enjoying a mini-vacation at home in Littleton, Colorado. She worked as a flight attendant for United Airlines but wasn't scheduled to fly again until early the next week. Her husband, Captain Jason Dahl, would spend September 11 piloting a United flight from Newark to San Francisco. After a brief stop in San Jose to visit his mother, Jason planned to return home to prepare for an anniversary trip with Sandy to London.

The phone rang that morning and it was a neighbor. Where was Jason?

"He's on a trip," Sandy said.

"Yes, but where? Where was he last night? . . . Have you watched the news? . . . Turn on the television. A plane crashed into the Trade Center."

Sandy flicked on the TV and saw a second plane hit the Twin Towers. She knew immediately it was a large commercial aircraft and wondered if it might have been one from United. Jason's flight was scheduled for an 8:00 a.m. eastern takeoff, so he would have been cruising safely over the Midwest by now. "That can't be him, because he left an hour or two ago," Sandy said. But she worried she might have had friends on the flight in New York.

"Go and look up Jason on the computer," the neighbor said. "What flight number is he?"

Sandy checked and found that he was on Flight 93. She assured her neighbor that "he was well past New York and that *couldn't* have been him," but she kept watching out of fear for friends and coworkers. "I was just mortified, because these are my people," Sandy said later.

A third plane rammed into the Pentagon, crushing the outer rings. Then a fourth plane went down in Pennsylvania. She saw footage of "a big, black burning hole in the ground" and decided it didn't make sense. She'd never seen a crash landing like that. *Where was the plane? Where were the parts?*

Like other family members, she was in denial. The media speculated that this might be Flight 93, and Sandy's first response was "that's ridiculous." It set off an agonizingly slow chain of events. Reports rolled in, neighbors called for updates. It began to sink in on her that the speculation might be true.

Matt Dahl, Jason's fifteen-year-old son from his first marriage, called from school, petrified. Father and son were close. When Matt was three years old, he had placed some small rocks inside a colored box and given it to his dad as a present. Jason carried the "Box of Rocks" with him on every flight.

"Where's Dad?"

"I don't know exactly, Matt."

"What's his flight number?"

"I don't know."

"Yes you do."

Sandy was trying to be protective, but Jason's son deserved an answer. She said she'd looked it up and it might be Flight 93, the same one the news reports were claiming had crashed in a field in rural Pennsylvania. Matt started crying. Sandy tried to calm him, reminding him his dad was a good pilot—that he could have crash-landed the plane and might just be hurt. But she was as confused as anyone.

Sandy then called United Airlines, called the Denver Flight Office, called everyone. No one could help her. Media reports soon confirmed that the plane down in Pennsylvania was indeed Flight 93. She went into shock and stared at the television "like a zombie." Neighbors started arriving at her house, but she wanted to avoid the commotion, walking outside by herself, sitting on the hood of her car, trying to sort it all out.

Then the phone rang again. It was a United Airlines supervisor in Denver.

"Sandy, I have to tell you bad news . . ."

In Danville, California, Carole O'Hare was up early for what promised to be a monumental day in her life. Her mother, Hilda Marcin, was booked on Flight 93 out of Newark, but it wasn't a typical vacation trip to the

West Coast to visit family. At age seventy-nine, Hilda was moving to Danville to live with Carole and her husband, Tom.

Carole was fixing breakfast at 6:00 a.m. when the TV flashed the harrowing news of a plane that hit the World Trade Center. She froze.

"I panicked," Carole later recalled. "I thought, 'Oh, my God, my mother is flying.'"

Like many nervous relatives with loved ones in the air, Carole telephoned the airline. A representative told her that as far as United knew, the flight was proceeding normally. It was good to hear. At that point, in fact, Flight 93 *was* proceeding normally. Carole called her sister, Betty Kemmerer, in New Jersey, and the two of them decided to stay in touch until the plane landed safely. Betty had driven her mom to the airport that morning and helped her with her four suitcases. She told herself to remain calm. But reports of more hijackings and more crashes had them on edge; Betty admitted, "I had a very, *very* eerie feeling."

The two sisters were talking on the phone and both watching CNN when a graphic on the bottom of the screen said United 93 had gone down in rural Pennsylvania.

"We both just lost it together," Carole said. "I went outside, screaming.

"I called my husband at work. Everything changed at that moment. Everything."

The very next day, Carole picked up the mail to find Hilda's first pension check had arrived at her new address in Danville.

―⁓―

Family and friends left forty-four messages on Mark Bingham's cell phone, starting within minutes of the first plane hitting the Twin Towers. Some weren't even sure he was flying that day. They just knew he was in New York. They wanted to make sure he was safe.

"Hey, Mark, this is Dad. Just calling to see how you're doing. I'm looking at this big wreck. Man, I hope you're not too close to that. Give me a call when you can."

"Hey, Mark. Amanda. Where are you? Call me, please. Bye."

"Hey, Mark. It's Ken. I am absolutely in shock right now. I just can't get over this. What's happening? I'm in Walnut Creek. Why don't you call me here

. . . But, my God, this is just devastating. I just can't believe this. Anyway, give me a call. Bye."

Mark had called his mother, Alice Hoglan, at 9:37 a.m. from an Airfone near the back of Flight 93. He reported the hijacking but didn't have time for much else before the line went dead. Alice called him back twice, leaving messages both times—a frantic mom trying to reach her son. Mark's cell phone was destroyed in the crash, but Alice later obtained the security passcode, retrieving all the unheard messages left that day.

In her first message, Alice was flustered enough to miscalculate East Coast time by an hour (she said it was 10:54 instead of 9:54 a.m.) and to suggest the plane would be used as a "target" rather than a "weapon." It was understandable under the circumstances. Following Mark's call, she gathered information from news reports. She wanted to pass it on.

Mark, this is your mom. It's 10:54 a.m. The news is that it's been hijacked by terrorists. They are planning to probably use the plane as a target to hit some site on the ground. If you possibly can, try to overpower these guys if you can, 'cause they'll probably use the plane as a target. I would say go ahead and do everything you can to overpower them, because they're hell-bent. Try to call me back if you can. You know the number here. Okay, I love you sweetie. Bye.

Her next message was more of the same—haunting, desperate, bewildered. Other calls were from family friends, fraternity brothers, work colleagues, rugby teammates. Everyone was worried, searching for some solace. Would he please call them back?

"Hey, Mark, it's Todd. Can you give me a call and let me know that you're OK when you get a chance? I'm watching all this (crap) on the news. OK, bye."

"Hey, Mark. It's Jim. It's 3:30 on Tuesday and I'm really praying you're OK, buddy. I'm worried. Anyway, call me, you know, somewhere. Leave me a message, anywhere, any time. I don't care. Just let me know you're OK. Thanks. I hope you're OK. Bye."

"Mark, this is Tom. I was just giving you a call. I wanted to see if you're OK. I heard your name or someone with your name mentioned on the news, and I just wanted to try to get a hold of you. Anyway, I'll try and reach you later. Bye."

Forty-four messages. And no one on the other end. The silence was deafening.

———◆———

Kenny Nacke had been out of touch that morning, on assignment for the Baltimore County police department. When the news came, it hit him hard.

Joey Nacke was the big brother he'd idolized as a kid, his partner in shenanigans. The bond between the brothers was a solid one, and it ran deep. At first Kenny was in denial about Joey being on the plane. As the day wore on and the facts rolled in, "I could feel the hair stand up on the back of my neck." The cop in him wanted to know the details.

Kenny and his wife drove to Ocean City, Maryland, to console his parents, then on to New Hope, Pennsylvania, to spend two days with Joey's grieving boys. Their next stop was Somerset. The Nackes were among the first families to arrive, pulling into the Seven Springs Mountain Resort on Friday, September 14. Seven Springs had been designated as the official family headquarters by United Airlines. That night they attended an emotional candlelight vigil with members of the public at the Somerset County Courthouse.

Kenny noticed players and coaches from the Pittsburgh Steelers standing in the back and got choked up. He and Joey had spent part of their childhood in Monroeville, Pennsylvania, just outside of Pittsburgh, and Joey had been a Steelers fan. "They were all there," Kenny said. "Jerome Bettis. Kordell Stewart. Coach Bill Cowher. The owner, Dan Rooney." He was startled when Pro-Bowlers Bettis and Stewart stopped by to speak with him afterward and pay their respects.

Distracted for a moment, he looked around and couldn't find his parents. Little did he know they were already on the bus with special guests. "I got there and I see my mom and dad with Dan Rooney and his wife and Coach Cowher and his wife," Kenny said. "They were all sitting on the bus, holding hands. And that's when it really hit me. I lost my brother, but everyone in this nation lost something that day. The loss was great for everyone." On 9/11, personal tragedy merged with public trauma—everyone was connected, and everyone shared in the grief.

The first visit by family members to the crash site wasn't scheduled until Monday; Kenny had other ideas. On Saturday morning, September 15, he approached a Pennsylvania state trooper, identified himself as a fellow officer, told him about his fallen brother—and asked a favor. Could he see the site, even briefly, on behalf of his parents?

"My parents were very Roman Catholic," Kenny said. "They believed Joey's soul was there. They wanted me to place a flower there or something." He knew it was a high-profile criminal investigation—an international terrorist incident, in fact—under the direction of the FBI. He knew he was asking a lot. The trooper went inside his command post and made the request. Kenny received clearance.

They put him in a state police car and drove him toward the site. His heart was pounding. He got emotional when they turned onto Lambertsville Road. "Every state trooper that we passed saluted the car," Kenny told me, shaking his head. "We got to a dirt road and they were all lined up, saluting me."

They didn't make it all the way to the crater because that was a protected crime scene. Some would also consider it holy ground. They took Kenny to an overlook about two hundred yards from the impact site. The recovery work stopped for a moment, out of respect. He placed a flower there in honor of Joey—a gesture of important symbolism for his mom and dad.

A group of uniformed officials from the state police, the FBI, the NTSB, and other agencies gathered around him, brothers in arms. They told him to shed his tears now so he could be strong for his parents and his family. "Then we all got down on one knee together and said a prayer," Kenny said. It was the first day of his long healing process.

———

United Airlines set aside two days for family members of passengers and crew to visit the crash site—Monday, September 17, and Thursday, September 20. Private memorial services would be held nearby. For Todd Beamer's wife, Lisa, pregnant and now the single mother of two young sons, the trip didn't sound appealing. As she described in her book, *Let's Roll! Ordinary People, Extraordinary Courage,* her first reaction was: "Nope, no way! I'm not going. I don't need to see that."

Then she had a sudden change of heart: "If I don't go now I probably never will and I may regret it someday," she realized. "If I go, it can't be much worse than what I've already experienced." Her words strike at the heart of what must have been a confusing part of the grieving process for the families of the victims of Flight 93. Their loved ones would forever rest at this site, but the horror of seeing it—and the shock of realizing how little there was to see—could be too overwhelming to bear.

In a car on the Pennsylvania Turnpike, Lisa dealt with this conflict—the desire to be at the place where her husband perished but the fear of what staring into that abyss might trigger. "Why am I doing this? What do I hope to see?" Lisa wrote. "Am I going to be able to handle it? Or is it going to be the final straw that sends me over the edge?"

The bus ride from Seven Springs took just more than half an hour, rolling through picturesque farmland and past small towns with neat rows of modest houses that are the fabric of rural Pennsylvania. Like Kenny Nacke before them, the family members were overwhelmed by what they saw. People lined the roads in silent tribute. Some waved. Others held signs. WE HONOR THE HEROES. NEVER FORGET. GOD BLESS AMERICA. "It was an incredibly moving sight," wrote Lisa. The reaction of the citizens of Somerset County was an echo of what was happening in New York City and Washington, DC, and a microcosm of what was happening around the country.

In tiny Shanksville, there was a large sign with the names of all forty passengers and crew. Police officers stood at attention, saluting. The buses took them to the same overlook where Kenny had prayed on Saturday. More salutes. They peered down on the hallowed ground where their loved ones died as American heroes.

Hay bales set under a canopy at the overlook became a makeshift temporary memorial—a place to meditate and ponder and mourn. Lisa Beamer left an Oracle pen, a Chicago Bulls hat, and a bag of M&Ms in honor of Todd. Lyz Glick left a "Got Milk?" poster—Jeremy drank a lot of milk—and sunflowers, their wedding flower. The family of Toshiya Kuge brought a Japanese flag. Scattered around were photos and books, poems and notes, stuffed animals and baby shoes.

The next stop was a special memorial service a few miles away at Indian Lake Lodge. Rick King and other volunteer firemen in dress uniforms manned the receiving line as the buses pulled in. Lynne Cheney, wife of the vice president, addressed the families at the September 20 service; she then took time to shake the hands of all the firemen. Then Rick heard someone say, "Which one is Rick King?"

He determined later that it was Jeremy Glick's mother, Joan. Rick was startled that someone actually knew his name. He figured it might have appeared in media reports about the first day at the crash site. Through tears, she wanted to know what he'd seen. It was a question he dreaded—a question he wasn't sure how to answer.

"I thought to myself, 'What do I do?'" Rick recalled. He could take the easy way out and tell her he hadn't seen much. Or he could tell her the truth. After debating it only briefly, he felt he owed her an honest response. "Without getting into any graphic detail, I told her what I saw," he said. "She thanked me. She hugged me. And she moved on."

Betty Kemmerer's family arrived in time for the courthouse vigil on Friday and stayed for the first organized service on the 17th. She will never forget the shock and utter sadness of her first view of the crash site from the overlook. Hers was a different experience than most; Betty wasn't staring at the final resting place of a child or a sibling. Hilda Marcin was her mother.

"The first thing I thought was, 'This is not the way I thought my mother would die,'" Betty said. "It was a horrific scene: A giant crater in the ground with all the stuff hanging from the trees and plane parts all over the ground. Just horrible. I always thought my mother would have a heart attack and I would bury her in a cemetery. But to have this happen and to not know if I was even going to have anything back to bury ..."

Some of the family members left flowers on or near the hale bales. But Betty didn't dare. Her thrifty mother always told her that buying flowers was a waste of money, "and she always thought it was cruel to the flowers if you cut fresh flowers." Betty wasn't going to disobey her, especially now. "If I had put flowers there for my mom, she probably would have been hollering at me from afar that I'm spending money unnecessarily on her behalf." Even in her grief, Betty allowed herself a little smile.

One of the families had an especially solemn journey to Pennsylvania. The week had been doubly tragic. Seventy-four-year-old John Talignani was already in despair as he boarded Flight 93 that Tuesday morning, traveling to attend a memorial service in California for his stepson, who died in a car crash on his honeymoon. Now, two other stepsons were driving east—heading to Somerset County to memorialize John. The compounding of grief for the family must have been almost too much to bear.

Individual services to honor the passengers and crew were held around the country and around the world. There were services for Tom Burnett in both California and Minnesota, his native state; one for Waleska Martinez in Puerto Rico; another for LeRoy Homer in Hamilton, Ontario, Canada, his wife's hometown. It was at the same church where LeRoy and Melodie were married. In Hawaii, more than three hundred people gathered to celebrate the life of Georgine Corrigan. It was a cross-section of America that died on that plane.

On September 20, Lisa Beamer traveled to Washington, DC, to attend President Bush's nationally televised address to a joint session of Congress. The president paid tribute to her husband and his heroic actions nine days earlier at the top of his speech:

In the normal course of events, presidents come to this chamber to report on the state of the Union. Tonight, no such report is needed. It has already been delivered by the American people.

We have seen it in the courage of passengers, who rushed terrorists to save others on the ground—passengers like an exceptional man named Todd Beamer.

President Bush then asked everyone to welcome Lisa Beamer, and the audience stood up and erupted into sympathetic applause.

Family members were invited to the White House the next week to meet privately with the president. There were interviews and speeches and TV specials about the heroes. Gordie Felt, whose brother, Ed, had made the cell phone call to 9-1-1 from the back of the plane, and who had instantly become a part of the historic record of Flight 93, quickly realized that life had changed permanently for all of them.

Gordie had the unimaginable task on September 11 of calling his mother to deliver the news that her oldest son was dead. Steadfast in the face of tragedy, he volunteered as an unofficial spokesman for the families in those early days. He addressed the media at Seven Springs on September 17 after the first visit to the crash site. He and others, including Tom Burnett's wife, Deena, and Mark Bingham's mother, Alice Hoglan, were thrust into unfamiliar public roles, speaking with a new purpose—to honor the memory of the heroes of Flight 93. "Our loss was very, very personal, very raw," Gordie said, "and yet we felt an obligation to our loved ones to make sure their stories were told."

It would become both a burden and an opportunity. They had to share their grief with the world.

CHAPTER TWELVE

The FBI Investigates

The probe into the September 11 attacks on the United States was the largest investigation ever undertaken by the Federal Bureau of Investigation. Thousands of agents chased leads around the country and the world, confirming identities of the hijackers, delving into finances, and untangling a web of deceit that led back to al-Qaeda training camps in Afghanistan. Special agents and evidence response teams sifted through rubble at the crash sites, searching for incriminating data. Some of the Bureau's top investigators were dispatched to the open field in Pennsylvania.

From the start the Flight 93 site was considered the key to the case. The violent collapse of the Twin Towers and the fiery wreckage at the Pentagon had pulverized much of the available evidence from the first three flights. Those planes literally embedded themselves into massive buildings. By contrast, the smoldering crater in Stonycreek Township and its surrounding debris field offered infinite possibilities.

Todd McCall, former Supervisory Special Agent of the FBI's Evidence Response Team in Quantico, Virginia, pulled into Somerset County on September 12. "To me," he later recalled, "Flight 93 was *the* most important aspect of the 9/11 investigation."

After crashing at the literally incomprehensible speed of 563 mph, about two-thirds of the shattered aircraft drove into the unconsolidated earth of the reclaimed strip mine. One agent said the back of the plane "accordioned" onto the middle. But the front had broken off and been propelled forward by the sheer force of the impact—airplane parts and other material lobbed into the branches of the hemlock trees and beyond. Flight 93 had been carrying more than fifteen hundred pounds of mail to the West Coast. When it crashed and imploded, paper and small debris drifted to Indian Lake, about a mile and a half downwind. Lightweight paper items even were found as far as New Baltimore, eight miles away.

"There was no evidence coming out of the World Trade Center obviously, and they had a huge fire at the Pentagon, and so a lot of that evidence was essentially destroyed," said the FBI's Bob Craig, Senior Team Leader of the Pittsburgh Division's Evidence Response Team. "Our crash, however, was essentially a flash fireball that didn't last very long." The fireball was followed by an enormous plume of smoke and dust and debris. They knew this was their best chance to solve the extraordinarily complex puzzle of September 11.

Airline travel in the United States was discontinued until further notice (planes would remain grounded until September 13), so agents were forced to hop in their cars and drive to the scene. Wells Morrison, from the FBI's satellite office in the Mon Valley, about fifty-five miles to the west, was among the first to arrive that morning. The *Pittsburgh Post-Gazette* reported that twenty agents were on-site during the day on September 11 and thirty more rolled in that night. FBI Evidence Response Teams from Pittsburgh, Cincinnati, Chicago, Cleveland, Detroit, Indianapolis, Louisville, and even Knoxville (five hundred miles away) were assigned to the investigation. Andrea Dammann, special agent from the Pittsburgh office, was assigned the task of supervising their efforts. The sense of urgency among the wide and diverse force was palpable.

"One of the things that made this crash site so productive from an evidence recovery standpoint was that we did not have the tons and tons of debris that they had at the World Trade Center and at the Pentagon," Morrison said. "We didn't have tons of concrete and steel girders. We had an airplane that flew into the ground and the earth that had fallen on top of that."

Among their main objectives was to find the "black boxes"—the flight data recorder and the cockpit voice recorder—that would be instrumental in unlocking clues to the mysteries in the air. Agents were already aware of the phone calls made from the flight to Deena Burnett and Lyz Glick, and of Ed Felt's desperate report of a hijacking to Westmoreland County 9-1-1, but they needed more tangible evidence to assemble a case. They would be working in the coming days to identify the hijackers, locate their weapons, and collect the human remains. So much debris had lodged in the branches of the hemlocks that the Bureau brought in arborists to climb the trees.

A nose axle had been flung furiously down the slope, landing just beyond the banks of a sediment pond—about three hundred yards from the crater. Most of the debris was found between the crater and the pond. The heaviest chunk of evidence was a thousand-pound engine fan. The largest was a piece of the fuselage measuring about six feet by seven feet. Investigators identified random parts of the engine nacelles, an engine hub, a fuel stick, an accessory gearbox, an entry door latch, and a pivot from an overhead luggage bin. A first responder said much of the rest looked like "confetti." They found rivets and wires and scattered personal belongings—a shoe here, a pocketbook there. Two Bibles. A seat belt. Pieces of flesh. A tooth.

Agents covered the field, patrolling shoulder to shoulder, searching for anything connected to the crash. "They would line up and walk it and pick up anything of size," Bob Craig said, "anything that was readily visible, that you could see from a standing position." Then they doubled back and repeated the process on their hands and knees.

FBI evidence teams were assigned to specific zones: the crater; the "halo"—their name for the area around the crater; the hemlock trees.

Hundreds of Pennsylvania State Police officers also were dispatched to the site, setting up a security perimeter to protect the crime scene and provide additional manpower to assist the FBI in the investigation. One of them was Corporal Louis Veitz, the unit supervisor for the Forensic Mapping Unit. The tragedy hit a little closer to home for Veitz than most; he once lived in Stonycreek Township.

Like many of the officers and agents, Veitz was used to dealing with death and tragedy, all kinds of horrific settings. But this one was different. It became incredibly personal and emotional. "You start finding personal belongings, you start to put faces to the people that used to be in that airplane," he said. "You get mad. You get upset. You feel terrible. Then you try to go back to the task at hand until you find the next piece of clothing or pocketbook. In one instance, we found the captain's wings. And you find pictures, family pictures, and that's what makes it hard.

"We actually found money that was still intact. Just the outer edge of the bill or bills was charred but the rest was intact, which kind of gives you an impression of the intensity and the brevity of the flash that would have occurred. I can remember finding pocketbooks with family pictures in it [*sic*], clothing, someone's shoe."

Agents and officers knew there still was a significant amount of material from the crash located above their heads, suspended in the branches of the hemlocks. They reached out to Penn State University in State College to enlist two arborists who could climb the trees and retrieve the debris. Mark Trautman and Ben Haupt were technically "tree surgeons" who also participated in tree-climbing competitions. They would provide invaluable service to the investigation, the FBI, and the country.

"I've never seen the amount of shrapnel, all on one side of the trees," Trautman said. "We were thinking, 'How are we going to climb these trees?'" The two men wore protective covering similar to all the investigators at the site, but Trautman remembers their Tyvek suits getting torn apart with each attempt. "We'd come out of a tree and our Tyveks would be ripped to shreds," he said. "We'd go back out and [each] get another one." They kept going, men on a mission.

But the arborists from Penn State weren't used to being part of a criminal investigation, and they certainly weren't used to identifying human remains. Unfortunately, that became an essential and difficult part of their task throughout the next four days. They were instructed to notify an agent or a state trooper any time they came upon remains. The two men found "a lot of stuff" up in the trees—much more than could be spotted or even imagined from the ground.

"Ben came across some remains on the first day, and it was pretty large remains," Trautman said. "And he broke down." Not everyone working the site was accustomed to death scenes. What stunned both of them was that veteran FBI agent John Larsen of the Chicago Division had the same response to the discovery. "Agent Larsen broke down with him. I don't know if he did it just to let us know that everybody's human, but that was something to see a man of his experience break down with Benny. As agent Larsen said, 'Hey, you have a good cry once in a while, it helps you out.'"

The investigation took a grinding emotional toll on all the partici- pants. But in unexpected ways, it also gave them motivation. Agent Todd McCall from Quantico was a veteran of some of the FBI's most grisly cases in recent years—the Branch Davidians at Waco, Texas, in 1993; the Oklahoma City bombing in 1995; the bombing of the US embassy in Tanzania in 1998. He'd endured it all. But McCall remembers driving past an elementary school on one of the early days of the Flight 93 probe and seeing flags flying in the schoolyard. The next day, there were more flags. The next day, painted signs in the windows—salutes to the heroes, thank-you messages to the first responders. His emotions kept building.

Finally, on the day McCall was scheduled to leave the crash site, headed back to his post in Virginia, "I couldn't drive by that school with- out stopping." He approached the school's principal to tell her how much he and the other agents appreciated the grassroots support, and he wanted to make sure all the students and teachers got the message. "Why don't you tell them yourself?" the principal suggested. Before he knew it, she handed him a microphone for the school's PA system.

This wasn't McCall's comfort zone, but he had no choice. "Boys and girls, ladies and gentlemen, I'm just one of the FBI agents working the crash site," he said in his brief and impromptu broadcast, the first such speech of his long and distinguished career. "And all the flags and all the things that you've done that we've seen here on a daily basis . . . we just really appreciate it."

With that, the veteran G-man headed down the hallway, determined to get back on the road before he started choking up—until he noticed a commotion all around him.

"Dozens of kids came flooding out in the hallway," he said, startled. "They were clapping."

The admiration went both ways.

At 3:15 p.m. on September 11, President George W. Bush met with senior advisors on a secure video teleconference and declared, "We're at war." George Tenet, director of the Central Intelligence Agency, reported "with near certainty" that Osama bin Laden and al-Qaeda were behind the attacks. Descriptions from callers on the planes indicated that the hijackers were Middle Eastern. Jeremy Glick, likely influenced by growing up during the terrorism scares of the 1980s, called them "Iranian."

The FBI obtained the Flight 93 manifest and quickly found four names of interest: Jarrah, Ghamdi, Haznawi, and Nami. But the manifest didn't really prove anything—agents needed to uncover evidence that physically placed those four men on the plane. The rural field in Somerset County was productive in that regard, yielding specific identification documents for three of the hijackers within days after the crash. Investigators found a Lebanese passport for Ziad Jarrah, a Saudi passport for Saeed al Ghamdi, and a Saudi Arabian Youth Hostels Association Identification card for Ahmed al Nami—all hauntingly strewn among the hemlock trees, where the shattered cockpit had landed. Jarrah's passport was extensively charred from the crash, but the chief forensic document examiner for the US Department of Justice determined that it was genuine. Other items located nearby included handwritten flight instructions, a blank check from Saeed al Ghamdi, a small spiral notebook with English/Arabic translations, and a torn paper card in the name of "Ziad Jarrah."

Agents also recovered fourteen pieces of knives at the site, including "part of a Leatherman multipurpose tool," an "open partial Leatherman tool," and a "multipurpose utility tool with knife blade exposed." Credit card receipts from the investigation in Florida had confirmed that the September 11 hijackers purchased at least four Leatherman Wave Multitools at major retail outlets in addition to other knives for the attacks. Multiple callers from Flight 93 told loved ones that the assailants wielded knives as weapons in their midair assault. The evidence was adding up.

One more discovery directly tied the Flight 93 hijackers to al-Qaeda operatives on other flights that morning. Investigators located the first page of a handwritten letter in Arabic that implored the hijackers to pray and indicated a willingness to die in the name of Allah. Similar letters were found in connection to two other flights—a full four-page version in the rental car of Flight 77 hijacker Nawaf al Hazmi at Dulles International Airport and another version in the suitcase of mission leader Mohamed Atta. Atta's suitcase never made it onto American Airlines Flight 11 after his early morning connection from Portland, Maine. He no doubt believed the letter and other suitcase contents, including his will, would have been destroyed when Flight 11 hit its target.

On September 14, the FBI officially released the names of all nineteen hijackers, including Jarrah, Ghamdi, Haznawi, and Nami. Agents utilized credit card and banking records connected to the men to help complete the list. Jarrah's rented red Mitsubishi Galant—the same one stopped for speeding by Maryland State Police two days before the attacks—was found in the parking lot at the Newark Airport; the speeding ticket was still in the glove compartment. Six airplane training videos were discovered at the Florida apartment he shared with Haznawi. A SunTrust Bank VISA check card in the name of Ziad S. Jarrah was picked up at the Flight 93 crash site. Taken as a whole, the evidence was extensive—and damning.

The "black boxes" from Flight 93 were still considered wholly essential to the case, and the search for those two items remained a priority in the first week of the investigation. The nickname endures even though the flight data recorder and the cockpit voice recorder aren't black. They are painted bright orange, for high visibility, especially in a pile of wreckage— or a crater.

The first breakthrough came at 4:20 p.m. on Thursday, September 13, as workers with heavy equipment excavated the ground around the impact site, gouging wider and deeper than the original crater. "We're digging down, digging down, digging down," Bob Craig said, "and the folks on the rim spy a flash of orange. And everybody jumps up and waves." The excitement was palpable, and for good reason. They'd found the flight data recorder buried fifteen feet beneath the surface.

The recorder collects every detail from the operation of a flight— speed, direction, altitude, and other data essential to unraveling the chaos in the air. Once analyzed by the National Transportation Safety Board, it would reveal the sudden drop in altitude when the hijackers attacked the cockpit, the precise moment when Jarrah turned the plane to the southeast, and his manic actions in the final minutes as he rocked the wings and pitched the nose up and down. It also confirmed that he was indeed heading to Washington, DC. At 9:55:11 a.m., just before the passenger revolt began, Jarrah had dialed the navigational code for Reagan National Airport into the aircraft's flight computer.

For the FBI and NTSB, it was one box down, one to go. None of the black boxes were recovered from Flights 11 and 175 at the World Trade Center sites, and only the flight data recorder yielded information from Flight 77 at the Pentagon. Agents needed more answers. Finding the cockpit voice recorder from Flight 93 would deliver unique and invaluable insight into the actions on board the plane that morning—and perhaps into the inner machinations of the plot itself.

They did not have to wait long. One day later, at 8:30 p.m. on Friday, September 14, in the lurking late-summer darkness of Somerset County, investigators working under spotlights caught another glimpse of orange. The cockpit voice recorder was even deeper—twenty-five feet beneath the surface—but prying it out of the reclaimed strip mine in the dark was wholly necessary. Agent Todd McCall had been correct in his assessment. Having crashed in an open field as opposed to striking giant landmark buildings, Flight 93 was able to provide more compelling evidence than any of the other three hijacked flights.

~~~

Americans love conspiracy theories. In the case of the September 11 attacks, those theories began spinning on September 12. The World Trade Center was brought down by planted explosives; the Pentagon was hit by a missile; Flight 93 was either shot down or it landed mysteriously in Cleveland—and let the passengers off. Websites, blogs, and Internet videos sprung up to insist the entire operation was an inside job by the US government. As was the case with the JFK assassination almost forty years earlier, the theorists couldn't even get their conspiracies straight.

The most prominent conspiracy theory about Flight 93 was that the aircraft had been tracked by the military and shot down over Somerset County. Ordinary Americans, frazzled by the superpower's sudden vulnerability, wondered whether the Air Force had taken decisive action and lashed out against al-Qaeda while the country was under attack. It was difficult for some to imagine that the most powerful military in the world had been caught unaware and rendered impotent by nineteen young zealots from the Middle East. But it had. The 9/11 Commission, FBI agents, and local investigators overwhelmingly refuted the shoot-down theory, and more than ten years later, there is no credible evidence that Flight 93 was shot down.

The biggest problem for proponents of such a theory is timing. Flight 93 crashed at 10:03 a.m. Officials from the Northeast Air Defense Sector (NEADS) weren't even notified that the plane had been hijacked until four minutes after it was already down—10:07 a.m. An order by Vice President Dick Cheney to shoot down unresponsive aircraft threatening Washington, DC, wasn't issued from the White House bunker until at least 10:10 a.m. (an aide to Cheney said it was between 10:10 and 10:15 a.m.). Press Secretary Ari Fleischer, flying with President Bush on Air Force One, recorded in his notes that the president told him at 10:20 a.m. he had given shoot-down authorization. Audio tapes confirm the order did not reach NEADS until 10:31 a.m. They were all too late.

It had been a bewildering morning for the Federal Aviation Administration and the North American Aerospace Defense Command (NORAD). Stunned air traffic controllers struggled to process information about unprecedented hijackings and crashes in real time. The story seems clear to us now through the prism of history—four planes, four targets, a precisely coordinated attack—but on the morning of September 11, with 4,500 planes in the air, it was a jumble of confusing and seemingly impossible reports and transmissions. There were rumors of multiple hijackings, most of them false alarms, including one about Delta Flight 1989 over Ohio at the same time Flight 93 was in that airspace. (Flight 1989 eventually *did* land in Cleveland). In a 2006 *Vanity Fair* story, journalist Michael Bronner wrote, "For the NEADS crew, 9/11 was not a story of four hijacked airplanes, but one of a heated chase after more than a dozen potential hijackings—some real, some phantom—that emerged from the turbulence of information that spiked in the first 100 minutes of the attack and continued well into the afternoon and evening."

Controllers tracking Flight 93 discussed the possibility of requesting some sort of military assistance as early as 9:36 a.m., just one minute before Flight 77 hit the Pentagon. But such an inquiry regarding a commercial airliner with American citizens on board had to work its way up the FAA chain of command. This was an achingly slow process, especially under circumstances none of them had faced in their careers—and amid other rumored hijackings. It was not until thirteen minutes later, at 9:49 a.m., that an official at the Air Traffic Control Command Center in Herndon, Virginia, suggested to FAA headquarters that someone should make a decision about requesting military assistance.

FAA Headquarters: They're pulling Jeff away to go talk about United 93.
Command Center: Uh, do we want to think, uh, about scrambling aircraft?
FAA Headquarters: Oh, God, I don't know.
Command Center: Uh, that's a decision somebody's gonna have to make probably in the next ten minutes.
FAA Headquarters: Uh, ya know everybody just left the room.

It was a stunning statement, especially in retrospect. Confusion was rampant across the system. Shortly before 10:00 a.m., the Command Center even told FAA headquarters that it briefly lost track of Flight 93 somewhere over Pittsburgh. But visual reports started arriving from other aircraft in the area, and at 10:01 a.m., the Command Center relayed information that a pilot had seen Flight 93 "waving his wings." The pilot had most likely seen evidence of Jarrah's attempt to knock the passengers off balance. Flight 93 crashed at 10:03 a.m., but NEADS headquarters did not receive word of its fate from the FAA until the following transmission at 10:15 a.m.

NEADS: I also want to give you a heads-up, Washington.
FAA (DC): Go ahead.
NEADS: United nine three, have you got information on that yet?
FAA: Yeah, he's down.
NEADS: He's down?
FAA: Yes.
NEADS: When did he land? 'Cause we have got confirmation—
FAA: He did not land.
NEADS: Oh, he's down? Down?

FAA: Yes. Somewhere up northeast of Camp David.
NEADS: Northeast of Camp David.
FAA: That's the last report. They don't know exactly where.

Flight 93 was 125 miles from Washington, DC, less than twenty minutes of flying time, when it plunged to the ground in Stonycreek Township. But the 9/11 Commission wasn't sure the military could have shot down the hijacked aircraft even had it continued unencumbered on its path toward the US Capitol. Two armed F-16 fighter jets scrambled from Langley Air Force Base in Virginia were circling the city on combat air patrol shortly after 10:00 a.m., but the pilots had not been briefed on details of the threat they were facing and had no information on Flight 93's location.

At 10:10 a.m., they still had "negative clearance to shoot." The commission specifically questioned whether NORAD would have been capable of preventing the final attack had Flight 93 ever reached Washington airspace. In a report that was critical of the military's performance, it wrote:

NORAD officials have maintained that they would have intercepted and shot down United 93. We are not so sure. We are sure that the nation owes a debt to the passengers of Flight 93 . . .

NORAD and the FAA were unprepared for the type of attacks launched against the United States on September 11, 2001. They struggled, under difficult circumstances, to improvise a homeland defense against an unprecedented challenge they had never before encountered and had never trained to meet.

Back in Somerset County, some observers reported seeing a small plane circling the crash site shortly after Flight 93 went down. This led to rumors that it was an F-16. In reality, a Dassault Falcon 20 business jet, owned by the VF Corp. of Greensboro, North Carolina, was descending to land at the Johnston-Cambria County Airport when Cleveland Air Traffic Control asked the pilot to drop to 1,500 feet to look for smoke from the crash site. VF Corp.'s director of aviation, David Newell, provided confirmation and details in an interview with *Popular Mechanics,* which produced a book titled *Debunking 9/11 Myths.* "The FAA asked them to investigate and they did," Newell said. "They got down within 1,500 feet of the ground when they circled. They saw a hole in the ground with smoke coming out of it. They pinpointed the location and then continued on."

The only military plane in the area was an unarmed Air National Guard C-130H cargo plane that was heading to Minnesota from Andrews Air Force Base. It was flying at 24,000 feet and was seventeen miles away when it reported seeing "black smoke" less than two minutes after the crash.

Multiple witnesses saw Flight 93 intact in its final moments. No one reported seeing a midair explosion, or seeing the plane break apart before the crash. Rodney Peterson, an auto mechanic at a car dealership in nearby Boswell, was startled when he saw the plane's wings dipping sharply to the right and left. "If they were fighting with the hijackers," he told the *New York Times,* "I guarantee it happened right here." Terry Butler was working at Stoystown Auto Wreckers on US Route 30, about four miles from the crash site, when he saw the low-flying jetliner gain altitude and then disappear over a tree line. The *New York Times* reported on September 14 that "Mr. Butler and Mr. Peterson said they saw no other plane near the jetliner and no smoke or fire coming from it."

Lee Purbaugh, working a blowtorch at the Rollock scrap metal company on a hill overlooking the strip mine—just his second day on the job—was the closest witness to the crash site. He stared in disbelief as the plane whizzed over his head and made its final fatal dive into the open field.

"The plane was not shot down," the FBI's Wells Morrison said bluntly. "It did not explode. It flew into the ground."

The evidence to support his claim was overwhelming—from the flight data recorder, which charted the flight path and details; from the cockpit voice recorder, which confirmed the passenger revolt and the terrorists' intent to crash the plane; from the phone calls to loved ones; from the 9/11 Commission investigation of the military's preparedness and actions; from eyewitness reports. Beyond all that, there was common-sense testimony from first responders on the ground. Had Flight 93 been shot down, the plane would have started coming apart in advance of the crash, and pieces of debris would have fallen along the flight path leading to the impact site. They found nothing.

"There was no debris in the flight path until the crash site," said Wally Miller, the Somerset County coroner, who spent more time tramping the ground there than anyone else in the country. "It was all found from the impact site and beyond." Miller didn't base his claim solely on personal observation, or on the statements of FBI and state police investigators who worked the site. He also was talking about local citizens with hunting rifles.

"Small-game hunting season started a few weeks later and if you know anything about western Pennsylvania, you know the woods around here were going to be swarming with people," he said. "Especially here in Somerset County. You're talking hunters' haven. If there was debris out there on the flight path, debris out there anywhere, those guys would have found something. Someone would have said something. You couldn't have kept it quiet."

From an investigative standpoint, Bob Craig wasn't taking any chances. Early in the probe, the thirty-year FBI veteran asked the Pennsylvania State Police to take their helicopter along the flight path to see if there was anything "suspicious." They did, and saw nothing. Then Craig and others organized a detail to conduct a shoulder-to-shoulder sweep from the crash site to the top of a long sloping hill that was in Flight 93's direct route. It was a distance of several hundred yards. The agents and officers dutifully walked back and forth, up the slope and back, looking for anything man-made. They came back empty-handed.

"We essentially eliminated the first couple hundred yards of ground space before the plane impacted the ground," Craig said. "We found nothing associated with the aircraft."

Conspiracy theorists continued for years to promote a shoot-down scenario, but Jack Shea, the special agent in charge of the Pittsburgh Division of the FBI on September 11, said, "The facts just didn't support their position."

The excavation and recovery effort had been a massive operation. The original crater created by the crash was thirty feet across and as much as fifteen feet deep. Workers with heavy equipment had enlarged it by more than twice the size to eighty-five feet by eighty-five feet and twenty-seven to forty feet deep. During the first week, someone asked Bob Craig how far they would keep digging. "We're going to chase this until there is nothing to be found," he said.

They uncovered debris thirty-five feet beneath the surface but went five feet deeper, just in case. They followed the trail wherever it led. A solid "high wall" from the old strip-mining operation was still intact underground, near the edge of the hemlock trees, so "nothing was going to go beyond that," Craig said. But they dug as far as they could in all other directions. They searched for final, elusive clues, more pieces of airplane shrapnel.

The FBI concluded its investigation of the Flight 93 crash on September 24, announcing that it had recovered 95 percent of the Boeing 757. All of the shattered plane parts were collected in Dumpsters and returned to United Airlines, with the exception of the flight data recorder and cockpit voice recorder.

The reclaimed strip mine in Stonycreek Township that for two weeks served as an active crime scene in the largest terrorist attack in American history was officially signed over at that point to the local coroner. For the next four years, as cleanup work continued and plans for a national memorial were developed, the crash site would fall under the jurisdiction of Somerset County native Wallace E. Miller.

CHAPTER THIRTEEN

The "Hick" Coroner

It did not take long after arriving at the crash site on the morning of September 11 for Wally Miller to understand the enormity of his task. "I stopped being coroner after about twenty minutes," he said. Not only were there no survivors, there were no bodies. In the few seconds that it took Flight 93 to crash and shatter and implode, the old Diamond T strip mine in tiny Stonycreek Township had been transformed into a giant burial ground.

So Miller put on his other hat: funeral director.

He grew up the son of a mortician and became one himself, taking over his dad's business and serving the people of Somerset County long before they elected him to public office. The Miller Funeral Home on Tayman Avenue prides itself on compassion and gentle touch. He estimates that in an average year he will arrange and oversee 125 services and burials. Very few people can operate in that environment. Even Miller admits, "I *do* know a little about grief."

The right man in the right place at the absolute worst time, Miller became a beacon in the darkness for the families of Flight 93. He calls himself "just a country coroner, just a hick, just a guy trying to do his job," but those who were struggling with horrific loss under a national media spotlight saw him as much more: He was their new friend and confidant. Lyz Glick could have been speaking for all of them when she said, "Wally Miller was the nearest thing to a hero the crash investigation had produced."

When the FBI handed Miller jurisdiction of the crash site on September 24, the families were foremost in Miller's mind. He'd already met many of them on their trips to Somerset County immediately after the crash, providing his home and cell phone numbers and encouraging them to call at any time. They did. The impact site was off-limits to the general public—a hastily assembled chain-link fence surrounded the original debris field—but Miller would personally escort family members to the area he considered sacred ground. For most of them, it was the start of a long, arduous healing process. Gordie Felt called him "an absolutely fierce advocate for the families in our time of need."

"At one point…I called his number, expecting an answering machine," Melodie Homer said. "And he answered the phone. It was maybe 11 or 12 at night. I didn't realize he would actually answer the phone, but he answered my question even though I woke him up. It could have been a lot worse had he not been the type of person that he is."

Miller understood that the families wanted and needed closure. The goal was to identify remains from all forty passengers and crew members. But he knew it would be difficult. He estimated that the combined weight of all forty-four people on board, including the four hijackers, was about 7,700 pounds. Most of the remains had been vaporized on impact. In time, investigators and volunteer searchers at the crash site would recover what Miller calculated to be just more than 8 percent of that total—650 pounds.

Sixteen of the passengers and crew members were identified in the first few weeks by either fingerprints or dental records. The first was Waleska Martinez, an employee of the US Census Bureau; the government had her fingerprints on file. An agent combing the site for evidence also found a tooth that was traced to Jeremy Glick. Others would have to be identified by using DNA samples provided in those early days by the families.

A temporary morgue was set up at the Pennsylvania National Guard Armory in nearby Friedens, where teams of experts—forensic pathologists, radiologists, dentists, X-ray technicians, fingerprint analysts—examined the fragmented remains. Additional samples were sent to the Armed Forces Institute of Pathology's DNA identification laboratory in Rockville, Maryland. Slowly, patiently, they began to make headway. The process was grim, disturbing—but necessary.

Ziad Jarrah
MOUSSAOUI TRIAL EVIDENCE

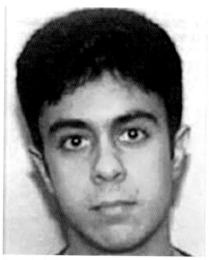

Saeed al Ghamdi
MOUSSAOUI TRIAL EVIDENCE

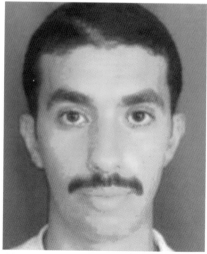

Ahmed al Haznawi
MOUSSAOUI TRIAL EVIDENCE

Ahmed al Nami
MOUSSAOUI TRIAL EVIDENCE

Among the items found at the crash site were Saeed al Ghamdi's visa (above) and a Saudi Arabian Youth Hostel Association ID card belonging to Ahmed al Nami (below).

MOUSSAOUI TRIAL EVIDENCE

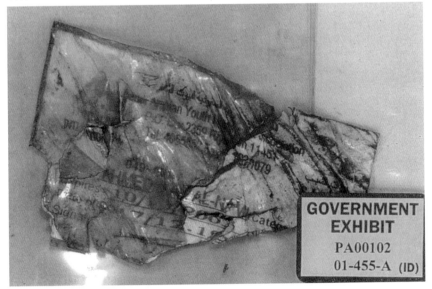

A bandanna found at the crash site. Passengers reported that the hijackers wore red bandannas during the attack.

Aerial view of the Flight 93 impact site. Note the haunting outline of the plane near the burned-out hemlocks.

The largest piece of the plane discovered at the crash site was this section of the fuselage.

Part of one of the engines was found by investigators in the crater.

The cockpit voice recorder contained the sounds of the last half hour of the flight, including the passenger/crew insurrection. It was found on September 14.

The flight data recorder provided vital information such as altitude, speed, and direction. It was discovered in the crater on September 13.

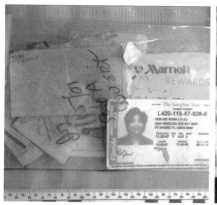

Personal effects of flight attendant CeeCee Lyles, including her driver's license, were found in the wreckage at the crash site.

MOUSSAOUI TRIAL EVIDENCE

Flight attendant CeeCee Lyles

MOUSSAOUI TRIAL EVIDENCE

From left, coroner Wally Miller; Flight 93 family members Alice Hoglan, Lisa Beamer, and Lyz Glick; and interviewer Katie Couric at the crash site in 2002.

MARY JANE KIEHL PHOTO

From the earliest days after the crash, visitors placed personal items on a fence at the temporary memorial.

CHUCK WAGNER PHOTO

Featured guests at the dedication of the Flight 93 National Memorial on September 10, 2011, were (front row, left to right) President George Bush, Laura Bush, President Bill Clinton, Jill Biden, and Vice President Joe Biden.
CHUCK WAGNER PHOTO

Dignitaries walking past the Wall of Names at the dedication of the national memorial included, from far right, Vice President Joe Biden, Jill Biden, President Bill Clinton, President George Bush, and Laura Bush.
CHUCK WAGNER PHOTO

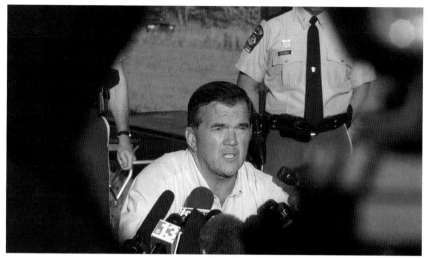

Pennsylvania governor Tom Ridge addressed the media on September 11, 2001.
Ridge later became the first Secretary of Homeland Security.
ARCHIE CARPENTER PHOTO

Investigators, including Pennsylvania State Police officers, at the impact site on
September 11, 2001.
ARCHIE CARPENTER PHOTO

A tribute to passenger Todd Beamer at one of the temporary memorials. It was Beamer who uttered the famous battle cry, "Let's roll."
ARCHIE CARPENTER PHOTO

Hilda Marcin's Flight 93 boarding pass, found at the crash site, was returned to her family.
COURTESY OF CAROLE O'HARE

Passenger Tom Burnett
COURTESY OF BEVERLY BURNETT

Passenger Jeremy Glick
COURTESY OF LYZBETH BEST

Hilda Marcin, 79, was the oldest passenger on board Flight 93.
COURTESY OF CAROLE O'HARE

Deora Bodley, 20, was the youngest passenger.
COURTESY OF DEBORAH BORZA

Passenger Ed Felt
COURTESY OF SANDRA V. FELT

Flight attendant Lorraine Bay
COURTESY OF EDWIN R. ROOT

The door of the Hoover family garage was rattled off its hinges by the force of the impact.

Debris from the crash was littered around Barry Hoover's cabin nearby.

Shattered airplane debris and jet fuel at the crash site.
COURTESY OF WALLACE E. MILLER AND ARLENE MILLER

The burned-out hemlock trees just beyond the impact site.
COURTESY OF WALLACE E. MILLER AND ARLENE MILLER

Small pieces of the airplane were evident in the crater.
COURTESY OF WALLACE E. MILLER AND ARLENE MILLER

Coroner Wally Miller (right) and other workers carry bins of items recovered at the crash site.
COURTESY OF WALLACE E. MILLER AND ARLENE MILLER

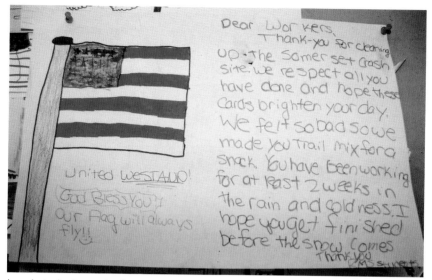

Local students made signs to support the first responders and volunteers.
COURTESY OF WALLACE E. MILLER AND ARLENE MILLER

Flowers and other mementos were left on hay bales at the western overlook in the early days after the crash. This is where family members first viewed the impact site.
COURTESY OF WALLACE E. MILLER AND ARLENE MILLER

Volunteers, many from local and regional fire departments, scan the field as part of the secondary recovery effort in October 2001.
COURTESY OF WALLACE E. MILLER AND ARLENE MILLER

Coroner Wally Miller addresses firemen and other volunteers who helped search the area around the crash site for debris and remains.
COURTESY OF WALLACE E. MILLER AND ARLENE MILLER

Somerset County residents placed signs, flags, and other items at one of the early temporary memorials.

TIM LAMBERT PHOTO

Flags, wreaths, and other items at one of the first temporary memorials in tiny Shanksville.

TIM LAMBERT PHOTO

Dumpsters were reserved for specific items at the crash site.
TIM LAMBERT PHOTO

View from the back of a United Airlines 757, showing Airfones on the seat-backs of the middle seats. Flight 93 passengers used Airfones to call loved ones and report details of the hijacking.
NICHOLAS YOUNG PHOTOGRAPHY

"I'm not naive enough to believe we'll get everything, but we'll try to get everything we possibly can," Miller told reporters. "When you have a plane traveling at 500 miles per hour, I think you understand what the scenario is."

Lean and angular at six-foot, four-inches tall, Miller commanded the field with a congenial manner that reflected his style as a funeral director: calm, considerate, and resolute. A visiting reporter said his face resembled "a young, shaven version of Abe Lincoln." The forty-four-year-old native of the borough of Somerset (population: 6,700) wasn't used to being on this kind of national media stage, and he certainly wasn't comfortable dealing with the corporate types and Washington bureaucrats who were an inevitable part of the Flight 93 aftermath. But he found a genuine kinship with the families. Miller knew that the public nature of their tragedy was bewildering, that most of them were still disconsolate and grieving deeply as September turned to October. He wanted to make sure they had a voice in any decision ever made about the crash site.

With no resources to hire additional staff, Miller turned to professional friends to assist him—including Denny Kwiatkowski, the coroner of nearby Cambria County, and Dr. Dennis Dirkmaat, a forensic anthropologist from Mercyhurst College in Erie. He also enlisted his wife, Arlene, to run a makeshift office coordinating their efforts and his cousin, Mark Miller, who had important connections as the director of support services at Somerset Hospital. On the coroner's first day in charge of the field, they made a chilling discovery. "Denny looked over at one of the piles that was left and he saw a jawbone with four or five teeth in it," Miller said. It was readily apparent that, despite painstaking effort, the FBI and state police had not recovered all the human remains from the crash.

Wally Miller was determined to have all those remains collected and removed before taking family members on tours of the impact site. Up to that point, they had been allowed no closer than an overlook that was two hundred yards away. The place was still considered a crime scene until the FBI concluded its investigation on September 24. Miller didn't want to risk any relative experiencing the trauma of having to see a finger, a chunk of flesh, a flap of skin. He recruited the services of the Southwest

Pennsylvania Emergency Response Team to canvass the site, and that group—volunteer firemen and other first responders from thirteen counties—came back with what he estimated to be an additional 150 pounds of remains. "That was significant, because the final total was only about 650 pounds from everyone on board," Miller said. They went back two or three more times before he was convinced that all the human bone and tissue had been recovered.

"They found some debris, too," the coroner said, "but nothing bigger than a pop rivet holding two pieces of aluminum."

In October, Miller made his next key decision: Before opening the area to family members, he wanted to backfill the crater and cover it with six inches of topsoil. It was the coroner's mandate to restore a crime scene to its original condition once an investigation was completed—but he also believed, in his heart, that it was the right thing to do. The site was the final resting place of the forty men and women who acted heroically in their final moments. They deserved more than a gaping hole in the ground. Just beyond the crater, a ring of burned-out hemlock trees had been felled in the weeks after the crash and chipped into piles of sawdust. It was not long before the old Diamond T landscape started to look much as it had on September 10.

The family and friends of Captain Jason Dahl arrived in early November, led by Jason's wife, Sandy, and his best friend and fellow pilot, David Dosch. They brought a bottle of wine with them and asked Miller how close they could get to the impact site. He decided the time was right.

"It was a pretty neat story," Miller said, "because they wanted to drink a toast to Jason on his birthday. I said, 'Why not?' So I let them go down there."

David had purchased the bottle of port for Jason from a winery in New Zealand. It was from 1957, the year both he and Jason were born. The two pilots had started at United on the same day, and the plan was to drink the special New Zealand port on the day of their retirement. But things had changed.

"So we took that bottle of port and we opened it up," Sandy Dahl said, "and we poured a little, tiny bit in each glass."

With the Somerset County coroner looking on, they raised a toast to the pilot of Flight 93.

—◦—

During those weeks, whenever a passenger or crew member was identified, it was up to Miller to notify the next of kin. Even for a man used to handling death scenes and presiding at burials, it was a gut-wrenching task. Reactions ran the emotional gauntlet. Closure wasn't always an easy thing; he knew that from experience. But he believed these people deserved the facts.

The phone rang at Lorne Lyles's home late on the evening of September 23. It was only twelve days after his wife, CeeCee, had called him from the plane, screaming as the passengers charged the cockpit. The wounds were still open, still raw. "Wally called me and said they had positively identified CeeCee," Lorne said. "I lost it again. I was by myself. I called my mom. She calmed me down."

A little more than a month later, near the end of October, Melodie Homer received her call. The young widow wondered what part of LeRoy's body had been recovered. "Wally asked me if I really wanted to know," she wrote in her book, *From Where I Stand*. "I could tell by the tone of his voice that I wouldn't want to know, so I declined." She sat on the steps of her doorway one more time and started to cry. It was the kind of heartbreak that was repeated over and over, not only from coast to coast but also across the world—from Germany, home of Christian Adams, to Japan, home of Toshiya Kuge.

With his background as a funeral director, Miller knew there would be other emotional challenges facing the families, especially young mothers with small children. Many of them were dealing with explaining death to someone for the first time. In Cranbury, New Jersey, Lisa Beamer struggled to explain to her three-year-old-son David that his daddy wouldn't ever be coming home.

Lisa did her best, told him Daddy was with Jesus, but she wasn't sure he understood until two of Todd Beamer's relatives visited a few days later. Little David was giving a tour of the house when they came to a big bedroom and one of them automatically asked, "Is this your mommy and daddy's room?"

David told them no. "This is just my mommy's room now because my daddy is gone."

Another necessary but heartrending job was to return the personal effects collected at the site—at least those that could be directly linked to individual passengers and crew. United Airlines had hired Douglass Air Disaster Funeral Directors out of Los Angeles to coordinate funeral arrangements for the victims and also to gather and distribute their belongings to the families. There were shoes, driver's licenses, work credentials, credit cards. And at least three wedding rings.

One ring belonged to Andrew "Sonny" Garcia. It was inscribed ALL MY LOVE, 8-2-69. In mid-December, the ring was returned to Sonny's wife, Dorothy, at her home in California. She also received his wallet.

Another ring was returned to Melodie Homer in New Jersey. She was surprised, since the ring wasn't marked with names or dates—in fact, no one from the FBI ever had asked her about it. But there it was, arriving just before Christmas, along with the dog tags LeRoy kept on his key chain. She cried again. "The inscription inside was the Bible verse we had chosen for our wedding ceremony: 'The greatest of these is love,'" Melodie wrote. "The only explanation I could imagine was that it had been found on LeRoy's hand." The speculation made sense. The first officer was the only African-American male on board Flight 93.

The third ring once belonged to Hilda Marcin's husband, Edward. A former welder and police officer, Edward passed away in 1979. Hilda had placed the ring in a Ziploc bag along with some of her favorite jewelry and packed it for the trip to California. "It was just an unusual design, so I knew what to look for," Betty Kemmerer said. "The jewelry probably was scattered all over the place. But we got quite a bit back." Betty found yet another keepsake among the unclaimed family items listed in a catalog. She came across her own graduation picture from the Class of 1963 at Irvington (New Jersey) High.

One of the most astonishing discoveries was the virtually intact badge and credentials belonging to Richard Guadagno, who worked for the US Fish and Wildlife Service at the Humboldt Bay National Wildlife Refuge in California. These were found dangling among the hemlocks, in what Miller described as an area of high debris concentration. They were returned to Richard's parents in New Jersey. "It just looked like it wasn't damaged or hadn't gone through much at all, which is so bizarre and ironic," said his sister, Lori. "But everything takes on a special meaning, especially when there's so little that you have."

The quest to identify human remains—still the most important task—continued well into December. By the end of the month, thanks to the diligent work of many specialists, all forty passengers and crew members had been accounted for—either by fingerprints, dental records, or DNA matches. Miller achieved his goal of giving each family a small sense of closure on December 19, more than three months after the crash, when analysts positively identified the remains of the last passenger, Joe DeLuca. There were four other sets of remains that were not able to be identified because of the lack of DNA samples, and they were turned over to the custody of the FBI. Those, of course, belonged to the hijackers.

From the beginning, Miller had wanted to bring family members together in one large setting to update them on the facts of the case. Scattered across the country and the world, they'd begun to slowly pick up the shattered pieces of their lives. Communication with such a diverse group of people had been difficult. He thought they deserved more information than they were receiving.

It took weeks of negotiations to sort through the red tape, pick a date, select a reasonably convenient site, and book travel and lodging, but the meeting finally was set for February 23 at the Hilton Hotel in Woodbridge, New Jersey. Arlene Miller, Wally's wife, helped him handle all the arrangements. Representatives of thirty-six of the forty families—eighty-eight people in all—made the trip. Some simply had not been ready for the details of the crash in the weeks immediately after September 11. Others had asked a few random questions, gathered basic information, learned specifics about their own loved ones—but had no clear sense of the big picture. Now, five months out, more of them wanted answers. Lyz Glick wrote about it in her book, *Your Father's Voice*, admitting, "I was surprised at my own curiosity."

Groups of them had been together before for ceremonies at the crash site, but this was the first time so many had congregated in the same room for a tutorial on the investigation. Miller narrated a slide show, talked about the speed and angle of the plane on impact, and visually walked them through the crater and the hemlocks and the sediment pond—"things we didn't know," Sandy Dahl said. He talked about the debris field, the locations of the human remains. He talked about the extraordinary efforts of local volunteers to reclaim every possible item.

"A lot of it was Wally in his role as funeral director, letting us know everything that had gone on," said Debby Borza, whose daughter, twenty-year-old Deora Bodley, was the youngest person aboard Flight 93. "You had a lot of emotional family members in that room. You can't even imagine the emotion. Wally spent all day with us. The poor guy went through four shirts, sweating. He tried to answer all of our questions. I'm sure it wasn't easy."

Miller's talk included a lot of numbers and raw statistics. Most of them, Lyz Glick said, were "grim." More than fifteen hundred samples of human remains had been recovered at the site, but many of them were so small and in such poor condition that even DNA testing wasn't possible. Miller told them that the distribution of remains wasn't logical because of the utter violence of the crash. "A little bit of a person might turn up at the mouth of the hole," Lyz remembered him saying. "Then, a half-mile away, a little more of that person would be found."

The FBI had caught wind of the meeting and wanted to attend, hoping to interview as many family members as possible. Agents were gathering evidence for future cases on terrorism, including the pending trial of Zacarias Moussaoui, the al-Qaeda operative who was arrested one month before the attacks. The chance to speak with so many relatives in a single day was an overworked investigator's dream. Miller had wanted this to be just about the families—basic, comfortable, casual—but the coroner of Somerset County didn't have the authority to banish the FBI. What he could do, however, was issue a friendly warning. "I told those guys that if they showed up, the family members would only talk to them about one thing," Miller said. "They wanted to hear the cockpit voice recorder."

The cockpit voice recorder had been a sore spot for months. The families were aware that the recording existed and were repeatedly frustrated by the authorities' refusal to allow them to hear it. Chaotic and unclear as the audio may have been, they believed they deserved a chance to understand what their loved ones had experienced, and Miller agreed. The FBI was reluctant to release such "evidence" before using it to prosecute Moussaoui or other terrorists. Making it even worse for the families, the decision to withhold the recording was framed by the Bureau as a way to "protect" them. They were told that hearing the tape might create too much emotional trauma.

Lyz Glick wasn't buying it. She knew Deena Burnett and others had been working to get access to the recording since shortly after the attacks in September. During the question-and-answer session at the end of the Woodbridge meeting, Lyz was determined to have her say. She rose to her feet and "berated" the FBI.

"You're telling us we can't listen to this because it's too terrible a thing for the families to hear?" Lyz said. "Where does the FBI get the right to judge that? I can tell you that everything terrible that could happen to me has already happened. The terrible thing was losing my husband and having to live with it."

The room broke out in applause.

"I'm telling you, the place erupted," Miller said.

The FBI didn't relent—at least not yet—but a supervisor told them the request would be seriously considered.

⁓

The session with Miller in Woodbridge had a liberating effect on many of the family members. They had been together in a large gathering for the first time since the memorial services in the days immediately following the crash. The emotions were still fresh, the losses still bitter and gnawing, but the knowledge they gained there enabled many of them to better process the events of September 11—and the role of their loved ones in the battle for Flight 93.

As the six-month anniversary approached in early March, Lisa Beamer, Lyz Glick, and Alice Hoglan agreed to travel to Somerset County to appear on NBC's *Today* show. Reports of their loved ones' dramatic phone calls from the plane had turned the three family members into frequent interview subjects and, in some ways, media stars. Todd Beamer's "Let's roll" had became the phrase that defined the passenger uprising for the general public—Neil Young even used it for a song title about the attacks. Before the interview, Lisa and Lyz took a private tour of the site with Miller. At one point, the topic turned to personal effects recovered by investigators. Some already had been returned to family members, but most were still being held by the FBI at a hangar nearby. Lyz was especially curious if Jeremy's wedding ring had been found.

Miller dutifully made a call to ask if it was included in the inventory of items. It was not.

"So what am I getting back?" Lyz asked.

"A credit card," he said. "It got melted some, but it's mostly intact."

It was far less than many families would receive. Lyz half-joked that if the ring didn't turn up, she would be back that summer with her metal detector.

"Hey, I'll help you look," Miller said, laughing.

"Deal," she said.

"I wouldn't be surprised if you both don't wind up down here digging like two crazy lunatics," Lisa Beamer said.

Alas, the search party never materialized and the ring was never found, but the point had been made once again. The "hick" coroner of Somerset County would crawl around on his hands and knees, if necessary, to help the families.

CHAPTER FOURTEEN

The Tape

Deena Burnett wasted no time asking federal authorities to release the tape of the cockpit voice recording from Flight 93. She had made her first request on the afternoon of September 11. "Even then," Deena wrote in her book, *Fighting Back*, "I felt that the families deserved to know what really went on up there, and I wanted to hear the tape for myself."

Deena found a staunch ally in Congresswoman Ellen Tauscher, and the two women made multiple requests of FBI director Robert Mueller to hear the recording—writing letters, making phone calls, sending faxes. Still, by early 2002 the only response Deena had received was a warning that hearing the recording could be detrimental to their mental health. "I believed their concern to be insulting," she said.

Melodie Homer also was pressuring the FBI. The first officer's widow had been through a jarring experience on November 15, 2001, when ABC's *Primetime Live* played—without forewarning—the brief Air Traffic Control recording from the cockpit during the hijacking. It was the first time she'd heard the voice of her husband, First Officer LeRoy Homer, yelling "Get out of here!" and "Mayday!"

"Words cannot explain how painful it was to hear this on a national broadcast," she wrote. Hoping to avoid a similar situation with the thirty-one-minute cockpit voice recording, she wrote a letter to Director Mueller, asking to hear the tape or to read the transcript in a private setting. Her request was denied. She was told she would not find "comfort in the recording."

Melodie found that to be unacceptable and composed another letter on March 4:

No one has any idea what a victim's family would find comforting, and unless your husband left for work on September 11, 2001, never to return, leaving you with a ten-month-old baby, you have no idea how I feel. When you receive 2.6 percent of your husband's remains six months after the last time you saw him, then maybe you can decide what is or what is not comforting. Until then, it is very arrogant of you or your agency to presume anything.

She told Mueller in the letter that if the Bureau didn't cooperate, she was going to take her case to the courts—or to the media.

Unable to make headway either, Deena Burnett considered traveling to Washington herself to address the FBI in person. Instead, she dashed off one more letter to Mueller from Tauscher's office on March 20, faxing it as well as sending it by overnight mail and requesting a face-to-face meeting with the director sometime in April. This time, the response was instantaneous.

Deena received a voice mail on the afternoon of March 21 saying Mueller had reconsidered and would allow the families to hear the recording. Melodie got the same message at the same time from a local FBI agent. Their pressure and resilience had clearly changed the FBI's mind.

The meeting was scheduled for April 18 at the Hyatt in Princeton, New Jersey. Family members of the crew would hear the recording in the morning, followed by relatives of the passengers in the afternoon. They were asked to sign confidentiality agreements because the contents of the tape would be evidence for the upcoming Moussaoui trial and other legal cases. They also were asked to provide "victim impact statements," describing how the loss of loved ones affected the survivors. The FBI was trying to maximize its access to the families.

The afternoon session with the passengers' families was scheduled from 1:30 to 5:30. A number of them arrived early and ate lunch in the hotel restaurant. As emotional and important as the day would become, one of Deena's most memorable moments came during lunch, when the wife of another passenger approached and introduced herself. It was Meredith Rothenberg, wife of Mark "Mickey" Rothenberg, who had been seated one row behind Tom Burnett in first class when Flight 93 left Newark.

Tom was in 4B, Mickey in 5B. Hijacker Ahmed al Haznawi was in 6B.

Deena recounted the story in *Fighting Back*. "I've wanted to talk to you," Meredith said. "I know your husband told you that a passenger was stabbed by the hijackers. I think it may have been my husband."

It was stunning. "Why do you think that?" Deena asked.

"Mickey was the kind of guy who would have interfered," Meredith said. ". . . He was a negotiator. It's what he did for a living. He would have tried to find out what they wanted and worked to achieve an end without violence."

Deena remembered that Tom had told her about a man who'd been stabbed. He'd tried to help him but couldn't get a pulse. He said the man appeared to be dead, the first passenger casualty in the battle for Flight 93. That explained why Mickey was the only passenger in first class who hadn't made a phone call. Now the two wives were sharing a moment before hearing the recording. Their emotions were on edge. But they were ready.

One of the great ironies of their day in Princeton came as they approached the large hotel banquet room. The families were required to pass through a metal detector. They were allowed to bring notebooks and pens with them, but everything else—cell phones, pagers, purses, cameras— had to be placed on a long table, which was then covered by a tarp. There were more than one hundred people in the room, sitting in what one remembered as "uncomfortable blue chairs." Dave Novak, one of the US attorneys prosecuting the Moussaoui case, opened the proceedings with an explanation of what they were about to hear. He said a transcript would be displayed on a large screen to help them understand the words through the muffled noise and static.

"We listened along through headsets," Debby Borza told me. "There were captions on the screen. We took notes, but they weren't going to let us have copies of the transcript."

Everyone listened for sounds of their loved ones, especially during the chaos at the end. Deena said she recognized Tom's voice shouting, "In the cockpit!" Lyz said she heard Jeremy's "judo grunt." Kenny Nacke sensed the familiar rage of his older brother, Joey. "There's a phrase in there that I hear—that's Joey," Kenny said. "It was pure rage. I've seen it.

I've heard it. I've been chased by it." Others didn't make any connections amid the tumult. One family member thought it was impossible to identify individual voices. Several believed that "some people heard what they wanted to hear."

Kenny, a police officer by trade, was asked about screams from a voice in Arabic; he was asked if he could decipher an attack on the hijackers themselves.

"Oh, yes, you hear it," he said. "You hear one guy getting the living s*** beat out of him."

By the end, he concluded, the hijackers were not just confounded but terrified.

"Once the passengers and crew were able to do what they did, the hijackers' mission was a failure," Kenny said. "They weren't going to get to their target. It was like, 'what do we do now?' You don't think that ran through their mind? You hear them say 'Allah' a whole bunch. I mean, there were forty pissed off people coming at them . . ."

The hardest part for the families was that they knew the end of the story. They knew the screams and static would turn to silence. And yet some of them found a fragile solace in hearing evidence of their loved ones' courage. The recording couldn't give them closure or clarity, but it gave them context. There was a certain mythology that had developed in news reports about the desperate and heroic counterattack by the passengers and crew. Now those closest to the victims could hear it and almost feel it for themselves.

"This was as close as I could be to my daughter in her final moments," said Derrill Bodley, Deora's father.

"They sounded like the heroes people are saying they were," said Christine Fraser, Colleen's sister.

Mark Bingham's mother, Alice Hoglan, attended the meeting with her brother, Vaughn, and one of Mark's closest friends, Spence Kelly. Spence and Mark had run with the bulls in Spain together just that summer. Alice described the day in Princeton as "excruciating" for the families, but she never doubted that it would be a worthwhile experience to hear the replay of final moments. No longer would the final moments of their loved ones' lives be available only to anonymous attorneys and investigators.

"The cockpit voice recorder, even though it was technically flawed and difficult to hear, was just the most dramatic thing," Alice told me. "It was thirty-one minutes on a continuous loop, and the last ten minutes were really telling. It was extremely loud as they attacked the cockpit—an escalating crescendo of male voices, probably half a dozen guys. At one point you even hear Jarrah telling his buddy to hold up the ax.

"Deena Burnett tells me she heard Tom's voice. That started the cockpit chant— 'In the cockpit!' —that got picked up by several others. I'm sure I heard Mark's voice, too. Kimi Beaven said she heard Alan's voice, his accent. They were all doing it together. It was a sustained assault that went on for several minutes."

That sustained assault eventually withered and the voices went silent, but Alice had found a sense of heroic grandeur in the fury of the doomed passengers. "I was so grateful that Mark was able to spend the last few moments of his life on his feet, fighting, with a bunch of other guys, doing his level best to save the people around him."

Meredith Rothenberg knew from the start that she would not hear Mickey's voice on the tape. The knife attack in first class had taken place almost immediately after the hijackers seized control of the plane. Mickey never would have known about the phone calls or the attacks on the World Trade Center, never would have known about the daring plan to charge the cockpit. And yet she went home believing that he was part of the passenger uprising.

"I think it was a story of extreme bravery," Meredith said. "I don't think he was a victim. I don't think that the terrorists decided to pick out an innocent person sitting in first class and say, 'maybe the right way to start this is just to stab somebody.' I believe that he stood up or indicated in some way that he could think of a deal they could make—because, after all, before [September 11], any hijacking was a negotiation. It was about money. It wasn't about murder."

Her husband paid with his life, but that sent a powerful message— and maybe helped focus the rest of the passengers. The five other regular passengers in first class, including Tom Burnett and Mark Bingham, would have witnessed the assault on Mickey from just a few feet away. Some may have been splattered with blood. They undoubtedly would have passed on the shocking information about his death and its sudden implications to the others in the back of the plane.

Viewing the events through their own prisms, many other family members found comfort among the chaos. Betty Kemmerer knew that her seventy-nine-year-old mother would not be up front flailing away at Ahmed al Nami or ramming a food cart into the cockpit. But Hilda Marcin had the gentle touch of a grandmother and a teacher's aide. Two other passengers, Donald Peterson and Jean Hoadley Peterson, had spent their retirement years doing volunteer work and crisis counseling. People with those unique skills could have provided invaluable service in the back of the aircraft when terror was unleashed at 35,000 feet.

"I think all forty [people] on that plane had a specific job to do that day," Betty said, "whether it was remaining in their seats while somebody took on the hijackers or consoling someone else who was upset. I think everyone worked together as a team. My sister and I said that one of the things our mother probably would have done would be to maybe take Nicole Miller under her wing, because she was the (college student). We often said that she probably was just calming these people down."

There were likely as many different reactions and emotions as people in the room.

Lyz Glick had been on the phone with Jeremy on September 11 until the midair revolt began, so she had a dramatically different perspective than most of the family members in attendance. Lyz didn't stay around for the tape to end. She chose to leave the room.

"I was re-living what had happened and I didn't want to wait until it went silent," she said. "I'd had enough details from Wally about the way the plane impacted. I couldn't . . . I just needed to be alone. And scream."

Wally Miller was in Princeton that day, but the FBI wouldn't allow him in the room. It seemed wrong that Miller couldn't accompany the families for such an important moment. He'd been their leading advocate, the man who'd arranged the first meeting in Woodbridge, the one who'd told the Bureau about their unrelenting interest in the tape. But the FBI had its rules. "I tried to get Wally inside," Debby Borza said. "The man had done so much for us, so much to help make this happen. He should have heard it."

"Some day," Miller was still saying more than ten years later, "I'd really like to hear that cockpit tape."

❦

If Wally Miller committed any errors in his handling of the Flight 93 case, they stemmed from his inexperience in dealing with the national news media. He did not realize that some of his comments in the early days would unwittingly fuel conspiracy theories.

He'd done plenty of local interviews throughout the years, explaining an auto fatality to the *Somerset Daily American* or providing background on a story to WJAC-TV in nearby Johnstown, but he wasn't prepared for the invasion of national reporters who showed up for regular news briefings in the days and weeks following 9/11. Miller was earnest in his efforts, providing as much information as possible while protecting the privacy of the families. He wanted to help people understand the unfathomable carnage. There were times he tried to achieve it by painting vivid verbal pictures.

Struggling to explain the devastation at the site, he told a reporter from the *New York Times*, "It was as if the plane had stopped and let the passengers off before it crashed."

Emphasizing a similar point to another news outlet, he said, "It looked like somebody just dropped a bunch of metal out of the sky."

The conspiracy folks ignored the other relevant details he provided and shifted into overdrive. They spun those few out-of-context quotes into an incredible tale of government cover-up and media fraud. Some theorized that a plane crashed with no passengers. Others said a plane didn't crash at all.

Miller sighed. "I was just trying to illustrate that there weren't many remains," he said. Conspiracy theories were the furthest thing from his mind. He had death certificates to issue, families to console. "I didn't even hear a lot about the conspiracy stuff at first," he said, "but some people read those quotes and figured I was just some country dumb-ass." Others thought someone in the government was lording over him, telling him what to say.

On another occasion, Miller told the media, "I have not, to this day, seen a single drop of blood." More conspiracy furor ensued. *No blood? Did that mean no passengers? Maybe no plane?*

"People back then just didn't understand the physics of it—the level of fragmentation that occurred because of the sheer speed of the plane," Miller said. "A plane with more than 5,000 gallons of jet fuel hit the ground at more than 500 miles an hour, the crash ignited a fireball that burned very hot, and thousands of small pieces of debris got kicked up in the air and exposed to the elements. The bodies got vaporized. Of course there was no blood."

As winter turned to spring, the kids he coached on the track team at Somerset High told Miller they were seeing him all over the Internet, including on conspiracy blogs and antigovernment websites.

He got used to hearing about it and became something of a minor celebrity on YouTube.

"For years," he said, "the conspiracy nuts kept coming after me." In the summer of 2012, a large envelope arrived in the mail at the family funeral home. It was addressed to "WALLACE MILLER: THE MAN WHO KNOWS TOO MUCH."

Miller remained staunch in his belief that the family members should play a key role in any decision about the future of the crash site. A history buff who was awestruck by the nearby Civil War battlefields at Gettysburg and Antietam—"you can feel the history when you walk those fields"—he worried that the sacred ground in Stonycreek Township could be commercialized or picked over by relic hunters if the families didn't get involved. He was both surprised and pleased when a government official told him in late 2001 that the effort to turn the site into a national park would be fast-tracked. It wouldn't take fifty or a hundred years. It might take only ten. "But I still thought it made sense for the families to organize, to give themselves a seat at the table," he said.

He planted the seed during the initial meeting with the families in Woodbridge. That was the first time any of them contemplated the idea of a formal organization. Their loved ones had recognized the strength in numbers during those frantic final thirty minutes aboard Flight 93. Now the families reached the same conclusion. As a group, they could exert *real* influence over the acquisition of land and creation of a memorial at the site.

Three of them were appointed to an interim board of directors: Larry Catuzzi, father of Lauren Grandcolas; Jennifer Price, daughter of Jean Hoadley Peterson and stepdaughter of Donald Peterson; and Betty Kemmerer, daughter of Hilda Marcin. The first achievement of the "Families of Flight 93" was working with community leaders and local and national politicians to successfully lobby the federal government for a memorial in Somerset County. That part of the process happened quickly. On September 24, 2002—barely a year after the crash—President Bush signed the Flight 93 National Memorial Act into law.

Other entities became involved in the decadelong memorial effort, including the Flight 93 Advisory Commission, the Flight 93 Memorial Task Force, the National Park Service, and the National Park Foundation, but the family organization played an important role in the design, creation, funding, and completion of a permanent tribute to the forty heroes.

"Wally always felt we had to organize ourselves to have a voice in the process," Kenny Nacke told me. "A lot of us weren't thinking that far ahead, but he was—and he wanted to make sure we had a role. Of all the many things he did for the families, that was maybe the most important. He saw the value of a memorial. He gave us the strength to form an organization."

In Miller's mind, he'd done nothing out of the ordinary. He'd become, by happenstance of history, the caretaker of a graveyard containing the scattered remains of the first combatants of the twenty-first-century War on Terror. He knew the passengers and crew had earned their rightful spot in the pantheon of American heroes. He wanted the plot of land to be preserved for posterity.

Even in their grief, family members came to understand and accept the historic significance of the place. Deena Burnett made her first trip to the crash site in late April 2002 and admitted she found a "strange peace" as she gazed across the rural landscape. Her husband had been an avid student of military history. His office was adorned with busts of Abraham Lincoln, Theodore Roosevelt, and Winston Churchill. Tom Burnett admired the fortitude and fearlessness of the soldiers who fought at Gettysburg in July 1863. He told Deena he wondered if he ever could display that same kind of courage in the face of death.

"What a fitting way for Tom to die," she wrote. "He didn't die sitting behind a desk at a publicly traded corporation. He didn't die watching TV in his recliner at his suburban home. He died fighting as a citizen soldier. What a fitting place for him to come to rest—an open field within a forest, so very similar to the Gettysburg battlefields which so fascinated and inspired him."

Miller, too, recognized a strong military component in the story of Flight 93, a spirit of patriotic defiance by ordinary citizens that had its roots in the local militia units that volunteered for service in the Revolutionary and Civil Wars. Back then they were farmers and blacksmiths and country preachers, coming together for a common cause, to form or preserve a nation. Now they were corporate executives, salesmen, college students, judo champs. "It's my opinion that those people aboard Flight 93 on September 11 became a militia unit of their own—they made that conscious choice," the coroner said. "They began the day as regular citizens traveling to the West Coast. They ended as soldiers fighting in the skies above western Pennsylvania.

"They were special people, patriots. Think of it. Other than the Revolutionary War and the Civil War—or Pearl Harbor—where else but Somerset County did Americans die trying to defend their homeland?"

CHAPTER FIFTEEN

"A Common Field One Day . . ."

It was not long after the carnage ended in New York City and Washington, DC, that citizens from across the country began to converge on the two metropolitan tourist centers. Some came to gasp and gawk at the devastation. Others came to pray and pay their respects. These weren't your typical visitors looking for Times Square or the Lincoln Memorial. You could see it in their eyes in those months after 9/11; they were drawn instead to the site of something tragic, something historic—something bigger than all of them.

New York and Washington had the infrastructure to handle the sudden influx: the transportation systems, the hotels, the restaurants. But it was a different story in the tiny town closest to the spot where Flight 93 had crashed. Shanksville, Pennsylvania, was home to 245 hearty citizens, several churches, a country store, and a fire department. It had no director of tourism. It *had* no tourism. On September 24, less than two weeks after the attacks, a local volunteer named Donna Glessner was packing boxes of donated items at the fire hall when a car with out-of-state plates rolled tentatively into the driveway on North Street. Much to her surprise, a woman got out to ask if she could take a picture of the fire truck that had answered the call on September 11.

How about that? Glessner thought to herself. *A tourist in Shanksville.*

The arrival of outsiders was not much more than a trickle at first—curiosity seekers, news junkies, angry patriots. It took persistence just to find the place. Anyone pulling off the Pennsylvania Turnpike at the Somerset exit still had to make a winding twelve-mile drive on two-lane roads, past the Friedens Lutheran Church and the Stoystown American

Legion Post 257—and often behind slow-moving coal trucks—to get within range of the crash site. Unlike New York and Washington, there wasn't much to see but an open field. But the crowds grew.

It was somehow fitting that the first unofficial "memorial" to the passengers and crew of Flight 93 was handmade by a local citizen. On September 15, Judi Baeckel, Shanksville's acting postmaster, desperate to do *something*, placed a plywood sign on the lawn of her home on Bridge Street, near the borough's main intersection. It read: Shanksville Remembers the Heroes of Flight 93. Soon, residents and out of towners were scrawling their own heartfelt messages to honor the passengers and crew. They began to leave flowers, wreaths, candles, American flags—often one on top of the other. As the items piled up, Judi had to scramble to find seven other plywood boards to accommodate all the tributes. Flight 93 had struck a chord in this bucolic patch of rural America.

"Shanksville may be a little town," student John Chaves said in a speech at the Shanksville-Stonycreek School on September 16, "but it's big enough for the whole world. Whoever needs us, we're there for them."

The crash site—still considered a crime scene—was off-limits to the public, but visitors soon found their way to another area on Lambertsville Road in Stonycreek Township that served as a "media village" during the FBI's two-week investigation. The location was a few miles closer than Judi's makeshift shrine in Shanksville, and yet it still offered no view of the impact crater or the burned-out hemlocks. That didn't seem to matter. "What we found was that people were drawn to this place," Donna Glessner said, "even if they couldn't really see anything yet." Pins, patches, note cards, and other items—some patriotic, some religious, others more subtle—were placed on several hay bales positioned at the site. Standing sentry were a flag pole, erected by the Pennsylvania Department of Transportation, and a wooden cross, requested by the FBI and placed by the congregation of the Somerset Alliance Church.

The tributes quickly became symbols of a larger local storyline developing about Flight 93. It was no longer just about a hijacked Boeing 757 that crashed in Somerset County on 9/11. It was about the reaction the crash created—the visceral outpouring of emotion. The County Commissioners held a meeting on October 10 to discuss the historic importance of the many items being left at the sites and the sudden spike in tourism. On hand were Joanne Hanley of the National Park Service, representatives of Congressman John Murtha's office, the mayor of Shanksville, the Stonycreek Township supervisor, United Airlines representatives, members of the Historical and Genealogical Society of Somerset County, and Coroner Wally Miller.

Out of that gathering came the very raw idea for a national memorial to honor the passengers and crew.

The first step was to approve the care and collection of the tributes at the impromptu memorials. The assignment was given to the county historical society and its curator, Barbara Black. Black, a resident of Shanksville, had rushed home from her job on the morning of September 11, fretting about her grandson who was attending school just beyond the crash site. The experience was very personal. Now, barely a month after the crash, Black would start carving several hours out of her work week to retrieve, clean, store, and catalog the items. She still was responsible for her full-time day job at the historical society, so she recruited and trained a team of local volunteers to assist with the project.

During the next ten years, as local officials and eventually the National Park Service created three different temporary memorials for the public, Black and her team oversaw the collection of more than forty thousand items left behind by people from across the country and across the world.

"A lot of people left items of obvious meaning—flags, photos, patriotic pins," Black remembered. "But what's so amazing is that there were so many items where the meaning wasn't so obvious. There's a kitchen serving spoon. It was left at a chain-link fence at one of the memorials, so it wasn't as if it dropped out of a car in the parking area. What does that mean? You're really tempted to make up all kinds of stories, to make a connection to someone on the plane. A tribute to someone who liked to cook? Maybe something from their grandmother? It's a mystery we can't solve. Baby shoes? What do *they* mean? We'll never know what or why."

Black was determined not to make any individual judgments while scouring the hay bales and fences at the various sites. Every item, no matter how obscure or out of context, was collected, cleaned, and recorded for posterity. A student of human behavior as well as history, she knew that people often place tributes at meaningful locations for no broader purpose than "simply to leave something of themselves." That might explain a pen, a business card, a piece of jewelry. "Jewelry is very personal," Black said. "And the message is, 'I was here.' It's pretty fascinating to see the depth of the items we found."

On November 2, 2001, a new temporary memorial was opened on Skyline Road, about four hundred yards from the spot where Flight 93 had gone down. It was the first time since the immediate hours after the crash that regular citizens could view the impact site. The challenge for visitors was to decipher what had happened in an otherwise serene country setting. In Manhattan, you could see the enormous piles of steel and shattered concrete that used to be the World Trade Center; you could feel how the city had become more alert and somber. In Washington, you could witness the damage and reconstruction at the wounded Pentagon—and the increased security everywhere. But in Somerset County, the only vista was an unremarkable open meadow off in the distance, framed by a semicircle of singed hemlock trees. It was perplexing, and the visitor had no context. *Which direction had the plane been traveling? Where did it actually crash? Where were the remnants found?*

Barbara Black was on the front lines of this new reality, mingling with the public during her periodic visits. There were days when she expected to spend five minutes collecting tribute items left on a forty-foot fence erected at the site. Instead, she would be there for several hours, answering questions, listening to stories. Some people were curious about the details, the timing, the aftermath. Others just wanted to talk. She was the only person around who looked to be in a position of authority.

Mostly, though, the visitors were left to figure things out on their own. There were no tour guides, and Black's time was limited. Donna Glessner stopped by one day while running errands with her son and overheard a few onlookers talking about the crash. Some thought the plane might have come down in a nearby pond. Others believed a natural depression in the landscape was the impact crater. One man theorized that a scrap yard still in operation on an opposite hillside contained the actual pieces of the wreckage. All the speculation was wrong.

"It really bothered Donna," Black said. "Not just that people didn't have the correct information . . . but that no one was even greeting them when they arrived. Donna said, 'Barbara, we can't have people coming to our community and not be taken care of. They leave and they've had no contact with anyone here. This isn't right.'"

The next Sunday, Glessner stood up in church and asked for volunteers to help work at the memorial.

Glessner and her sister, Kathie Shaffer, hoped they could recruit ten people to donate their time on weekends. They got seventeen. Virtually everyone lived within a ten-mile radius of the crash site; it became a hometown effort. The first training session was held on January 26, 2002, when Kathie's husband, Shanksville fire chief Terry Shaffer, informed them of the few details about the flight that were known at that time. Black gave them pointers on making presentations to random visitors. "I remember how strange it felt to put yourself out there as an authority when we really knew so little," Glessner said. "It was very much grassroots. But it filled a void." These volunteers soon became known as the "Ambassadors" of the memorial.

Other folks contributed in their own unique ways. Chuck Wagner, a Shanksville resident who had operated heavy equipment during the investigation, knew that it was almost impossible for first-time visitors to determine where the plane had crashed. So he placed a flag on the chain-link fence closest to the actual site. Chuck later became the unofficial photographer and volunteer custodian of the temporary memorial. Eric and Tammy Pearson, who lived three hours away in Birdsboro, Pennsylvania, and owned a slate company called Simply Slates, created forty slate angels with the names of the passengers and crew. Students from the Spring Valley Bruderhof community in nearby Fayette County built benches that allowed visitors to sit and rest—and perhaps linger a bit longer at the site—while paying their respects.

In 2008 the temporary memorial was moved a short distance across the road because of an issue with the private landowner. Just more than a year later, it was moved again—to a bluff above the crash site known as the western overlook, where the FBI established its original command post in 2001. This was the same spot where the families had gathered in those early days to see the final resting place of their loved ones for the first time. It had all come full circle.

No matter the location, visitors continued to flock to the temporary sites and to leave tributes to honor the passengers and crew. Of the tens of thousands of items collected by Barbara Black and her team, a few were especially poignant. Tom Walker of Homer City, Pennsylvania, left a purple heart he'd received when his helicopter was shot down in Vietnam. Local students from Shanksville and Stonycreek Township placed a toy airplane inscribed with the words, "Thank you for saving our lives and not hitting our school." Stephen Rouda of the Los Angeles City Fire Department penned a phrase that was soon adopted as part of the mission statement of the permanent memorial: "A Common Field One Day, A Field of Honor Forever."

Most dramatic of all was a seemingly insignificant brick that was broken in half. It might have been discarded shortly after being discovered in 2008 had it not been accompanied by a special note that caught a volunteer's attention:

This brick is from the compound of Taliban leader Mullah Mohammed Omar in Kandahar, Afghanistan. On October 20th, 2001, US Special Operations Forces attacked and seized the compound. It is now used as a US base from which attacks are launched against the Taliban and al-Qaeda. Placed here in tribute to the first warriors of the Global War on Terror by members of the 19th Special Forces.

The passengers and crew of Flight 93 had become an inspiration even to America's finest soldiers.

⸺•⸺

Paul Murdoch was flipping through the pages of an architectural journal late in 2004 when his eye caught an advertisement about a national design competition. It intrigued him.

Folks in his home state of Pennsylvania were in the early stages of developing a permanent memorial to the passengers and crew of Flight 93. The founder and president of Paul Murdoch Architects in Los Angeles thought it sounded like a worthwhile project for his firm to explore.

"We were looking for a way to give back after September 11," he said, "and those people on the plane inspired us."

The challenge for Murdoch was timing. Designs for Stage I of the competition were due by January 11, 2005. The architect and his staff were so late to the process that they didn't even have time to visit the crash site before submitting their original entry. But Murdoch may have had a built-in advantage. Although he grew up outside Philadelphia in the eastern part of the state, he'd spent considerable time camping and hiking in the Laurel Highlands, a four-county region in rural southwestern Pennsylvania that included Somerset. He'd gone canoeing at Ohiopyle State Park and visited Frank Lloyd Wright's architectural masterpiece at Fallingwater. He felt a kinship with the area. He knew the land.

Murdoch determined almost immediately that a traditional monument would not work. It would interrupt the pastoral serenity and be dwarfed by the sprawling, 2,200-acre landscape designated for the national memorial. The idea he developed was to incorporate the features of the land into an understated memorial that would honor the heroism of the victims while fitting comfortably against the backdrop of "this special part of the state." It was not a concept that would be appropriate for New York City or Washington, DC. That was the whole point.

It also meshed with the project's mission statement, which sought to blend the desire to honor the passengers, serve the public, and respect the landscape.

Murdoch joined more than a thousand other entries in a competition that drew interest from forty-eight states and twenty-seven countries. The designs came pouring into Somerset County from all talent levels. "We wanted to create an open dialogue about what the memorial could be," said Jeff Reinbold of the National Park Service, "and we hoped to get designs from both professionals and the guy down the street at his kitchen table." They did. But many struggled to capture the legacy of an event that shook the national foundation, one that was equal parts tragic and heroic.

As the competition developed, Murdoch added Nelson Byrd Woltz Landscape Architects of Charlottesville, Virginia, to his team. The centerpiece of their proposal was the topography itself—a large, bowl-shaped landform with natural ridges to the north and west that encircles the crash site. A curving walkway of native red maple trees leading to the viewing area would be framed by forty memorial groves of trees. A white marble wall designed to mark the flight path would bear the names of the forty passengers and crew. At the entrance to the park, visitors would be greeted by a ninety-three-foot-high Tower of Voices with forty wind chimes, commemorating the sound of wind and voices on the plane in those final moments.

"This was not a memorial on the National Mall or something commemorating an event that happened somewhere else in the world," Murdoch said. "It was where the crash occurred. It was already a place of sanctity.

"What we tried to do was frame it up—set up a series of experiences for the visitors when they arrive there and not pre-empt it or overwhelm it with the design. We didn't want to get in the way. What happened on September 11 was very much rooted in the land there."

The competition was held in two stages and judged by two panels made up of design professionals, project partners, local residents, and nine family members of the passengers and crew. The involvement of the families was considered essential to the process. One family member in particular, Ed Root, cousin of flight attendant Lorraine Bay, brought impressive credentials as a historian to the process. He'd been a member of the Gettysburg Battlefield Preservation Association, served as president of the Civil War Roundtable of Eastern Pennsylvania, and was working on a book about three Massachusetts regiments who helped repel Pickett's Charge. Perhaps more than most, he felt the weight of history on his decision.

"One thing that struck me early on is that every day in this country people lose their lives—military, first responders, people showing tremendous heroism, courage, sacrifice," Root said. "But you can't have a memorial to everything. So what makes this one worthy? I came to the conclusion that Flight 93 really showed a difference in philosophy between a free society and a totalitarian society. The terrorists obviously were more than willing to sacrifice their lives. For our people, for my cousin, the thing they valued *most* was life.

"And look at the makeup of the people on that plane. They weren't all Americans. There was a man from New Zealand. There were people from

Germany and Japan—our greatest enemies in World War II. It speaks to democratic values and the philosophy of the Western world. I thought that made it worthy of an excellent memorial."

Paul Murdoch's proposal for the site, titled "Crescent of Embrace," was one of five entries selected for the final stage of the competition. Others came from groups based in Berkeley, California; Austin, Texas; Columbus, Ohio; and Toronto, Canada. Six members of the Families of Flight 93 were on the final panel that deliberated for three days before making its recommendation to the Flight 93 Advisory Commission. Murdoch was declared the winner, having received the majority of the votes.

The concept for the new Flight 93 National Memorial was unveiled to the public in Washington, DC, on September 7, 2005, with more than fifty friends and relatives of the passengers and crew in attendance. According to the Associated Press, they "gave a standing ovation to the design." Christine Fraser, whose sister, Colleen, was a passenger on the flight, said, "It was very important for me for the area to retain its simplicity." Calvin Wilson, brother-in-law of First Officer LeRoy Homer, added, "The design did a good job of incorporating the landscape. It was important for us not to disturb the sanctity of the site. It really harnesses the spirit of our forty heroes."

The international design competition had been a remarkable public process. After receiving more than one thousand entries from across the country and the world, the project partners brought together design professionals, local residents, educators, and still-grieving family members to reach a consensus on a national memorial within four years of the attacks. The final step was for the National Park Service and the US Department of the Interior to give their blessing to the design. Once that happened—and it happened quickly—they were well on their way to creating a permanent tribute to the passengers and crew of Flight 93.

Or so they thought.

A controversy began to broil shortly after Murdoch and park officials arrived back in Somerset County for the fourth anniversary on September 11, 2005. Someone alerted Murdoch to a blog that focused on the name of his entry, "Crescent of Embrace." The blogger pointed out that a crescent was a symbol of Islam. Murdoch was accused—of all things—of creating a shrine to the terrorists.

It was not the first time members of the jury had heard such a claim, but they had dismissed it as nonsensical. "Everyone sort of rolled their eyes," Ed Root said. "No one was going to build a Flight 93 memorial that honored the hijackers." But the controversy gained momentum in the blogosphere, and it caught the attention of Colorado congressman Tom Tancredo, who openly questioned the design.

In time, a West Coast blogger named Alex Rawls became the strongest voice of the opposition, creating a website and writing a book that asserted "Murdoch's mosque" was a cleverly disguised terrorist memorial, that the proposed ninety-three-foot Tower of Voices was an Islamic sundial, and that the site had been designed to intentionally point toward Mecca. Furthermore, he claimed that the memorial wall would feature forty-four glass blocks—one for each person killed on the plane, including the four hijackers.

Murdoch and the families were stunned.

"They were somehow reading things into the design that weren't even close to our intentions," Murdoch said. "It was bewildering."

Nonetheless, National Park Service officials, the Advisory Commission, and the Families of Flight 93 believed the best way to confront the hysteria was to meet it head on. They contacted religious and academic experts to examine Rawls's claims. The conclusion reached was that none of them had credence. At the same time, Murdoch sought to disarm the critics with a pre-emptive strike of his own. He decided to make several refinements, including expanding the crescent into a circle, and he began to refer to the design as the "Circle of Embrace" (although, by this time, the official name was already the "Flight 93 National Memorial"). He didn't want a sideshow controversy to overshadow the memorial effort.

"The landform of that bowl at the crash site, that *circle*, is what we always were working with," Murdoch said. "And it was so obvious that everything was already oriented toward the crash site, to put the focus on the hallowed ground."

Some critics thought the use of red maple trees to frame the site gave it the look of a red crescent that could be seen as a symbol of Islam. So Murdoch added several other species of trees that are native to the Laurel Highlands. His expanded circle would have breaks in two places—one to mark the flight path and the other to mark the crash site. The alterations were symbolic in nature and did not distract from his original intent to feature the raw landscape in a one-of-a-kind memorial. He believed they would satisfy "all but the fanatical fringe."

But Rawls, who had a website to promote and a book to sell, would not back off. And his criticism of the design got support from a most unexpected source—Tom Burnett Sr., one of the family members who had been part of the Stage II jury. Burnett's public opposition gained media exposure for the cause, even though no other family member spoke out in a similar manner. It helped keep the controversy alive.

"It's really revolting to me, this whole thing," Burnett said in an interview with the *New York Times*. "It's an insult to my son and all the others."

Rawls and Burnett appeared on a Fox television show where Burnett called the design "terribly tainted" and asked to have the jury reconvened. He thought the other family members were "misguided." But those efforts got less and less traction as the Families of Flight 93 organization fired back, voicing loud and official support for Murdoch and his work. "It's actually offensive that anyone would think the memorial would be created for any other reason than to honor the passengers and crew," said Gordie Felt, who served two terms as president of the family group.

That opinion was underscored in a letter to Congressman Tancredo in November 2007. The Families of Flight 93 reiterated their belief in the design and reaffirmed their decision with a unanimous vote of the board of directors. In a follow-up public statement in May 2008, Felt said, "after having evaluated the objections to the design, we have found no merit in their claims." He confirmed that the project partners were moving forward with a design "that was selected through an open and democratic process."

It had been a long and often exasperating effort, one fraught with deep emotion for those who had lost loved ones on the flight. There still would be sporadic howls of discontent throughout the final few years of funding and construction—and even beyond. But the National Park Service and the Families of Flight 93 had overcome any substantive opposition to the design. They were now moving toward the anticipated completion of the new national memorial by the tenth anniversary on September 11, 2011.

"The controversy was a distraction but, other than a couple of weeks here and there, it really didn't set us back at all," said Joanne Hanley, superintendent of the memorial for the Park Service, who had shepherded the various parties through the peaks and valleys. "There was never a doubt in any of our minds about Paul's design. The whole thing was just bizarre. It was good to move on."

But even with the design controversy behind them, there was one remaining obstacle facing the families and their partners. The 2,200 acres designated for the national memorial were owned by eight different individuals and companies. They still had to acquire the land.

❧

Tim Lambert hadn't been to Somerset County in fifteen years, but he knew he owned property near the edge of a reclaimed strip mine near Shanksville. The land had been passed down through the family since the 1930s. Lambert vaguely remembered picking raspberries there as a boy and playing among the hemlock trees.

Those memories came flashing back on the morning of September 11. Lambert was heading to his job as a part-time radio reporter for WITF in the state capital of Harrisburg when news broke that a plane had crashed in rural southwestern Pennsylvania. It was possibly connected to the rash of attacks that morning on New York City and Washington, DC. Details were imprecise, but one dispatch indicated that the crash site could have been Shanksville.

"Holy crap," Lambert said he thought to himself. "That's where my dad grew up. And that's pretty close to our land."

He didn't know how close until he checked his voice messages later that night.

"I don't know if you saw the video of the crash in Somerset County," his dad said, "but those are *our* trees."

Lambert had wanted to cover the story. Now he was part of it. Four other people owned stone cabins located in the hemlocks, just beyond Lambert's property line, and had even more direct connections to the site. Three companies controlled large parcels of land in the area that eventually would be needed for the national memorial.

"It was a strange feeling," Lambert said, "but I think we knew right away that this was something that was bigger than all of us."

The Reverend Larry Hoover owned one of the stone cabins and used it as a getaway retreat on holidays or weekends. Reverend Hoover was at the St. Andrews Lutheran Church in nearby Boswell when he heard about two planes hitting the World Trade Center. It was not long before he got a phone call from the Shanksville Fire Department about another plane crash—this one near his place in the woods.

"All of a sudden, your life is turned upside-down," Rev. Hoover told the *Somerset Daily American.* "For me it all seemed impossible, that a plane could come down on your property. There were so many emotions going on. I was struck by the magnitude of what happened there."

Access to the site was restricted for almost four years, until August 2005, when Wally Miller released it back to the original eight landowners. Miller, who held the site as a death scene, had conducted periodic sweeps to collect any small debris that may have turned up or fallen out of the trees, but by late July 2005, he reported that "the volume [of items found] has dropped off considerably, to the point that I now feel it's appropriate to close my involvement in the case." It was then that the National Park Service and the Families of Flight 93 could begin their efforts to obtain the 2,200 acres needed for the national memorial.

The process took time. The first large parcel of more than 900 acres was purchased by the family organization from PBS Coals Inc. of Somerset in March 2008, but other negotiations stalled on several fronts, including one with Svonavec Inc., a coal and quarry company that controlled 275 acres. Several people close to the talks believed that deals with five private landowners and one more commercial property could not move forward until an agreement was reached with Svonavec Inc., which owned the actual crash site. The growing delay became cause for concern.

In the back of everyone's mind was the goal designated for the dedication of the new memorial: the ten-year anniversary.

The logjam began to loosen when Secretary of the Interior Ken Salazar visited Somerset County in June 2009 to meet directly with the landowners. Salazar's personal involvement, the establishment of a deadline, and the looming threat of eminent domain got negotiations started in earnest. Agreements were reached quickly with the five individual landowners, including Lambert—who earlier had announced he would donate six of his acres closest to the site.

"There was a sense of inevitability to it all," Lambert told me. "I'm not sure the other landowners understood that at first, but I'd lived and worked in Gettysburg. I know what happens when the government wants land for a memorial. We were going to have to sell. It was going to happen.

"But the bottom line for me was having a role in preserving the history of the site for future generations. The story of Flight 93 and what those people did on that plane is bigger than all of this other stuff. In the end, I think, we could all hold our heads high. Was it frustrating? Sure. There's no book to read on what you're supposed to do if a national tragedy occurs on your land."

On August 31, Salazar announced that the federal government had reached agreements with all eight landowners to complete the memorial site. Settlements already were in place for seven of them, including the Kordell family, which owned the Rollock scrap yard that overlooked the crash site. And the eighth, Svonavec, was now on board. The Somerset-based company had agreed to turn over its land to the Park Service while allowing the courts to establish fair compensation.

In all, the government would pay more than nine million dollars for the land that would become the national memorial.

Tim Lambert's 163 acres had been in the family for eighty years, but he felt a sense of accomplishment in completing the transaction. He'd also done some award-winning work as a reporter during the process. As a landowner, he'd been given special access to the site and had produced unique and insightful reports featuring Wally Miller and Kenny Nacke. "I felt good about telling a story that's now part of our nation's history," Lambert recalled.

The Hoover family, which owned two of the four cabins in the woods, also recognized and appreciated its unexpected role in the memorial effort. "In a small way, I am part of a much larger thing, larger than myself, larger than my family," Barry Hoover told the *Somerset Daily American*. "There are times you have to put others first. This is one of those times.

"After that plane crashed, we became only stewards of the land. It didn't feel like my ground on day two. It's a strange feeling when you are walking on your own property and you feel you are trespassing."

The groundbreaking ceremony for the Flight 93 National Memorial took place on November 7, 2009. Secretary Salazar was there, along with assorted other dignitaries, but the focus was on four young family members who helped ceremonially turn the dirt.

Campbell Peterson, age thirteen, and his brother Peyton, age nine, were grandchildren of Donald and Jean Hoadley Peterson. Justin Nacke, age twenty-one, was the nephew of Joey Nacke. Sarah Wainio, age twenty-two, was the sister of Elizabeth Wainio. Their presence was powerful and symbolic. It spoke to how things—inevitably, always—move forward.

"Having those children there was the thing that brought me to tears," said Debby Borza, whose daughter, Deora Bodley, was the youngest person on Flight 93. "Afterward, someone from the media asked me if it was a day that re-opened all the wounds. 'No!' I said. 'Didn't you see who represented the families? Those young people are the future of this memorial.'"

And yet the project partners still faced a daunting task. The National Park Service now had twenty-two months to build an entire national memorial from scratch. Unlike similar efforts already under way in New York City and Washington, DC, there was no infrastructure in place near the crash site, no road network, no water and sewer system. One estimate was that the memorial in rural Somerset County would attract 300,000 visitors a year. "In essence," said Jeff Reinbold, "we were creating a small town on our own."

They also had to raise more funds. The project was estimated to cost sixty million dollars at its inception in 2005, but at the time of the groundbreaking, they still needed fifteen million dollars of private money to reach their goal. The first phase of the design, featuring the memorial plaza and the marble Wall of Names, would be targeted for the tenth anniversary. Other elements, such as a visitors center and the Tower of Voices, would be phased in later.

"Originally many people thought the funds would just pour in," Reinbold said. "But we realized very quickly that we faced some challenges that they didn't have at the other sites."

Many residents of New York City had died in the crashes at the Twin Towers. Many with ties to Washington, DC, and the federal government perished at the Pentagon. But no one from Somerset County was on Flight 93. There were forty families scattered across the country and the world, working to get to know one another during a very difficult period in their lives, and to develop a level of trust with the government. It took time to get going.

"[S]ome of the foundations and corporations from Pittsburgh helped us out," Reinbold said, "but it was clear that a lot of the funding would need to come from many small donations. This would be a significant grassroots process."

From a national perspective, Flight 93 by then had become the forgotten story of September 11. Many media reports referred to the events of that day as "the attacks on New York and Washington" and mentioned "a field in Pennsylvania" only as an afterthought. Video footage focused almost exclusively on the fiery crashes at the Twin Towers and the horrific destruction at the Pentagon. Viewers rarely saw distant and unremarkable images of the smoking crater in Stonycreek Township. It just didn't make for powerful TV.

Former secretary of homeland security Tom Ridge and Pennsylvania governor Ed Rendell offered a gentle reminder to the country in an op-ed that appeared in the *Washington Post* on the day of the groundbreaking. "Flight 93 is sometimes eclipsed in our memories of that dark day by the images of the Twin Towers falling or the dark smoke billowing from the Pentagon," they wrote. "That there are no images of the U.S. Capitol or the White House in flames is most likely a testament to the actions of the people on board Flight 93."

The partners in the project would not be deterred. The National Park Service, the Families of Flight 93, and the Flight 93 Advisory Commission worked with the National Park Foundation and others to tap government and corporate sources—and the public, as it often does, came through. Individual donations as small as five and ten dollars added up. Eventually, more than 100,000 people contributed to the cause.

———

Construction progressed, and the target date of September 11, 2011, finally looked achievable. They had withstood design controversies, land squabbles, funding shortfalls, and assorted other obstacles. A remarkable grassroots effort that had begun in the bleak days after the crash with local residents Judi Baeckel, John Chaves, Barbara Black, Donna Glessner, Kathie Shaffer, Chuck Wagner, Rick King, Wally Miller, and others was about to culminate in a magnificent tribute to one of the most heroic acts in the country's history.

"Pearl Harbor didn't ask to be bombed," said Henry Cook, president of the Somerset Trust Company and a member of the Stage II jury. "The crossroads of Gettysburg didn't ask for two armies to meet there. It just so happens that Flight 93 crashed [here]."

Challenged by history and happenstance, the people of Somerset County had answered the call.

CHAPTER SIXTEEN

Ten Years Later

By nine o'clock on the morning of Saturday, September 10, 2011, bumper-to-bumper traffic extended well more than a mile on a newly constructed entrance road from US Route 30 to the Flight 93 National Memorial. Cars inched along the curving roadway. Drivers craned their necks. The dedication ceremony was scheduled for 12:30 p.m., and thousands of regular citizens had arrived early. They were there to pay witness to history.

Representatives from the National Park Service and the Families of Flight 93 designed the tenth-anniversary weekend as a three-day event. Saturday would be a celebration of sorts, the dedication of the memorial and the unveiling of the Wall of Names. Sunday would be a solemn program to commemorate the anniversary. Monday would be a private funeral service for the families. The magnitude of what had happened here was evident in the guest list for the weekend: three presidents of the United States, the sitting vice president, the first Secretary of Homeland Security, the governor of Pennsylvania, and 780 family members of the passengers and crew.

The vision that Paul Murdoch developed on a one-board drawing in 2005 came to life against the backdrop of the hemlocks. The marble Wall of Names was striking in its simplicity, and it gave visitors their first clear sense of the direction of the flight path. A seventeen-ton sandstone boulder marked the crash site. A granite walkway starting at the entrance to the memorial plaza allowed members of the public to come within a hundred yards of the spot where Flight 93 had gone down. Part of the magic was that the rest of the field still looked much as it had at 10:02 a.m. on September 11, 2001.

"This is a place where you don't view the memorial; you inhabit it," Reinbold said. "You are part of the memorial when you are here . . . that was central to Paul's idea for this project. You see the fields. You feel the sky."

Eight inches of rain fell the week before the dedication, soaking the ground around the memorial and turning unpaved parking lots into quagmires. It was one final logistical challenge for the National Park Service staff. The gates opened late and traffic snarled. Trucks brought in gravel as makeshift parking spaces were arranged on the fly. Shoes and boots were stuck in the mud. No one among the early morning visitors voiced an objection.

———

Two former presidents, George W. Bush and Bill Clinton, joined Vice President Joe Biden at Saturday's historic dedication ceremony, which drew a crowd of more than four thousand people—larger than the population of almost every town in Somerset County.

Bush set the tone for the day by invoking the memory of another president on a different historic field in Pennsylvania: Abraham Lincoln and the Gettysburg Address.

"Many years ago, in 1863, another president came to dedicate a memorial in this state," Bush said. "He told his audience, 'In a larger sense, we cannot dedicate, we cannot consecrate, we cannot hallow this ground. The brave souls who struggled there consecrated it far above our poor power to add or detract.'

"He added, 'The world will little note, nor longer remember what we say here, but it can *never* forget what they did here.'"

Almost 150 years later, those words still resonated in a lot of places, maybe more so in rural Pennsylvania.

The Flight 93 story was intensely personal for Bush. He had been in office for less than eight months when al-Qaeda struck on 9/11. The repercussions of the attacks and their aftermath would reshape the future of his administration—and haunt his legacy. He'd been reading to schoolchildren in Sarasota, Florida, when the first two planes struck the World Trade Center. In the space of just more than an hour, nearly three thousand people died on the American homeland. The first glimmer of hope on a day of unthinkable darkness for the United States came in the skies directly above the spot where the forty-third president now stood. Bush said:

> *With their selfless act, the men and women who stormed the cockpit lived out the words, "Greater love hath no man than this, that a man lay down his life for his friends." We'll never know how many innocent people might have been lost, but we do know this: Americans are alive today because the passengers and crew of Flight 93 chose to act, and our nation will be forever grateful.*
>
> *The forty souls who perished on the plane left a great deal behind. They left spouses and children and grandchildren who miss them dearly. They left successful businesses and promising careers and a lifetime of dreams they will never have the chance to fulfill. They left something else—a legacy of bravery and selflessness that will always inspire America.*

Bill Clinton had personal connections of his own to events leading up to that day. He was in office in 1998 when al-Qaeda bombed the US embassies in Kenya and Tanzania, and he responded by launching an unsuccessful cruise missile attack against bin Laden. Two years later, still on his watch, al-Qaeda struck the USS *Cole* off the coast of Yemen. Clinton's wife, Hillary, a US senator at the time of the attacks, represented thousands of New Yorkers who died in the World Trade Center, including 343 New York City firemen. The actions of the passengers and crew were an inspiration at a time of intense grief and soul-searching.

Clinton said:

> *They gave the country an incalculable gift. They saved the Capitol from attack. They saved God knows how many lives. They saved the terrorists from claiming the symbolic victory of smashing the center of American government.*
>
> *They allowed us to survive as a country that could fight terror and still maintain liberty and still welcome people from all over the world,*

from every religion and race and culture, as long as they shared our values . . . all because ordinary people, given no time to decide, did the right thing.

Biden, a US senator for thirty-six years before becoming vice president in 2009, brought another unique perspective to the dedication ceremony. He had been in the nation's capital with other members of the Senate and House of Representatives for a scheduled joint session of Congress on September 11, 2001, and his own life may have been saved by the insurrection of the passengers and crew. It is not surprising then that Biden had developed a special affinity with the memorial in Somerset County. His speech was probably the most dramatic of all those delivered at the September 10 event. Biden was no stranger to personal tragedy himself, having lost his first wife and one-year-old daughter in 1972 when their car was broadsided by a tractor trailer. He addressed the families most directly.

"We know, and I know, that no memorial—no words, no acts—can fill the void they left in your hearts," Biden said.

My prayer for you is that ten years later, their memory is able to bring a smile to your lips before it brings a tear to your eye. And I hope you take comfort in knowing that a grateful nation understands that your loved ones gave their lives in pursuit of the noblest of earthly goals: defending their country, defending their families, sacrificing their lives so we could live ours.

They didn't know the horror that awaited them, but they confronted unimaginable fear and terror with a courage that has been summoned by only the truest and rarest of American heroes—forty names etched on each of those panels on the wall, the Wall of Names. But more than that, their names are going to be, as President Bush said, etched forever into American history.

None of them asked for what happened. They didn't board that plane to fight a war. But when they heard the news, when they found out what happened in New York, they knew that they were going through something more than a hijacking. They knew it was the opening shot in a new war. And so they acted. They acted as citizen patriots have acted since the beginning of our country. They stood up and they stood their ground. They thought, like Captain Parker said at Lexington—and I quote him—"If they mean to have a war, let it begin here."

Jack Shea and Andrea Dammann, two FBI agents who helped lead the investigation at the Flight 93 crash site, raised the first flag at the national memorial. Fittingly, it was the same flag that had flown over the Capitol on September 11.

When the formal ceremony ended, family members walked together along the Wall of Names, some of them reaching out to touch the eight-foot-high marble panels, or to lay flowers and wreaths. Many were overcome with emotion. Alice Hoglan could be seen tracing the letters of the name of her son, Mark Bingham. Others paused and bowed their heads.

Gordie Felt, who had spoken from the podium on behalf of the families, described the unveiling of the memorial as a "tremendous and symbolic gesture that showed how much the forty heroes meant to the country." He was pleased that he would always have a place to "visit and spend time with my brother." Patrick White, cousin of passenger Joey Nacke, noted the symbolism of rain and darkness giving way to sunshine for the dedication ceremony. Ilsa Homer, mother of First Officer LeRoy Homer, told a reporter she had imagined a quiet conversation with her son at the Wall of Names.

She said she could hear him asking, "Mom, this isn't for us, is it?"

~⁓~

The tenth-anniversary ceremony on Sunday had a profound impact on Tom Ridge, one of the featured speakers. Ridge had been standing on the same spot ten years earlier—almost to the hour.

The governor of Pennsylvania in 2001, Ridge was visiting his hometown of Erie in the far northwestern corner of the state when the state police tracked him down on the morning of the attacks. All air traffic in the United States had been grounded by the FAA and the Department of Transportation, but Ridge received special permission to fly by helicopter to the state capital in Harrisburg, then on to the crash site somewhere near Somerset. He was not prepared for what he saw.

Ridge had served in Vietnam and experienced the gory devastation of a military battlefield. He'd visited federal and state disaster sites as a congressman and governor. He expected to see twisted pieces of the wings and fuselage, random piles of mangled airplane debris, and human bodies, or at least body parts. All he could make out from the air was a smoldering hole. The totality of the destruction was frightening.

"Nothing I'd done before in my life," he said, "including my time as an infantry staff sergeant, prepared me for this encounter with tragedy and evil."

Ridge's life changed almost instantly. With much of the federal government's attention focused on New York and Washington, he became the principal authority figure at the Flight 93 site. He spoke at one of the early gatherings of the families in Somerset County the week after the crash. Then a call from Andy Card, chief of staff for President Bush, took the governor's career down a path he never anticipated.

On September 19, he was asked to leave Harrisburg for Washington to accept the newly created position of assistant to the president for homeland security. Ridge accepted—and eventually joined the Cabinet as the first Secretary of the Department of Homeland Security. He was no longer just a detached observer, a state leader providing solace and comfort. He was now enmeshed in the story himself.

That difference in perspective from the other speakers was evident in Ridge's personal and powerful oration on the tenth anniversary. Influenced by what he'd experienced at the site in 2001, he didn't address his comments solely to the family members in attendance, or to the crowd, estimated at five thousand people, or to a national television audience. He spoke instead directly to the passengers and crew of Flight 93.

"And so you, our forty heroes," Ridge began,

on this special September morning, may I take a few moments to speak of you, and to you, as you sit beside us here. Beside your family, friends, and fellow citizens. Upon soft and sacred earth. Under now peaceful skies. Throughout a land where your last loving embrace of your nation profoundly moved our hearts ten years ago—and still does, ten years on.

Ten years ago, many of us stood upon a nearby field. We were angry and heartbroken. As the days and weeks and months unfolded, your story to us became known.

And we wondered. Would we, could we—had we been in your place—shown the same resolve, the same selflessness, the same astonishing valor?

Was this uniquely American?

Or uniquely you?

Or a unique combination?

Ridge paused at one point to look out at the thousands who had gathered near the crash site for this moment—regular folks, beckoned by history, leaning forward and straining to hear his words. He wondered if the families had any idea how many anonymous citizens had come to pay their respects. Breaking briefly from his prepared remarks, Ridge addressed the visitors and told them, "I think your presence today means almost as much to the families as the memorial itself." With that, the family members turned around and—stunned by the size of the crowd—gave them a spontaneous standing ovation.

But it was not long before Ridge returned to the original focus of his speech, the passengers and crew.

Ten years on, your actions still call to us—they remind us to be our best selves, to take care of one another, to honor and preserve the sheer will, the magnificence and the fortitude of the American spirit.

Ten years on, you remain an emblem of America's great glory— 230-plus years of liberty and self-determination—demonstrated at its highest regard and highest cost.

Your actions, the message it sent to all of us, helped us to remember one September . . . and many Septembers—that America is and must always be a resilient nation.

And we will long honor that role with the memory and guidance of forty good shepherds.

The tenth-anniversary ceremony had begun with a prayer by the Rev. Paul Britton, brother of passenger Marion Britton. The keynote speaker was John Hendricks, founder and chairman of Discovery Communications, where passenger Elizabeth Wainio had been an employee. Pennsylvania governor Tom Corbett and other local dignitaries joined Hendricks on the dais. Coroner Wally Miller had to choke back tears while reading a litany from the podium. "Take your time, Wally," family member Calvin Wilson called out from the audience.

Later that afternoon, President Barack Obama arrived to place a wreath at the crash site and visit privately with the families.

The memory many of the visitors took from the ceremony, though, was the raw power of Ridge's comments that morning. He delivered what the nearby Johnstown *Tribune-Democrat* described as a "speech for the ages," capturing with rare eloquence the full range of emotions on a sad, reflective, bittersweet anniversary.

"Forty Heroes, as you sit beside us here, we pledge to you that we will ensure that future generations know your names and your remarkable story, just as we have been privileged to do," Ridge had said.

"We are honored to share the legacy of people who made a difference, whose lives had great meaning . . . and who remain deeply missed."

—◦—

The final act was a private burial service for the families on the morning of Monday, September 12. Almost from the time he'd arrived here ten years earlier, Somerset County coroner Wally Miller considered this place a cemetery, the final resting spot of the passengers and crew. Now he would make it official.

Three caskets of intermingled but unidentifiable human remains from Flight 93 had been kept at a mausoleum in Windber, about twenty miles to the northeast. Miller always believed they should be buried at the crash site, but he didn't want to push the idea. That was the families' decision. He was relieved when a committee of family members approached him in 2010 with the idea to move forward with a burial and funeral service. "The question of where to inter came up," Miller said, "but in my mind there was no more appropriate place than right here—where the aircraft hit the ground."

All of the families had taken part in individual services for their loved ones across the country and across the world in the days and weeks after September 11. This event would be different. It would be a shared, communal service. Only 8 percent of the fragmented remains of the passengers and crew had been recovered from the crash site, which meant that 92 percent had either been vaporized or was still lodged somewhere deep in the earth of the reclaimed strip mine. Burying the three caskets here would provide another layer of closure for the families. Miller told them it might be the only cemetery in the world where there would be one funeral service with no additional burials allowed.

"People might be surprised by this, but I think it's fair to say that the families were more interested in the burial that weekend than anything else," Debby Borza said. "It was empowering in a way because it was just for us. We'd had to share our grief with the world for most of those ten years, on a very public stage—and that was understandable—but this would be one time, one day, where it was different. We could share that moment among ourselves."

The National Park Service had to agree to essentially close the memorial two days after it was opened to accommodate the service. But everyone understood. Attendance was by invitation only and the media was kept away. Miller, in his role as funeral director, planned an ecumenical service with a minister, a rabbi, a priest, and an ordained Buddhist. Pallbearers included Pennsylvania State Police and first responders who had been at the crash site on September 11. Uniformed military personnel stood guard at the caskets.

"They tiptoed around religion at the World Trade Center," Miller said. "There wasn't really a spiritual aspect [in the service] up there. This however, was going to be an actual *funeral service*. There was going to be a spiritual component and a military component, with a Somerset County honor guard carrying the flags. There would be a little slice of Somerset County. I wouldn't have it any other way."

The military aspect was important to Miller. He knew that four military veterans had boarded Flight 93 in Newark on the morning of September 11, but by 10:00 a.m., with the insurrection playing out in the skies above western Pennsylvania, he considered them all citizen-soldiers—an impromptu militia organized within minutes and fighting for their lives.

"As far as I'm concerned, there were forty veterans on board this aircraft," Miller told the families at the service. "They talk about Gettysburg, and about Lexington and Concord, and I agree with that. I can't imagine what must have gone on in that cabin. For everybody to get organized and do what they had to do under excruciating pressure was incredible. That's why there's a military component to this service. Please accept it as an honor to your loved ones."

A man playing a bagpipe had led the funeral procession to the crash site. After the service ended with a prayer and a benediction, the man with the bagpipe headed off into the hemlocks. Even when he no longer was in sight of the mourners, the sound of music from a distance still hung over the sacred ground. It was the final breathtaking moment of the weekend. "There wasn't a dry eye anywhere," Miller said, "including mine."

By law the funeral director had to wait until vaults were sealed before the burial process could take place. Many of the family members waited with him, lingering at the site, almost unable to leave. It was during this time that Kenny Nacke approached Miller with a request. A Nacke family tradition called for throwing a shovel of dirt onto a casket just before the burial. "Can we do that here?" Kenny asked. The answer was yes.

"So Kenny takes a full shovel of dirt and throws it on," Wally told me. "Then his cousins get involved. Then some other guys. The next thing you know, there are maybe fifteen to twenty guys throwing shovels of dirt. Nacke's really got a lather worked up. They actually might have covered all the caskets if the National Park Service hadn't stepped in because they had to re-open the park to the public. There were about five hundred cars waiting in line. We had to wrap it up. But it's something I'll always remember—the passion those guys had for this place, right down to shoveling dirt on the graves."

The end of the ceremony marked the end of Miller's official duties on the Flight 93 case. It was a bittersweet moment. For ten years in the dual role as coroner and funeral director, he had been an information source, sounding board, and grief counselor for forty disparate families linked together on a national stage by tragedy and unthinkable loss. He called them together for the first group meeting in New Jersey, hatched the idea for them to unite, and stood up to the FBI and other authorities when he thought they were being stonewalled. He took every phone call, answered every question. Now, though, as the caskets were covered and his formal role ended, he had one final message for the families.

"I told them I'm still only a phone call or a text away if they need me," Miller said. "We'll all move on in our lives, but the bonds we built together will never be broken. No matter what happens, they will always have a friend at the Miller Funeral Home in Somerset County."

CHAPTER SEVENTEEN

Legacy

More than ten years later, the legacy of Flight 93 comes down to something quintessentially American: the uncommon valor of the common man.

On one of the darkest days in US history, with unimaginable horror gripping the skies above western Pennsylvania, the passengers and crew on the hijacked Boeing 757 rose as one to confront a new breed of fanatical terrorist bent on destruction. That they failed in their ultimate mission—to land the plane safely and save their own lives—does not detract from the stoutness of their character or the raw heroism of their attempt.

Tom Burnett didn't know Christian Adams when they headed down the Jetway at Newark International Airport that Tuesday morning. Joe Driscoll didn't know Kristin White Gould. Todd Beamer may have introduced himself to Waleska Martinez as they settled into their seats in row ten, but these people were strangers, brought together by the random coincidence of history. They never suspected there were seething al-Qaeda henchmen in their midst. Sisters-in-law Jane Folger and Patricia Cushing likely walked unknowingly past Saeed al Ghamdi in his first-class seat in 3D. Flight attendant Wanda Green may have served tea to Ahmed al Nami.

But barely an hour later, the passengers and crew were all comrades in arms.

⁓

"Studying history serves democracy by highlighting contingencies," the columnist George Will once wrote. "Things did not need to turn out the way they did. Choices matter."

And they did for the innocent people on Flight 93. Had they been seized by fear or paralyzed by indecision—reluctant to take a risk that meant almost certain death—al-Qaeda would have destroyed the fourth of its iconic targets, reducing the magnificent dome of the US Capitol to ruins and killing another incalculable number of innocent people. Though 9/11 was an impossibly bleak day, Flight 93 stood out as a symbol of American resistence, something for the public to rally around. The actions of the passengers and crew shined a beacon through the darkness and began a sense of national healing—even as smoke still spewed from the Pentagon and the toppled Twin Towers.

Al-Qaeda zealots who later hailed Ziad Jarrah in a propaganda video as "Destroyer of the American Spirit" could not have predicted the response of US citizens faced with sudden, unprecedented terror in their homeland. It began with the first responders from New York City and Washington, DC, who roared to the scenes at the World Trade Center and the Pentagon. It continued with the residents of Somerset County who were drawn to the sound of the crash in those bizarre and bewildering first moments, followed by the firefighters, the ambulance drivers, the state police, the FBI, the forensic specialists, the arborists who climbed the trees, the ladies who baked cookies and brought blankets and jugs of water—and the regular citizens who opened their hearts and homes. In time, thousands of young people from around the country would volunteer for military service in a surge of patriotism not seen since the Japanese bombed Pearl Harbor. The American spirit, indeed.

Tom Ridge was among the first to address a renewed sense of national pride when he spoke from the steps of the Somerset County Courthouse on September 14. It was as though he anticipated the al-Qaeda taunt. "They didn't destroy our spirit—they rekindled it," Ridge bellowed. "They will not drive us apart—we have come together. And [they] did not, and we won't let them, take away our way of life. What appears to be a hole in the ground is truly a monument of heroism."

Jack Grandcolas of San Rafael, California, shared many of those same thoughts on his first visit to the scarred Pennsylvania countryside on September 17. His wife, Lauren, had called from the plane in the frantic moments after the hijacking, leaving a message to inform him about a "little problem" they were having. Her voice was calm, as if to assure him that everything would be okay. Now he was standing on the bluff overlooking the spot where Lauren and others had perished, taking the terrorists down with them. Yet he felt a strange and overwhelming peace.

"Love conquered hate in that field right there," Jack would say years later. "It really was the first victory against terrorism in our battle back, and it came over me that way. It wasn't easy to adjust to that . . . but that's what struck me about the place. It seemed like a divine location high upon the hills and in a beautiful rolling Pennsylvania [field]. It was a disturbed harmony—but in a way that hopefully will inspire."

In the original narrative patched together by reporters in those early days, the focus was on a group of four heroic men battling the terrorists—Todd Beamer, Tom Burnett, Mark Bingham, and Jeremy Glick. In time, though, it became apparent that others had to be involved in plotting, supporting, and executing the counterattack. No one on the plane sat there and waited to die. Some prayed. Some relayed information to loved ones and authorities on the ground. One boiled water to throw at Ahmed al Haznawi and Ahmed al Nami.

"It was the ultimate sacrifice," Jack Grandcolas said, "and they gave it unconditionally."

Not long after the crash, family members began to develop different ways to honor the heroism of their loved ones. Lisa Beamer and Melodie Homer completed the cross-country flights their husbands had intended that day, flying from Newark to San Francisco and bringing some closure. Many, including Lisa, Melodie, Lyz Glick, the Burnett family, and Sandy Dahl, started charitable foundations. The LeRoy W. Homer Jr. Foundation and the Captain Jason Dahl Scholarship Fund specifically support young adults who want to be professional pilots.

The sisters of Lauren Grandcolas teamed up to finish the book Lauren had started; *You Can Do It! The Merit Badge Handbook for Grown-Up Girls* was published in 2005. Kenny Nacke, a motorcycle enthusiast, organized a group that rode Harley-Davidsons from Newark to the San Francisco International Airport in September 2009, an event he dubbed Ride with the 40. Alma maters created memorial awards and activities, from the annual Thomas Burnett Day of Service at Oak Grove Middle

School in Bloomington, Minnesota, to the Deora Bodley Alumni Award for Service at La Jolla Country Day School in San Diego, California. Honolulu Community College (HCC) dedicated a memorial to honor the September 11 heroes, including Christine Snyder, who had attended classes at HCC.

All of this helped to salve the wounds—to a point. The efforts to memorialize the heroes could still not fill the enormous voids in many lives. Lori Guadagno felt so angry when she visited the crash site the first time in 2001 that she vowed never to return to Somerset County. "I just thought, That's it," Lori said. "That's a dark place. That's not really a good place for me." The healing took time.

She came back for the fifth anniversary in 2006 and began to recognize a kinship with the local community and a new connection with other family members. She saw why so many people—not just the families but hundreds of thousands of others—were drawn to this place where regular folks had battled al-Qaeda terrorists and become the twenty-first-century symbol for American resilience.

Lori continued to return often, became an ardent supporter of the Flight 93 National Memorial project, and spoke at a special educational program sponsored by the National Park Service on the eleventh anniversary. She had channeled her once-frayed emotions into something hopeful and positive.

"The memorial has taken something so horrible and so tragic and has turned it into something that can teach, can inspire, can transition," Lori said. "The first year I came back here, it was so traumatic for me. I was in an insulated bubble of sadness. But then I realized that something amazing had happened, something that needs to be shared. Chaos equals opportunity." That also is part of the legacy.

The reactions of others in the family group are as varied as the people themselves. Often it depends on personal perspective from the morning of the hijacking. Lyz Glick was on the telephone with her husband for almost twenty minutes—the longest continual connection to anyone on the plane, even before she handed the phone to her father right before the airborne assault began. It is impossible for her to relate that to others with a different experience.

On her occasional trips to the crash site, Lyz has looked at the sky and tried to picture the plane going down, imagining certain details, like the angle. She still has trouble with the utter violence of Jeremy's final moments. There is pride in his bravery, his cool determination to overcome the challenge of the terrorists, and yet she cannot avoid the "very anxious, uncomfortable dagger feeling in my heart" that accompany her visits to Somerset County. She knows that as every anniversary approaches she will see the story on the news or overhear a haphazard mention at the gym, "and I get that same stabbing feeling." She likens her emotions to a seesaw.

"I was on the phone with him while it was happening, so the first few years were pretty traumatic for me," Lyz told me. "I can grasp more things many years later, but it's almost like I have a post-traumatic obsessive compulsion with the violence. Grief changes. You learn to deal with the grief. A lot of my healing was not to think of the violence but to think of the person I loved and all the good things he left me with."

Foremost among them was a daughter, Emerson, who was three months old at the time of the crash. They have visited the memorial site together several times, including once when Emmy was five—after a boy at her school mentioned something about Jeremy dying when a plane hit a tower. "How do you explain that to a five-year-old?" Lyz said. So they got in their car and drove to Shanksville. Emmy was mostly fascinated by the tribute items people left behind.

It was a reminder that children too young to remember the events of that day will have a much different perspective on the legacy of September 11, the stories from that day, and of the memorial. "For her, it's like, 'Wow, my dad's name's here. That's pretty cool. They know who my dad is,'" Lyz said. "That has eased the burden, and has probably helped with my healing, too." When Emmy was in the fourth grade, she got an assignment to write a report about her hero. She chose her father, which brought tears to her mother's eyes.

Lyz has since remarried (as have several other widowed spouses, including Deena Burnett). Memories linger, but life must move on. In 2005 Lyz married Jim Best, who had been Jeremy's close friend and the best man at their wedding. They have had two children of their own. On

September 11 of each year, they all get together with the families of Jeremy's five brothers and sisters in the Catskills.

"[Emmy] actually loves September 11 because for her it's this great day where all her aunts, uncles, and grandma and everybody tell silly stories about Jeremy," Lyz said. "We go to lunch, go for hikes, just escape for the day. She's never known the loss in that sense. She doesn't remember the days where I cried all day. She doesn't know all the details of what happened on Flight 93, but I'm sure she will someday—when she's ready."

For much of the rest of America, the enduring images of September 11 are vivid snapshots of ghastly destruction—of a plane crashing into the World Trade Center, and of the crumbled outer wall of the Pentagon. It is different in rural Pennsylvania. For family members still faced with the competing emotions of pride and grief, the Flight 93 National Memorial stands now as a lasting testament to the valor and dauntlessness of the passengers and crew. There is a sense of nobility in the wind-swept field in Somerset County, where the tribute has been built into the landscape itself—the same landscape that essentially swallowed the plane.

A different story, a different memorial, a different legacy.

"This plane happened to have a certain significance to it that can ring forward as the silver lining to a very gray cloud of September 11," Jack Grandcolas said. "That's what I think keeps us walking on."

———

At the US Capitol on the morning of September 11, 2001, a seventeen-year-old congressional page named Nicole Eickhoff from Yorktown, Virginia, was reporting for her first day of work. She was nervous, excited, even jubilant. Why not?

Nicole was one of sixty-nine elite high school students who had been nominated by their local congressional representatives and selected to work at the Capitol that summer. It was a tremendous honor. The first day, though, promised to be a blur, especially with a joint session of Congress scheduled and a number of foreign dignitaries visiting the building.

Nicole and her new coworkers already had heard reports of plane crashes in New York City when they arrived in a small, L-shaped room known as the Cloak Room to wait for their first-day instructions from the page director. He entered the room and pulled out a cigarette. The moment is frozen in her memory.

"I will never forget him lighting that cigarette," Nicole said. "His hand was shaking, but his voice was calm. *'Get Out!'*"

Get out?

"That was it. That was it. There was nothing else, no other instruction, no other direction."

In another part of the building, Capitol employee Nellie Neumann was conducting a tour for nine members of the visiting British Parliament. Nellie had led them through the famous Rotunda and was helping to snap photos in the old Senate chamber, where the US Senate met from 1810 to 1859, when a policeman popped his head in the doorway and yelled, "Evacuate immediately!"

She knew it wasn't a fire drill. Nellie herded her guests down a nearby stairway to the first floor, got the attention of another group in the old Supreme Court chamber, and "fled out the east side of the Capitol." She came upon normally taciturn policemen who were agitated and frantically waving their arms. "Run for your life!" they shouted. "Run as far and as fast as you can!"

The Pentagon had been hit by Flight 77 just a few moments earlier. An outer section of the formidable building was badly damaged. Washington, DC, was now under attack—and another plane might be on the way.

Nellie and the others dutifully obeyed the commands. They ran. But as she made her way hastily across the plaza, she couldn't help but turn around for one brief look at the gleaming dome of the Capitol. "I fully expected it was the last look I would ever have," she said. "For all I knew, it was the last look I would have at anything before I was buried under the rubble."

As Nellie and the others scurried to relative safety, she could see the shocking sight of the center of the US military in flames. The Pentagon always had seemed so impenetrable, a virtual fortress. Now it reminded her of a wounded animal. She saw normally dignified members of Congress scrambling down the steps of the Capitol, feverishly trying to make calls on cell phones that were no longer working. And she saw shoes, empty shoes, seemingly everywhere, littered across the ground.

"I always wished I could have taken a picture of that scene," Nellie said. "It would have so graphically portrayed the terror that we were feeling. It was a beautiful day, and many of the women had worn sandals, but it is so difficult to run in sandals. So people literally kicked off their shoes and ran for their lives."

That there was no additional destruction in the nation's capital that day is a tribute to the quick thinking and bold bravery of the passengers and crew of Flight 93. The five thousand people who were working in the Capitol on September 11, 2001, are keenly aware of that now. They made it home safely. Life returned to normal. But the shock and uncertainty of that day—the fear and helplessness they all felt—would stay with them forever.

In 2005, when Nicole Eickhoff was a junior at the University of Virginia, she and her family made an emotional trip to the temporary memorial at the Flight 93 crash site in Somerset County. Nicole left a handwritten message in the visitors' book that was archived and later read by some of the workers at the facility. It awed them. Nicole's note underscored the legacy of Flight 93 from a completely different perspective—beyond the families, beyond the local residents. It quickly became one of the memorial's keepsakes.

> *September 10, 2005.*
>
> *My name is Nicole Marie Anne Eickhoff from Yorktown, VA. The heroes who gave their lives September 11, 2001 DID NOT DIE IN VAIN. One of the many lives they saved was mine. I was a U.S. House of Representatives page, and 9-11 was my first day of work. I was 17 years old. I was in the Capitol. Flight 93's passengers and flight crew were taking down my murderers. I thank them, and I have made a vow to live my life in gratitude of their sacrifice. I am now a 21-year-old 3rd-year (student) at the University of Virginia. I just thought that any family member of one of the heroes would like to know that I was here. I am grateful, and I know their sacrifice gave me life.*

Four years later, on September 11, 2009, a plaque honoring the passengers and crew of Flight 93 was dedicated in the east lobby of the

Capitol. Nellie Neumann soon began to include the lobby as a stop on her tours. Guests were encouraged to read the plaque, which listed the names of the forty heroes, with the following script:

In memory of the passengers and crew of United Airlines Flight 93, whose brave sacrifice on September 11, 2001 not only saved countless lives but may have saved the U.S. Capitol from destruction.

It still gives Nellie pause.

"I tell visitors that these were ordinary, everyday people who got on a plane on a Tuesday morning, planning to fly to California," she said. "Had they not taken the action that they did that day, we would not be standing here at the Capitol. I know I wouldn't be here."

———

During the ten years after September 11, far from the Capitol and the borders of Somerset County, the United States and its allies lashed out against the plotters and facilitators behind the attacks.

Mohammed Atef, al-Qaeda's military commander and the man who arranged the 1996 meeting when Khalid Sheikh Mohammed first proposed the Planes Operation, was killed by a US airstrike on his home in Afghanistan in November 2001. At the time, US officials suspected his involvement in the September 11 attacks but weren't yet aware of his specific role in the planning. Contemporary media reports mentioned his connection to the African embassy bombings in 1998 and to the strike on the USS *Cole* in 2000. Atef, also known as Abu Hafs, was considered the number 3 leader in al-Qaeda behind bin Laden and Ayman al Zawihiri. It was a significant blow against the terrorist network.

Ramzi Binalshibh, the plot's key facilitator, who wanted to be a hijacker pilot but couldn't get a visa, was captured in a morning raid in Karachi, Pakistan, on the first anniversary of the attacks—September 11, 2002. The arrest came only one day before the airing of an *Al Jazeera* TV special that featured taped interviews with Binalshibh and Khalid Sheikh Mohammed, which revealed, for the first time, specific details of the operation. After being nabbed by Pakistani authorities, a defiant, blindfolded

Binalshibh was photographed being paraded through a crowd. He underwent interrogation, was charged with war crimes, and was eventually sent to Guantanamo Bay.

Six months after Binalshibh was apprehended, Khalid Sheikh Mohammed, the mastermind who had started it all with his plan to fly planes into buildings, also was taken prisoner during a raid in Pakistan—this time in Rawalpindi, during the dark early morning hours of March 1, 2003. A photo of a disheveled KSM at the time of his capture was distributed around the world. He was in custody for three years and was reportedly subjected to extensive waterboarding before he was sent to Guantanamo Bay. KSM, Binalshibh, and others still were awaiting trial as of 2014. Among those also being held at Guantanamo were Mohammed al Kahtani, the alleged twentieth hijacker, and Ali Abdul Aziz Ali, who had assisted with funding and logistics.

The biggest breakthrough in the search for those responsible came almost ten years after the attacks, when US intelligence operatives tracked Osama bin Laden to a house in Abbottabad, Pakistan. Navy SEALs conducted a stealth raid into Pakistani territory in the wee hours of May 2, 2011, shooting and killing the al-Qaeda leader, one of his sons, and several others who lived in the compound. In announcing the news from the White House, President Obama said, "On nights like this one, we can say to those families who lost loved ones to al-Qaeda's terror, justice has been done."

Immediately, reporters sought out the reaction of family members to the stunning news from Pakistan. Lyz Glick remembers her phone ringing until two o'clock that morning. Responses varied. Some had moved on; some were relieved. Others felt at least an incremental feeling of closure. Many, such as Beverly Burnett, Tom's mother, praised SEAL Team Six and others responsible for the operation.

"We thank the military," Beverly told the Minneapolis *Star Tribune*. "We thank all of the young men who undertook this operation and didn't give up and found him. It's been a long time. And our military didn't give up. George Bush our president didn't give up, and neither did President Obama. It reminds us of the passengers and crew, especially our son. They didn't give up either. They fought to the very end."

Aside from the determined, decadelong assault on the men behind the plot, the long-term impact of September 11 and Flight 93 was that passengers would no longer react to terrorists on commercial airliners in the same way. Never again would they sit idly by while their lives were threatened. On December 22, 2001, passengers and crew members aggressively took down al-Qaeda member Richard Reid, who tried to ignite explosives in his shoe on American Airlines Flight 63 from Paris to Miami. On Christmas Day 2009, passengers and crew likewise helped to thwart Umar Farouck Abdul Mutallab, who tried to light explosives in his underwear on Northwest Airlines Flight 253 as it was approaching Detroit from Amsterdam. Both planes landed safely.

"Let's roll" wasn't just a slogan or a bumper sticker. It was a new call to action, and an essential and unmistakeable element of the legacy of Flight 93.

━━

In great deeds, something abides. On great fields, something stays. Forms change and pass; bodies disappear; but spirits linger, to consecrate ground for the vision-place of souls. And reverent men and women from afar, and generations that know us not and that we know not of, heart-drawn to see where and by whom great things were suffered and done for them, shall come to this deathless field, to ponder and dream.
—GENERAL JOSHUA CHAMBERLAIN, DEDICATION OF THE 20TH MAINE MEMORIAL, GETTYSBURG, 1889

Life would never be the same again in Shanksville or Somerset County. History had come calling, and once it does that, it never leaves.

From the earliest days after September 11, curious travelers would traverse State Route 281 through the sleepy hamlets of Friedens and Stoystown to connect with US Route 30, then turn right on Lambertsville or Buckstown Road, trying to find the crash site. The change brought by the influx of tourists was not always easy. Some locals resented it. Traffic eventually had to be re-routed to preserve local roads and neighborhoods that weren't designed for that kind of heavy use. But community leaders and many good-hearted citizens realized that things could never again be the way they were. As with Gettysburg before them, history had seen to that. The names of Shanksville and Somerset County had been etched for all time on the scroll of hallowed places where regular Americans had committed heroic deeds.

———

Reporters from local and national media outlets had converged on the crash site by the early afternoon hours of September 11, but a handful of local residents with no media credentials or experience were the first to record events on the morning of the attacks. One of them was Valencia McClatchey, a housewife from Indian Lake, who lived about a mile and a half from the old Diamond T strip mine. Val had gotten her husband off to work and was sipping her second cup of coffee when she saw the first crash at the World Trade Center on NBC's *Today* show. She followed the coverage intently for the next hour, until she heard the shocking "sudden surge" of an airplane engine.

"I caught just a quick flash of light," she said. "All of a sudden you just heard and felt a large explosion. I mean, the house shook violently. I was sitting very much on the edge of my sofa and the blast almost knocked me off balance."

Val ran to the door and could see smoke rising over the hill. Instinctively, she reached for her camera. The view through the lens was jarring—a black mushroom cloud rising over a neighbor's familiar red barn in the once-serene pastoral setting of Somerset County. With one click, Val took the first still photo of the aftermath of the crash of Flight 93.

"Oh, jeez, it's just smoke rising over the barn and the hillside," she said. "I didn't think it was anything of great importance." But a few days later, when local authorities inquired about photos or other evidence, she printed a copy for the Pennsylvania State Police and delivered her memory card to the FBI. She shared it with the public at a town meeting and showed it to a reporter from WTAE TV in Pittsburgh. The photo soon became a media and Internet sensation—as did Val herself. She spoke with ABC's *Good Morning America*. She remembers the photo appearing in the *Washington Post, Newsweek, Time, Reader's Digest,* and *U.S. News and World Report.* Internationally, there were inquiries from *Der Spiegel* in Germany and *Le Point* in France.

There was a downside to the attention. Conspiracy theorists questioned the validity of the photo and began pestering her with phone calls, e-mails, and even visits to her home. They challenged everything from the size of the mushroom cloud to the color of the smoke—asserting that it must have been doctored.

"Every time I've done any stories it goes online, and all these conspiracy theorists . . . call me and harass me," Val told the *New York Times.* All she had done was grab her camera when she heard the thunder of a plane crash nearby. She could not have imagined the interest or the backlash that would come as a result of her split-second decision.

In contrast to the harassment regarding conspiracies, McClatchey was honored for Outstanding Achievement for Amateur Photography by the International Society of Photographers, and her photo was displayed at the Smithsonian Institution in Washington, DC, and the National September 11 Memorial and Museum in New York City. The staff at the new Flight 93 National Memorial chose it as the first image visitors would see upon their arrival at the memorial plaza. A framed version also was presented to the crew of the USS *Somerset.*

Val named her photo *End of Serenity* because "the serenity of our country kind of died that day"—and because she knew Somerset County would never be the same. But while the frenzy that accompanied its release created a decade of distraction in her life, it never altered her view of the lasting impact of the story of Flight 93. "I see that red barn and that blue sky every morning I open my blinds," she said, "and there's not a day that goes by that I don't think, 'I'm still here to see it. A blink of an eye and I wouldn't be.'

"You have no choice but to thank those forty people for having the courage to stand up and fight for something," Val said. "I would have been the one sitting in the back . . . gritting my teeth and trying to make peace with my maker. They went down fighting."

It is a feeling that is shared by many of the local residents whose lives were changed that day, and who remain uncomfortable with their unexpected places in history. Rick King, the assistant fire chief, once spent an entire interview with a reporter from *New Republic* magazine without mentioning that he had been one of the first people to reach the crash site. He never sought the spotlight and always thought the focus should be on the passengers and crew. Years later, Rick said he still "can't even fathom" what those folks went through. "I can't imagine what was going through their minds or how they came to the conclusion . . . how they came together to do what they did. These people knew that if they didn't do anything, they were going to die, and if they did do something they were still probably going to die, but they did it anyway. To me, it's beyond anything I can comprehend."

The meaning of the story of Flight 93 had hit home almost immediately for the 490 students in grades K–12 of the little Shanksville-Stonycreek School, located less than three miles from the crash site. The school might have been in the flight path had the hijacked Boeing 757 stayed airborne just a few seconds longer. Students and teachers heard the noise of the impact and felt the walls of the building shake. As news spread of a nearby plane crash, parents arrived to rush their kids out of school.

In the days and weeks ahead, teachers had to answer many questions, especially from the younger children. Joyce Dunn, a first-grade teacher, would discuss it with her students whenever they broached the subject, talking about the courageous actions of the passengers and crew, talking about heroes. She couldn't be sure how much of it had sunk in until she glanced out on the school's playground one day.

The boys, she said, were "playing" Flight 93.

"And they always would be the heroes and they would be the ones to save the plane," Joyce said. "But, you know, it never crashed. They always saved it and they got rid of the bad guys. And they talked a lot about their courage and how brave they were. They decided to do something. They tried to overcome evil. They didn't just take it."

They didn't just take it.

The legacy that began that day lives on.

United Airlines Flight 93 Crew and Passengers

September 11, 2001

Flight Crew

Captain Jason M. Dahl
Age: 43
Residence: Littleton, Colorado
Occupation: Pilot, United Airlines

First Officer LeRoy Homer
Age: 36
Residence: Marlton, New Jersey
Occupation: Pilot, United Airlines

Lorraine G. Bay
Age: 58
Residence: East Windsor, New Jersey
Occupation: Flight Attendant, United Airlines

Sandy Waugh Bradshaw
Age: 38
Residence: Greensboro, North Carolina
Occupation: Flight Attendant, United Airlines

Wanda Anita Green
Age: 49
Residence: Linden, New Jersey
Occupation: Flight Attendant, United Airlines

CeeCee Ross Lyles
Age: 33

Residence: Fort Myers, Florida
Occupation: Flight Attendant, United Airlines

Deborah Jacobs Welsh
Age: 49
Residence: New York, New York
Occupation: Flight Attendant, United Airlines

Passengers

Christian Adams
Age: 37
Residence: Biebelsheim, Rheinland-Pfalz, Germany
Occupation: Export Director, German Wine Institute
Reason for flying: Business

Todd M. Beamer
Age: 32
Residence: Cranbury, New Jersey
Occupation: Account Manager, Oracle Corporation
Reason for flying: Business

Alan Anthony Beaven
Age: 48
Residence: Oakland, California
Occupation: Attorney, specializing in environmental litigation
Reason for flying: Business

Mark Bingham
Age: 31
Residence: San Francisco, California
Occupation: Owner, The Bingham Group
Reason for flying: Business

Deora Frances Bodley
Age: 20
Residence: San Diego, California
Occupation: Student, Santa Clara University
Reason for flying: Visiting friends

Marion R. Britton
Age: 53
Residence: Brooklyn, New York
Occupation: Assistant Regional Director, US Census Bureau
Reason for flying: Attending conference

Thomas E. Burnett Jr.
Age: 38
Residence: San Ramon, California
Occupation: Chief Operating Officer, Thoratec Corporation
Reason for flying: Business

William Joseph Cashman
Age: 60
Residence: West New York, New Jersey
Occupation: Ironworker
Reason for flying: Hiking trip

Georgine Rose Corrigan
Age: 55
Residence: Honolulu, Hawaii
Occupation: Antiques and Jewelry Dealer
Reason for flying: Visit with brother/business

Patricia Cushing
Age: 69
Residence: Bayonne, New Jersey
Occupation: Retired Service Representative, New Jersey Bell
Reason for flying: Vacation

Joseph DeLuca
Age: 52
Residence: Succasunna, New Jersey
Occupation: Business Systems Specialist, Pfizer Consumer Healthcare
Reason for flying: Vacation

Patrick Joseph Driscoll
Age: 70
Residence: Manalapan, New Jersey
Occupation: Retired Executive Director of Software Development, Bell
Communications
Reason for flying: Hiking trip

Edward Porter Felt
Age: 41
Residence: Matawan, New Jersey
Occupation: Computer Engineer and Technology Director, BEA Systems
Reason for flying: Business

Jane C. Folger
Age: 73
Residence: Bayonne, New Jersey
Occupation: Retired Bank Officer, Commercial Trust
Reason for flying: Vacation

Colleen L. Fraser
Age: 51
Residence: Elizabeth, New Jersey
Occupation: Executive Director, Progressive Center for Independent
Living
Reason for flying: Attending conference

Andrew (Sonny) Garcia
Age: 62
Residence: Portola Valley, California

Occupation: Owner, Cinco Group, Inc.
Reason for flying: Business

Jeremy Logan Glick
Age: 31
Residence: Hewitt, New Jersey
Occupation: Sales Manager, Vividence, Inc.
Reason for flying: Business

Kristin Osterholm White Gould
Age: 65
Residence: New York, New York
Occupation: Freelance Medical Journalist
Reason for flying: Visiting friends

Lauren Catuzzi Grandcolas
Age: 38
Residence: San Rafael, California
Occupation: Advertising Sales Consultant, *Good Housekeeping* Magazine
Reason for flying: Grandmother's memorial service

Donald Freeman Greene
Age: 52
Residence: Greenwich, Connecticut
Occupation: Executive VP, Safe Flight Instrument Corporation
Reason for flying: Hiking and biking trip

Linda Gronlund
Age: 46
Residence: Greenwood Lake, New York
Occupation: Manager of Environmental Compliance, BMW North America
Reason for flying: Business/vacation

Richard J. Guadagno
Age: 38
Residence: Eureka, California
Occupation: Manager, Humboldt Bay National Wildlife Refuge, US Fish and Wildlife Service
Reason for flying: Grandmother's hundredth birthday/visit family

Toshiya Kuge
Age: 20
Residence: Osaka, Japan
Occupation: Student, Waseda University, Tokyo
Reason for flying: Vacation

Hilda Marcin
Age: 79
Residence: Mount Olive, New Jersey
Occupation: Retired Bookkeeper and Teacher's Aide
Reason for flying: Moving to live with daughter

Waleska Martinez
Age: 37
Residence: Jersey City, New Jersey
Occupation: Supervisory Computer Specialist, US Census Bureau
Reason for flying: Attending conference

Nicole Carol Miller
Age: 21
Residence: San Jose, California
Occupation: Student, West Valley College, Saratoga, California
Reason for flying: Vacation

Louis J. Nacke II
Age: 42
Residence: New Hope, Pennsylvania
Occupation: Director of Distribution Center, Kay-Bee Toys
Reason for flying: Business

Donald Arthur Peterson
Age: 66
Residence: Spring Lake, New Jersey
Occupation: Retired President, Continental Electric Company
Reason for flying: Vacation

Jean Hoadley Peterson
Age: 55
Residence: Spring Lake, New Jersey
Occupation: Retired Registered Nurse and Nursing Teacher
Reason for flying: Vacation

Mark David Rothenberg
Age: 52
Residence: Scotch Plains, New Jersey
Occupation: Owner, MDR Global Resources
Reason for flying: Business

Christine Ann Snyder
Age: 32
Residence: Kailua, Hawaii
Occupation: Arborist and Project Manager, The Outdoor Circle
Reason for flying: Attended conference

John Talignani
Age: 74
Residence: Staten Island, New York
Occupation: Retired Bartender
Reason for flying: Stepson's memorial service

Honor Elizabeth Wainio
Age: 27
Residence: Watchung, New Jersey
Occupation: Regional Manager, Discovery Channel Stores
Reason for flying: Business

Sources:

www.nps.gov/flni/historyculture/upload/Biographies-Passenger-Crew.pdf

Pittsburgh Post-Gazette, October 28, 2001

Jere Longman, *Among the Heroes: United Flight 93 and the Passengers and Crew Who Fought Back* (New York: HarperCollins, 2002)

ACKNOWLEDGMENTS

I am indebted to the authors and researchers who first reported and pieced together the complex story of the September 11 attacks.

Chief among them is Jere Longman, reporter for the *New York Times*, who wrote the first book about Flight 93, *Among the Heroes*, less than a year after the crash, in 2002. His book is a rich resource, particularly on the backgrounds of the passengers and crew and the stories of their families.

Terry McDermott, reporter for the *Los Angeles Times*, wrote *Perfect Soldiers*, about the nineteen hijackers, and then co-authored *The Hunt for KSM* with Josh Meyer. Both provided groundbreaking insight on the plot and the plotters. Yosri Fouda of *Al Jazeera* landed the only interviews with plot mastermind Khalid Sheikh Mohammed and facilitator Ramzi Binalshibh before their capture and collaborated with Nick Fielding of the London *Sunday Times* on *Masterminds of Terror*. In 2011, Anthony Summers and Robbyn Swan produced *The Eleventh Day*, a comprehensive ten-year look at the attacks and their aftermath.

The National Commission on Terrorist Attacks Upon the United States delivered *The 9/11 Commission Report* in 2004. In addition to the report itself were detailed staff statements on topics ranging from "The Four Flights" to "Entry of the 9/11 Hijackers Into the United States" to "The Aviation Security System and the 9/11 Attacks"—all now available to readers and researchers online. Of particular interest is Staff Statement No. 17, titled "Improvising a Homeland Defense," dealing with the response that morning of the FAA and the military.

Many newspapers contributed to our understanding of the events, but two that stood out in their coverage of Flight 93 were the *Pittsburgh Post-Gazette* and the Somerset, PA, *Daily American*. The *Post-Gazette*'s special section of October 28, 2001, is a must-read for any Flight 93 researcher.

Jeff Reinbold, superintendent of National Parks for Western Pennsylvania, opened the Flight 93 National Memorial's considerable resources and agreed to multiple interviews, always providing encouragement for the project. Donna Glessner, Kathie Shaffer, and Barbara Black, staff members at the national memorial, were gracious with their time and insights and repeatedly accommodated my questions and occasional badgering. Joanne Hanley, who originally oversaw the memorial site for the National Park Service and who now does such great work for the Gettysburg Foundation (another passion of mine), also offered great background and perspective.

Wally Miller, the Somerset County coroner who took control of the crash site following the FBI's two-week investigation, and then developed such a close relationship with the family members, was unfailingly cooperative in my research and volunteered some never-before-seen photos for the book. One of the unforgettable experiences of my life will always be the day that Wally and Jeff Reinbold took me to the impact site and into the woods beyond. I truly felt that I was walking on sacred ground.

Family members Lyz (Glick) Best, Debby Borza, Beverly Burnett, Gordie Felt, Alice (Hoglan) Hoagland, Carole O'Hare, Kenny Nacke, Ed Root, and Patrick White graciously responded to my inquiries on a topic that even now remains heartrending. Many other family members granted compelling oral history interviews to the staff at the Flight 93 National Memorial. Four wives of those on board—Lisa Beamer, Deena Burnett, Lyz Glick, and Melodie Homer—wrote books that added immensely to the historic narrative.

Paul Murdoch, architect of the Flight 93 National Memorial, walked me through the intricacies of the competition and design process. Tom Ridge, governor of Pennsylvania on September 11, 2001, and later the country's first Secretary of Homeland Security, kindly agreed to write the foreword and provide his own unique insights.

Tim Lambert, a landowner at the crash site in Somerset County, who also did some award-winning radio reporting on the Flight 93 story, was gracious enough to share his memories and perspective. Chuck Wagner, a Shanksville resident who worked at the crash site, volunteered at the early temporary memorials, and later became the unofficial photographer for the Flight 93 National Memorial, provided some of his voluminous photo inventory. Archie Carpenter and Nicholas Young also kindly donated photographs.

My good friend Mike Fetchko introduced me to Uwe Stender, who agreed to become my agent for this project. Uwe offered invaluable guidance on a book proposal that was eventually accepted by Lyons Press.

Thanks especially to my editor at Lyons Press, Jon Sternfeld, whose advice, suggestions, gentle prodding—and, above all, patience—made it possible for me to complete such an improbable odyssey. When we started, Jon informed me that he tries to read one book a year about the September 11 attacks. I trust that we have fulfilled his quota for 2014.

Sources and Notes

Chapter One: Morning

1. *its scheduled departure time of 8:00 a.m.*, National Commission on Terrorist Attacks Upon the United States, *The 9/11 Commission Report*, p. 10.

1. *such as Tom Burnett, seated in 4B*, Flight 93 seating chart, USA vs. Moussaoui, Prosecution Trial Exhibits, Exhibit No. P200055.

1. Be busy with the constant remembrance, www.theguardian.com/world/2001/sep/30/terrorism.september113, "Last Words of a Terrorist," *The Guardian/The Observer*, September 30, 2001. The four excerpts in this chapter from the hijackers' instructions were published in the *Guardian*. The document had been released by the FBI and translated for the *New York Times* by Capital Communications Group, an international consulting firm, and by Imad Musa, a translator for the firm. There were several translations of this document with slightly different wording, depending on the translator, but the essential message was the same. Versions of the document were found by investigators in connection to three of the flights on September 11, including Flight 93.

2. *were scheduled to take off within a tight time frame of twenty-five minutes*, National Commission on Terrorist Attacks Upon the United States, *The 9/11 Commission Report*, p. 10. Flight 11 was scheduled to depart at 7:45 a.m. Flights 175 and 93 were both scheduled for 8:00 a.m. Flight 77 was scheduled for 8:10 a.m.

2. *The hijackings were to start about fifteen minutes after each flight was in the air*, Ibid., p. 245. Al-Qaeda's operational liaison, Ramzi Binalshibh, said that he and mission leader Mohamed Atta thought "the best time to storm the cockpit would be about ten to fifteen minutes after takeoff, when the cockpit doors typically were opened for the first time."

3. *sipped orange juice*, Jere Longman, *Among the Heroes*, p. 29.

3. "cleared for takeoff four left United ninety three," National Transportation Safety Board, Vehicle Recorders Division, *Air Traffic Control Recording, Transcript of ATC communications with a Boeing B-757 (United Airlines flight 93) which crashed near Shanksville, PA on September 11, 2001*, Specialist's Report by Joseph A. Gregor, December 21, 2001.

3. *Kristin White Gould, seated in 21C, was a freelance medical journalist*, Information about Kristin and other passengers in this chapter was gathered primarily from two sources: Longman's *Among the Heroes* and a *Pittsburgh Post-Gazette* special section published on October 28, 2001. Kristin was listed on the Flight 93 seating chart as Olga Kristin White. She was born Olga Kristin Osterholm (Longman, p. 227), and her first husband was named White. On the Flight 93 National Memorial's Wall of Names, her name is listed as Kristin Osterholm White Gould.

5. *Being the coroner in Somerset County didn't come with all the accommodations,* Author interview with Somerset County coroner Wally Miller, June 2012. Additional information on Somerset County came from www.co.somerset.pa.us.

5. *"We're thinking the pilot must have had a heart attack or something,"* Author interview with Wally Miller, June 2012.

7. *"how'd you like to be the coroner in New York City today?"* Ibid.

7. *Ed Ballinger was supposed to have the day off,* Oral history transcript with Ed Ballinger, Flight 93 National Memorial, interview conducted by Kathie Shaffer.

7. *worked paratrooper school at Fort Benning,* Ibid.

7. *just before 8:00 a.m. Eastern Daylight Time,* Ibid. Ballinger reported to work at 7:00 a.m. Central Daylight Time in Chicago.

7. *been assigned sixteen cross-country flights,* National Commission on Terrorist Attacks Upon the United States, *Memorandum for the Record, Ed Ballinger,* April 14, 2004, p. 1.

8. *sent to the cockpits using ACARS,* Oral history transcript with Ed Ballinger.

8. *'Ed, one of your flights appears to be not operating correctly,'* Ibid.

8. *"HOW IS THE RIDE?"* National Commission on Terrorist Attacks Upon the United States, *Memorandum for the Record, Ed Ballinger,* April 14, 2004, p. 4.

8. *At 8:46 a.m. American Airlines Flight 11 plowed into the North Tower,* National Commission on Terrorist Attacks Upon the United States, *The 9/11 Commission Report,* p. 7.

9. *"when a United flight dispatcher, Ed Ballinger, took the initiative,"* Ibid., p. 11.

9. *A supervisor later commended him for performing "expertly" under the circumstances,* Letter to Ed Ballinger from Joe Vickers, Manager Domestic DD Ops., September 24, 2001, UASSI100036098. According to the oral history Ballinger did with the Flight 93 National Memorial staff in 2007, he often asked himself if he could have done more or if he could have used different language in his texts. But the opinion of his superiors was that he had acted both expertly and heroically and had done all he could under unimaginable circumstances. He received a commendation letter on September 24, 2011, from Vickers, which said, "Please accept this sincere expression of gratitude for the fine performance you turned in during the disaster on that tragic day. Above all, you were affected most. At no time has anyone had to endure witnessing, over and over, on the overhead monitors, on news broadcasts, in newspapers and journals, the destruction of a flight for which they were responsible. Ed, as the events unfolded, you performed your job expertly and in a manner that even the 20/20 vision of hindsight can't find fault. I can't imagine the thoughts and emotions you feel being so deeply and personally involved with a tragedy of such epic proportions. Your professionalism, skill, and calm demeanor gave strength to those around you and to all the flight crews flying that day. Your contribution will never be measured because there is no scale that can measure such a significant contribution, made under such trying circumstances. Thank you, again." Ballinger retired a month after the attacks in October 2001.

9. *At 9:19 a.m. he began sending,* National Commission on Terrorist Attacks Upon the United States, *The 9/11 Commission Report,* p. 11.

9. *"BEWARE ANY COCKPIT INTROUSION [sic],"* National Transportation Safety Board, *Air Traffic Control Recording, Transcript of ATC communications with a Boeing B-757 (United Airlines flight 93) which crashed near Shanksville, Pa. on September 11, 2001;* also, 9/11 Commission Files: Misc. Communications From 4 Flights, UAL ACARS to 9/11 flights. This is the way Ballinger typed "intrusion" as he hurriedly composed his ACARS text message. Some previous reporting has used an edited version of the message.

9. *according to departure time and en-route progress,* National Commission on Terrorist Attacks Upon the United States, *Memorandum for the Record, Ed Ballinger,* April 14, 2004, p. 6.

9. *was received in the cockpit at 9:24 a.m.,* National Commission on Terrorist Attacks Upon the United States, *The 9/11 Commission Report,* p. 11. The sequence of all message times between Ballinger and the Flight 93 cockpit is included in this section of the report.

Chapter Two: Mastermind

10. *first made the wildly ambitious proposal,* National Commission on Terrorist Attacks Upon the United States, *The 9/11 Commission Report,* pp. 148–49.

10. *fighting alongside bin Laden,* Terry McDermott, *Perfect Soldiers,* p. 121.

10. *It was KSM's nephew, Ramzi Yousef,* Terry McDermott and Josh Meyer, *The Hunt for KSM,* pp. 45–48. The nephew's given name was Abdul Basit. He used an Iraqi passport in the name of "Ramzi Ahmed Yousef" to gain entry to the United States in 1992, and "Yousef" became his alias.

10. *built a bomb for three thousand dollars,* McDermott, *Perfect Soldiers,* pp. 132–33.

11. *Six people died,* Ibid., p. 133.

11. *"fifth battalion in the Liberation Army,"* Ibid.

11. *was born in Kuwait on April 14, 1965,* McDermott and Meyer, *The Hunt for KSM,* pp. 23–27.

11. *from the independent region of Baluchistan,* National Commission on Terrorist Attacks Upon the United States, *The 9/11 Commission Report,* p. 145.

12. *ripped down the Kuwaiti flag,* McDermott and Meyer, *The Hunt for KSM,* p. 26.

12. *joined a prominent Islamist group, the Muslim Brotherhood,* Department of Defense JTF-GTMO assessment, published online by the *New York Times,* the Guantanamo Docket, http://projects.nytimes.com/guantanamo/detainees/10024-khalid-shaikh-mohammed, p. 2.

12. *enrolled at tiny Chowan College,* National Commission on Terrorist Attacks Upon the United States, *The 9/11 Commission Report,* p. 146.

12. *North Carolina Agricultural and Technical State University,* Ibid.; North Carolina Agricultural and Technical State University website, www.ncat.edu.

13. *He graduated in December 1986,* National Commission on Terrorist Attacks Upon the United States, *The 9/11 Commission Report,* p. 146.

13. *"By his own account, KSM's animus toward the United States,"* Ibid., p. 147.

13. *"KSM's limited and negative experience in the United States,"* Peter Finn, Joby Warrick, and Julie Tate, "How a Detainee Became an Asset," *Washington Post,* August 29, 2009.

13. *introduced him to the Afghan warlord Abdul Rasaf Sayyaf,* National Commission on Terrorist Attacks Upon the United States, *The 9/11 Commission Report,* p. 146.

13. *sending him at first to the Sada camp,* Department of Defense, JTF-GTMO assessment, http://projects.nytimes.com/guantanamo/detainees/10024-khalid -shaikh-mohammed. KSM worked for the newspaper *al-Bunyan al-Marsus,* published by Abdul Rasul Sayaff's Islamic Union.

13. *learned of Ramzi Yousef's plan to attack inside the United States,* National Commission on Terrorist Attacks Upon the United States, *The 9/11 Commission Report,* p. 147; McDermott and Meyer, *The Hunt for KSM,* pp. 45–48.

14. *a radical Egyptian cleric named Omar Abdel Rahman,* McDermott, *Perfect Soldiers,* p. 132.

14. *Holland and Lincoln tunnels,* National Commission on Terrorist Attacks Upon the United States, *The 9/11 Commission Report,* p. 72.

14. *chose the World Trade Center,* McDermott, *Perfect Soldiers,* p. 130.

14. *KSM wired $660 at one point,* National Commission on Terrorist Attacks Upon the United States, *The 9/11 Commission Report,* p. 147.

14. *basic fertilizer bomb,* McDermott, *Perfect Soldiers,* p. 132.

14. *"carved out a nearly 100-foot crater several stories deep,"* www.fbi.gov/news/ stories/2008/february/tradebom_022608, 1993 World Trade Center Bombing; First Strike: Global Terror In America.

14. *"Yousef's instant notoriety as the mastermind,"* National Commission on Terrorist Attacks Upon the United States, *The 9/11 Commission Report,* p. 147.

15. *Khalid Sheikh Mohammed and Ramzi Yousef traveled to the Philippines,* McDermott and Meyer, *The Hunt for KSM,* pp. 60–68.

15. *"Bojinka,"* National Commission on Terrorist Attacks Upon the United States, *The 9/11 Commission Report,* notes to chapter 5, no. 7. It has been reported elsewhere that "Bojinka" was a Serbo-Croatian word for "big bang." However, in intelligence reports of interrogations of KSM, obtained by the 9/11 Commission, KSM said it was "a nonsense word he adopted after hearing it on the front lines in Afghanistan."

15. *simultaneous bombing of twelve US commercial jets,* National Commission on Terrorist Attacks Upon the United States, *The 9/11 Commission Report,* p. 147.

15. *came crashing down on January 6, 1995,* McDermott, *Perfect Soldiers,* p. 152.

16. *Yousef was tracked to Islamabad, Pakistan,* National Commission on Terrorist Attacks Upon the United States, *The 9/11 Commission Report,* p. 148.

16. *"Look, they're still standing,"* McDermott and Meyer, *The Hunt for KSM,* p. 79. In 1998, at federal district court in Manhattan, Yousef was sentenced to life plus 240 years in prison for his role as mastermind of the World Trade Center bombing. The *New York Times,* in its January 8, 1998, edition, quoted Yousef as saying, "I am a terrorist and I am proud of it."

16. *Abdul Murad, had developed his own idea,* McDermott and Meyer, *The Hunt for KSM,* p. 118.

17. *had not even seen each other since 1989,* National Commission on Terrorist Attacks Upon the United States, *The 9/11 Commission Report,* p. 148.

17. *a plan to hijack ten US domestic aircraft,* Ibid., pp. 149, 154. Additional details of the original KSM plot were drawn from McDermott and Meyer, *The Hunt for KSM,* pp. 117–18.

17. *in early 1999, bin Laden summoned,* McDermott and Meyer, *The Hunt for KSM,* p. 137.

17. *From now on, it would be known as the "Planes Operation,"* National Commission on Terrorist Attacks Upon the United States, *The 9/11 Commission Report,* p. 154.

Chapter Three: Forming a Cell

18. *ancient university in Greifswald,* www.uni-greifswald.de. The university was founded in 1456.

18. *he wore American jeans,* Mary Anne Weaver, "The Indecisive Terrorist," *London Review of Books,* September 8, 2011.

18. *They drove Mercedes automobiles,* Staff of *Der Spiegel* magazine, *Inside 9-11,* pp. 245–47.

18. *built his first plane out of Legos,* Ibid., p. 147.

18. *"I was afraid that he would crash,"* Marcus Walker and James M. Dorsey, "A Student's Dreams or a Terrorist's Plot," *Wall Street Journal,* September 18, 2001.

19. *"He was good-looking, flattered the girls,"* Staff of *Der Spiegel* magazine, *Inside 9-11,* p. 147.

19. *Toronto, Canada, or Greifswald,* McDermott, *Perfect Soldiers,* p. 50.

19. *"we drank so much beer we couldn't ride straight on a bike,"* Staff of *Der Spiegel* magazine, *Inside 9-11,* p. 190.

19. *was smitten by a striking dental student named Aysel Senguen,* McDermott, *Perfect Soldiers,* p. 51.

19. *"We had problems since the beginning,"* Dirk Laabs, "Testimony Offers Intimate Look at a Sept. 11 Hijacker's Life," *Los Angeles Times,* November 21, 2002.

19. *"They cooked meals together,"* McDermott, *Perfect Soldiers,* p. 51.

20. *"dissatisfied with his life up till now,"* Ibid., pp. 51–52.

20. *a religious leader named Abdul Rahman al Makhadi,* Weaver, "The Indecisive Terrorist," *London Review of Books;* McDermott, *Perfect Soldiers,* pp. 51, 53.

20. *aeronautical engineering at the University of Applied Sciences,* Weaver, "The Indecisive Terrorist," *London Review of Books.*

20–21. *"appears already to have had Hamburg contacts by this time,"* National Commission on Terrorist Attacks Upon the United States, *The 9/11 Commission Report,* p. 163.

21. *had landed an internship in Hamburg,* McDermott, *Perfect Soldiers,* p. 53.

21. *at 54 Marienstrasse,* Yosri Fouda and Nick Fielding, *Masterminds of Terror,* p. 77.

21. *Mohamed Atta arrived first, traveling from Egypt,* National Commission on Terrorist Attacks Upon the United States, *The 9/11 Commission Report,* p. 160.

21. *initially applying to Hamburg's University of Applied Sciences*, McDermott, *Perfect Soldiers*, p. 23.

21. *"He was a perfectionist,"* Fouda and Fielding, *Masterminds of Terror*, p. 80.

22. *had grown a beard and become even more detached*, McDermott, *Perfect Soldiers*, pp. 31–32, 34.

22. *Ramzi Binalshibh arrived in Germany*, Anthony Summers and Robbyn Swan, *The Eleventh Day*, pp. 272–73.

22. *before settling on Germany as his destination*, McDermott, *Perfect Soldiers*, p. 43.

22. *He couldn't hold a job*, Ibid., pp. 44–46.

23. *he packed his bags for the German city of Bonn*, National Commission on Terrorist Attacks Upon the United States, *The 9/11 Commission Report*, p. 162.

23. *Described by friends as a "regular guy,"* Summers and Swan, *The Eleventh Day*, p. 273.

23. *if he could transfer to a school in Hamburg*, McDermott, *Perfect Soldiers*, p. 56.

23. *"They seemed to know each other already when Shehhi relocated to Hamburg in early 1998,"* National Commission on Terrorist Attacks Upon the United States, *The 9/11 Commission Report*, p. 162.

23. *They dubbed the apartment* Dar al Ansar, Summers and Swan, *The Eleventh Day*, p. 278.

23. *Jarrah met Binalshibh at al Quds sometime late in 1997*, Weaver, "The Indecisive Terrorist," *London Review of Books*.

24. *She had an abortion*, McDermott, *Perfect Soldiers*, p. 80.

24. *"because my husband moved into a fanatic war,"* Ibid.

24. *transferring to a university in Bochum, near Dusseldorf*, INTELWIRE, Federal Bureau of Investigation, Translation of the interview conducted by German authorities of the girlfriend of Ziad Jarrah, September 18, 2001.

24. *"three or four times only,"* Ibid.

24. *at least several dozen participants*, Dirk Laabs and Terry McDermott, "Prelude to 9/11: A Hijacker's Love, Lies," *Los Angeles Times*, January 27, 2003.

24. *Among the most prominent*, National Commission on Terrorist Attacks Upon the United States, *The 9/11 Commission Report*, pp. 164–65.

24–25. *were employed in the paint shop of a Volkswagen plant*, McDermott, *Perfect Soldiers*, p. 58.

25. *a veteran of the Afghan jihad named Mohammed Haydar Zammar*, Ibid., p. 72.

25. *an active recruiter for al-Qaeda*, Weaver, "The Indecisive Terrorist," *London Review of Books;* House-Senate Joint Congressional Inquiry, 9/11 Report, July 24, 2003.

25. *no greater honor than to die for Allah*, National Commission on Terrorist Attacks Upon the United States, *The 9/11 Commission Report*, p. 163.

25. *"Ziad's own jihad was more aggressive, the fighting kind,"* Summers and Swan, *The Eleventh Day*, p. 274.

25. *and asked her to marry him*, Weaver, "The Indecisive Terrorist," *London Review of Books*.

25. *They never lived together as husband and wife*, McDermott, *Perfect Soldiers*, pp. 78–79.

25. *Jarrah's move toward extremism reached its peak,* Laabs, "Testimony Offers Intimate Look at a Sept. 11 Hijacker's Life," *Los Angeles Times,* November 21, 2002.

26. *men sang martyrdom songs,* Weaver, "The Indecisive Terrorist," *London Review of Books.*

26. *Atta ranted about what he described as a global Jewish movement,* National Commission on Terrorist Attacks Upon the United States, Staff Statement No. 16 ("Outline of the 9/11 Plot"), pp. 3–4.

26. *downloaded generic forms for jihadi wills,* Laabs and McDermott, "Prelude to 9/11: A Hijacker's Love, Lies," *Los Angeles Times,* January 27, 2003.

26. *One would shout, "Our Way!"* McDermott, *Perfect Soldiers,* p. 87.

26. *"The USA is not omnipotent,"* Summers and Swan, *The Eleventh Day,* p. 278.

26. *"must have the aim to free Islamic soil of any tyrant,"* www.usatoday.com, "Wedding Video Shows Sept. 11 Hijackers, Plotters," Associated Press, May 7, 2003.

26. *"The earth will shake beneath your feet,"* McDermott, *Perfect Soldiers,* p. 88.

27. *they left for Afghanistan,* Ibid., p. 89; Summers and Swan, *The Eleventh Day,* p. 278.

27. *to select a preliminary list of targets,* Staff Statement No. 16, p. 2.

27. *"leads to further exploitation of the Arab/Muslim peoples,"* USA vs. Moussaoui, Defendant's Exhibit 941, "Substitution for the Testimony of Khalid Sheikh Mohammed," p. 11. KSM was not available to testify in the Moussaoui trial for national security reasons, but he had been interrogated many times since his capture in March 2003. Lawyers compiled a fifty-eight-page document containing summaries of oral statements he made in response to extensive questioning.

27. *Bin Laden personally assigned the first four suicide operatives,* National Commission on Terrorist Attacks Upon the United States, *The 9/11 Commission Report,* p. 155.

27. *Abu Bara al Yemeni,* Ibid. Khallad was another of the names used by bin Attash.

27. *based on the potential for Yemenis to become economic migrants,* Lawrence Wright, *The Looming Tower,* p. 349.

28. *taking off from East Asia and blow them up in midair,* Staff Statement No. 16, p. 2.

28. *flight simulator computer games,* Ibid.

28. *they had volunteered for a martyrdom mission,* National Commission on Terrorist Attacks Upon the United States, *The 9/11 Commission Report,* p. 158.

28. *observe their security measures,* Staff Statement No. 16, p. 3.

28. *January 15, 2000,* Ibid.

28. *bin Laden abruptly cancelled the East Asia portion of the operation,* Ibid.

29. *"the pair could barely find their way out of LAX,"* Richard Miniter, *Mastermind,* p. 127.

29. *The two men moved to San Diego,* McDermott, *Perfect Soldiers,* pp. 189–90.

29. *A flight instructor at a small airfield,* Ibid., pp. 191–92.

29. *"they were like Dumb and Dumber,"* Summers and Swan, *The Eleventh Day,* p. 293.

29. *the Toba Kakar mountain range,* Weaver, "The Indecisive Terrorist," *London Review of Books.*

29. *The daily routine for recruits,* McDermott, *Perfect Soldiers,* pp. 172–73.

30. *summoned by bin Laden to a meeting at the House of Ghamdi,* Ibid., p. 178. There is speculation that Atta may have been in Afghanistan in 1998, which would have given al-Qaeda leadership a chance to assess him. For a period in 1998, his whereabouts were unknown. But there is no record of the trip, of course, and KSM has denied that he was in Afghanistan any time before late 1999.

30. *asked to pledge a* bayat *(oath),* Staff Statement No. 16, p. 4.

30. *Mohammed Atef, al-Qaeda's military leader, met with Atta, Jarrah, and Binalshibh,* McDermott, *Perfect Soldiers,* p. 180.

30. *Shehhi had left early,* Ibid., pp. 179–80.

30. *Bin Laden selected Atta as the leader,* National Commission on Terrorist Attacks Upon the United States, *The 9/11 Commission Report,* p. 166.

30. *bin Laden's headquarters at Tarnak Farm,* www.nbcnews.com/id/15082633/ns/us_news-security/t/video-showing-atta-bin-laden-unearthed. "Video Showing Atta, bin Laden Is Unearthed," October 1, 2006; Weaver, "The Indecisive Terrorist," *London Review of Books.*

31. *Jarrah appears to struggle,* www.youtube.com/watch?v=eQziDmMk88c, NBC "obtains" video of Ziad Jarrah, November 22, 2008.

31. *were sent to Karachi to meet with Khalid Sheikh Mohammed,* Staff Statement No. 16, p. 4.

31. *questioning by UAE authorities on January 30th,* National Commission on Terrorist Attacks Upon the United States, *The 9/11 Commission Report,* p. 496, note 97.

31. *to question anyone who might have traveled to the training camps,* Ned Zeman, David Wise, David Rose, and Bryan Burrough, "The Path to 9/11: Lost Warnings and Fatal Errors," *Vanity Fair,* November 2004.

31. *interrogated for four hours,* Weaver, "The Indecisive Terrorist," *London Review of Books.*

31. *a CIA spokesman denied to CNN,* http://edition.cnn.com/2002/US/08/01/cia.hijacker, "September 11 Hijacker Questioned in 2001," August 1, 2002. As authors Weaver and McDermott have noted, the date of the interrogation was wrong; it took place in 2000.

31. *the Western-style clothing he had favored when he first arrived in Germany,* Weaver, "The Indecisive Terrorist," *London Review of Books.*

31. *nom de guerre,* Fouda and Fielding, *Masterminds of Terror,* pp. 110–12. Atta's name was *Abu Abdul Rahman al Masri.* Each of the nineteen hijackers was assigned such a name, which Fouda referred to as a kunyah. He speculates that Jarrah (*Abu Tareq al Lubnani*) was named after Tareq Ibn Ziad, a

legendary Muslim warrior who once conquered North Africa and the area that is now Spain.

32. *"Don't ask me, it's better for you,"* McDermott, *Perfect Soldiers,* p. 187.

32. *Jarrah inspected German flight schools,* National Commission on Terrorist Attacks Upon the United States, *The 9/11 Commission Report,* p. 168.

32. *Atta sent e-mails to more than sixty US flight schools,* United States of America vs. Zacarias Moussaoui, United States District Court for the Eastern District of Virginia, Government Exhibit ST00001, 01-455-A, p. 21.

32. We would like to start training for the career of airline professional pilots, Ibid.

Chapter Four: Infiltrators

33. *into Newark International Airport on May 29, 2000,* National Commission on Terrorist Attacks Upon the United States, *The 9/11 Commission Report,* p. 223.

33. *flying to Newark from Prague in the Czech Republic,* Ibid., p. 224.

33. *checking out flight schools in the region,* Staff Statement No. 16 ("Outline of the 9/11 Plot"), p. 6.

33. *Atta bought a cell phone and Shehhi enrolled in a one-month English language class,* USA vs. Moussaoui, Government Exhibit ST00001, 01-455-A, pp. 23–24.

34. *inquired about obtaining both a private pilot's license and a commercial license,* USA vs. Moussaoui, Prosecution Trial Exhibits, Exhibit No. MM00741, Faxed application of acceptance for Ziad Jarrah, including photocopy of the application.

34. *on June 27, flying from Munich to Atlanta,* USA vs. Moussaoui, Government Exhibit ST00001, 01-455-A, p. 25.

34. *Kruithof labeled Jarrah "airline material,"* Oral history transcript with Arne Kruithof, Flight 93 National Memorial, interview conducted by Kathie Shaffer.

34. *"can switch from language to language and keep a good conversation going,"* Ibid.

34. *records show he was back at it on June 29,* USA vs. Moussaoui, Prosecution Trial Exhibits, Exhibit No. MM0750, General history for Ziad Jarrah, FFTC.

35. *check out the Airman Flight School, where one of bin Laden's personal pilots had once been a student,* Summers and Swan, *The Eleventh Day,* p. 294. In addition, they write, "As early as 1998, the FBI's regional office had been alerted to the large number of Arabs learning to fly in the area." Another al-Qaeda member later linked to the plot, Zacarias Moussaoui, would train at Airman in early 2001.

35. *a few hundred feet from where Jarrah was training,* McDermott, *Perfect Soldiers,* p. 195.

35. *They started classes on July 7,* USA vs. Moussaoui, Government Exhibit ST00001, 01-455-A, pp. 26–27.

35. *Binalshibh had applied for the same kind of tourist visa,* 9/11 and Terrorist Travel, Staff Report of the National Commission on Terrorist Attacks Upon the United States, pp. 11–12.

36. *failed to prove he was not an "intending immigrant,"* Ibid., pp. 12, 31, 73, 74, 118, 133, 141. "Few aliens were ever denied a nonimmigrant visa on grounds of terrorism in the pre-9/11 era—only 83 in fiscal year 2001" (p. 74); "Prior to 9/11, immigration inspections were not considered a counterterrorism tool. Rather, they were viewed in the context of travel facilitation." (p. 133); "Citizens of wealthy Persian Gulf nations or third country nationals from the Middle East with established lives in Germany were seen by State as good visa risks because they rarely overstayed the terms of their admission or sought to work in the United States." (p. 141).

36. *a bank statement, and a completed application form,* USA vs. Moussaoui, Prosecution Trial Exhibits, Exhibit No. MM00704, cover sheet of fax sent to Ramzi Binalshibh from Florida Flight Training Center, August 17, 2000.

36. *wired $2,200 to the school as a deposit,* Statement for the Record, FBI Director Robert S. Mueller III, Joint Intelligence Committee Inquiry.

36. *The other was in October from Berlin,* 9/11 and Terrorist Travel, Staff Report of the National Commission on Terrorist Attacks Upon the United States, pp. 13–14.

36. *"Please acknowledge that we cannot give you a visa,"* McDermott, *Perfect Soldiers,* p. 201.

36. *rented their own apartment in the nearby town of Nokomis,* USA vs. Moussaoui, Government Exhibit ST00001, 01-455-A, p. 25.

36. *"He was pretty social with them,"* Oral history transcript with Arne Kruithof.

37. *on the same day that December,* USA vs. Moussaoui, Government Exhibit ST00001, 01-455-A., pp. 27–28.

37. *each had accumulated approximately 250 flight hours,* 9/11 Commission Briefing, Flight Training, January 13, 2004, by John Allen, Deputy Director, Flight Standards Service.

37. *"the operational efficiency, 'feel,' and confidence to fly the aircraft into the intended target,"* Staff Statement No. 4 ("The Four Flights"), p. 5.

37. *Jarrah passed the test for his private pilot certification in September,* FBI, UA Flight 93 Investigative Team, "Ziad Jarrah," FBI03212, April 19, 2002.

38. *"and come back later to finish it,"* Oral history transcript with Arne Kruithof.

38. *Jarrah had compiled just one hundred flight hours by mid-November,* 9/11 Commission Briefing, Flight Training.

38. *All five trips were to Germany, and two included connections to Lebanon to see his family,* USA vs. Moussaoui, Government Exhibit ST00001, 01-455-A, pp. 36–38, 61.

38. *he even brought Aysel to Florida,* National Commission on Terrorist Attacks Upon the United States, *The 9/11 Commission Report,* p. 227.

38. *Counting a two-day pleasure trip to the Bahamas,* McDermott, *Perfect Soldiers,* p. 197.

38. *the equivalent of three full months,* USA vs. Moussaoui, Government Exhibit ST00001, 01-455-A, pp. 36–38, 61.

38. *Atta took two European trips of his own,* National Commission on Terrorist Attacks Upon the United States, *The 9/11 Commission Report,* pp. 227, 243–46; USA vs. Moussaoui, Government Exhibit ST00001, 01-455-A, pp. 59–60 (Spain).

39. *"so his father could see them before he dies,"* McDermott, *Perfect Soldiers,* p. 213.

39. *he trained on Boeing 727 and 737 simulators at the Aeroservice Aviation Center,* USA vs. Moussaoui, Government Exhibit ST00001, 01-455-A, p. 30.

39. *at an aviation center in Georgia,* Ibid., pp. 39–40.

39. *in June, at Hortman Aviation in Philadelphia,* Ibid., p. 54.

39. *enrolled at the US1 Fitness Center,* Ibid., p. 41.

39. *from kickboxing to knife-fighting,* USA vs. Moussaoui, Indictment of Zacarias Moussaoui, "Other Hijackers Take Gym Training," p. 9. According to the indictment, "Ziad Jarrah (#93) joined a gym and took martial arts lessons, which included lessons in kickboxing and knife-fighting."

39. *"He was learning to be in control,"* Elizabeth Neuffer, "Hijack Suspect Lived a Life, or a Lie," *Boston Globe,* September 25, 2001.

39. *at the al-Faruq training camp in Afghanistan,* Staff Statement No. 16, p. 6.

40. *told him to report to KSM,* Summers and Swan, *The Eleventh Day,* p. 299.

40. *traveled periodically to the United States since 1991,* Staff Statement No. 16, p. 6.

40. *taking English as a Second Language courses,* Statement for the Record, FBI Director Robert S. Mueller III.

40. *criticized his poor English,* McDermott, *Perfect Soldiers,* pp. 205–6.

40. *added his commercial, multiengine certificate in April 1999,* 9/11 Commission Briefing, Flight Training.

40. *Hanjour received his US visa on September 25, 2000,* National Commission on Terrorist Attacks Upon the United States, *The 9/11 Commission Report,* p. 226.

40. *introduced to a man in the United Arab Emirates named Ali Abdul Aziz Ali,* Staff Statement No. 16, p. 6.

40. *more than $100,000,* Statement for the Record, FBI Director Robert S. Mueller III. According to Mueller's statement, presented to the Joint Intelligence Committee Inquiry, "In July 2000, Marwan al Shehhi opened a joint checking account with Mohamed Atta at SunTrust Bank in Florida. From July 2000 through September 2000 this account received what appears to be the primary funding for the conspiracy: four money transfers totaling $109,500 from Ali Abdul Aziz Ali."

40. *Hanjour entered the United States on December 8, 2000,* Staff Statement No. 16, p. 6.

40. *had abruptly returned to the Middle East in June,* National Commission on Terrorist Attacks Upon the United States, *The 9/11 Commission Report,* pp. 222, 237. After Mihdhar heard the news of the birth of his first son in Yemen, the report says, "he could stand life in California no longer." He closed his bank account and transferred his car registration to Hazmi. He stayed in Yemen for

about a month and then returned to Afghanistan. He complained about life in the United States. KSM was said to be furious about Mihdhar's departure because he thought it might affect operational security, but bin Laden still wanted Mihdhar to be part of the attacks.

41. *at Pan Am International Jet Tech in Phoenix,* USA vs. Moussaoui, Government Exhibit ST00001, 01-455-A, p. 32.

Chapter Five: Final Preparations

42. *to identify additional young zealots who would fill out the hijack rosters,* Staff Statement No. 16 ("Outline of the 9/11 Plot"), p. 8.

42. *These would be the hit teams,* McDermott, *Perfect Soldiers,* p. 17. Although muscle hijackers has become the widely accepted term, McDermott's use of hit teams is more accurate.

42. *approved by bin Laden himself,* National Commission on Terrorist Attacks Upon the United States, *The 9/11 Commission Report,* p. 235.

42. *outlook changed dramatically after he attended a religious camp in the summer of 1999,* Charles M. Stennott, "Before Oath to Jihad, Drifting and Boredom," *Boston Globe,* March 3, 2002.

42. muscle hijackers, Staff Statement No. 16, p. 8.

42. *between September and November of 2000,* USA vs. Moussaoui, Government Exhibit ST00001, 01-455-A, p. 32.

43. *Nami, for instance, was only five-foot, seven-inches,* State of Florida, Department of Highway Safety and Motor Vehicles, Nami driver's license, DL/ID Number A455-001-77-447-0.

43. *"between 5'5" and 5'7" in height and slender in build,"* Staff Statement No. 16, p. 8.

43. *in order to camouflage the true intent of what their leaders had in mind,* National Commission on Terrorist Attacks Upon the United States, *The 9/11 Commission Report,* pp. 234–36.

43. *but the other twelve were from Saudi Arabia,* Staff Statement No. 16, p. 8.

43. *Most were unemployed and unmarried,* National Commission on Terrorist Attacks Upon the United States, *The 9/11 Commission Report,* p. 231.

43. *By now, Nawaf al Hazmi had been designated second in command,* Fouda and Fielding, *Masterminds of Terror,* p. 136; Summers and Swan, *The Eleventh Day,* p. 312.

43. *set up a new base in Paterson, New Jersey,* Staff Statement No. 16, p. 9.

44. *traveled to the United States in small groups between April 23 and June 29, 2001,* Statement for the Record, FBI Director Robert S. Mueller III; USA vs. Moussaoui, Government Exhibit ST00001, 01-455-A, pp. 42–51.

44. *where Hazmi was in charge,* Summers and Swan, *The Eleventh Day,* p. 312.

44. *"suggesting travel to a Russian republic,"* National Commission on Terrorist Attacks Upon the United States, *The 9/11 Commission Report,* p. 233.

44. *show that he worked out at the gym for twenty-eight of the next thirty-one days,* http://vault.fbi.gov/9-11%20Commission%20

Report/9-11-chronology-part-02-of-02, Working Draft, Chronology of Events for Hijackers and Associates.

44. *his five-foot, nine-inch frame,* Investigative Services Division, FBI headquarters, report on Saaed Al Ghamdi.

45. *shared a tribal affiliation with Ghamdi,* National Commission on Terrorist Attacks Upon the United States, *The 9/11 Commission Report,* p. 231.

45. *had memorized the Koran,* McDermott, *Perfect Soldiers,* p. 218.

45. *returned later to recruit other members of the clan,* Julian Borger, "Chilling, Defiant: The Video Suicide Message of a September 11 Killer," *The Guardian,* April 15, 2002.

45. *to ask about his mother,* www.globalsecurity.org/security/profiles/ahmed_al-haznawi.htm, profile of al Haznawi.

45. *"to send a message that has the color of blood,"* Longman, *Among the Heroes,* pp. 37–38.

45. *took cross-country surveillance flights between May and August,* USA vs. Moussaoui, Government Exhibit ST00001, 01-455-A, pp. 52–58.

45. *Jarrah, for instance, flew from Baltimore-Washington International Airport to Los Angeles on June 7,* Ibid., p. 55.

45. *and continued on to Madrid, Spain,* Ibid., pp.59–60; National Commission on Terrorist Attacks Upon the United States, *The 9/11 Commission Report,* pp. 243–44; McDermott, *Perfect Soldiers,* pp. 222–25.

46. *Bin Laden was pushing for the attacks to happen soon,* National Commission on Terrorist Attacks Upon the United States, *The 9/11 Commission Report,* pp. 244–45.

46. *"not easily spotted from the air,"* Fouda and Fielding, *Masterminds of Terror,* p. 127. They wrote, "The comparatively small building was not easily spotted from the air and was known to be well protected, so it was replaced by another spectacular target, Capitol Hill."

46. *while keeping the Capitol as an alternative,* National Commission on Terrorist Attacks Upon the United States, *The 9/11 Commission Report,* p. 248.

46. *that Jarrah's target was "Capitol Hill," meaning the Capitol,* Fouda and Fielding, *Masterminds of Terror,* pp. 127, 138.

46. *KSM also told investigators the target was indeed the Capitol,* USA vs. Moussaoui, Defendant's Exhibit 941, "Substitution for the Testimony of Khalid Sheikh Mohammed," p. 13.

46. *when the cockpit doors were usually opened for the first time,* National Commission on Terrorist Attacks Upon the United States, *The 9/11 Commission Report,* p. 245.

46. *They also had selected code names for the targets,* Fouda and Fielding, *Masterminds of Terror,* pp. 127, 138.

47. *Then the subject turned to Jarrah,* National Commission on Terrorist Attacks Upon the United States, *The 9/11 Commission Report,* p. 246.

47. *had bought him a one-way ticket,* Memorandum for the Record, Moussaoui Team Briefing, March 18, 2004, p. 2.

47. *"asks for a divorce, it is going to cost a lot of money,"* Staff Statement No. 16, p. 16.

47. *"send the skirts to Sally,"* Ibid.

47. *that he was merely an early arrival for a "second wave" of attacks,* Ibid., p. 17.

47. *at the Airman Flight School in Norman, Oklahoma,* Ibid.

47. *after receiving $14,000 from Binalshibh,* Ibid.

47. *He paid $6,800 in cash,* National Commission on Terrorist Attacks Upon the United States, *The 9/11 Commission Report,* p. 247.

48. *arrested on immigration charges,* Ibid. In December 2001, Moussaoui was charged with six counts of conspiracy in connection with the September 11 attacks. He became the first person tied to the plot who was tried in a US courtroom. He eventually pleaded guilty to conspiracy and was sentenced to life in prison in May 2006. www.cnn.com/2013/04/03/us/zacarias-moussaoui-fast-facts, Zacarias Moussaoui Fast Facts, April 3, 2013.

48. *were unable to get permission from headquarters to search his laptop,* McDermott, *Perfect Soldiers,* pp. 226–27; Neil A. Lewis, "FBI Agent Testifies Supervisor Didn't Pursue Moussaoui Case," *New York Times,* March 21, 2006.

48. *and Binalshibh was waiting for him when he landed in Dusseldorf,* Weaver, "The Indecisive Terrorist," *London Review of Books.*

48. *touched down at Miami International Airport on August 5,* USA vs. Moussaoui, Government Exhibit ST00001, 01-455-A, p. 61.

48. *The first semester commences in three weeks,* Fouda and Fielding, *Masterminds of Terror,* pp. 138–39.

49. *I will call you nearer the time,* Ibid., p. 139.

49. *paid for 1.3 hours of flight time at Airborne Systems,* USA vs. Moussaoui, Government Exhibit ST00001, 01-455-A, p. 68.

49. *visited the Oshkosh Pilot Shop in Miami,* Ibid., p. 69.

49. *Jarrah flew to Baltimore and checked into a motel in Laurel, Maryland,* Ibid., p. 70.

49–50. *"Two sticks, a dash, and a cake with a stick down—what is it?"* Fouda and Fielding, *Masterminds of Terror,* p. 140.

50. *All would be either 757s or 767s, which had almost identical cockpits,* Memorandum for the Record, Interviews of United Airlines and American Airlines Personnel, November 17–21, 2003, p. 2. According to the report, "The cockpits of the B757 and B767 are virtually interchangeable in their essential elements."

50. *The assignments and pilots,* National Commission on Terrorist Attacks Upon the United States, *The 9/11 Commission Report,* pp. 2–10, 32–33.

50. *KSM wanted to use twenty-five or twenty-six hijackers,* Staff Statement No. 16, p. 15.

50. *even with the return of Khalid al Mihdhar to the United States on the Fourth of July,* USA vs. Moussaoui, Government Exhibit ST00001, 01-455-A, p. 52.

50. *identifies no fewer than nine men who, over the course of the final year, were nominated to fill the position of the "twentieth hijacker,"* Staff Statement No. 16, p. 15.

51. *when a Saudi named Mohammed al Kahtani flew from Dubai through London to Orlando,* USA vs. Moussaoui, Government Exhibit ST00001, 01-455-A, p. 62.

51. *a sharp immigration official named Jose Melendez-Perez,* 9/11 Commission, 7th Public Hearing, January 26, 2004; Michael Smerconish, *Instinct: The Man Who Stopped the 20th Hijacker,* pp. 1–6.

51. *stating that he hoped to enter the United States on September 4 and planned to stay for "one week,"* 9/11 and Terrorist Travel, Staff Report of the National Commission on Terrorist Attacks Upon the United States, p. 31.

51. *a Saudi named Fawaz al Nashmi,* Katherine Shrader, Associated Press, "Al Qaeda Identifies Would-Be 20th Hijacker," (appeared in *Washington Post*), June 21, 2006.

51. *were reserved between August 25 and August 31,* USA vs. Moussaoui, Government Exhibit ST00001, 01-455-A, p. 71.

52. *two one-way tickets for $3,539.50,* Investigative Services Division, FBI Headquarters, Saaed al Ghamdi, FBI033235,033236.

52. *a one-way ticket in first class for $1,722,* USA vs. Moussaoui, Chronology of Events for Hijackers, 8/16/01–9/11/01, Ahmed al Haznawi.

52. *in the first row of first class for $1,621.50,* Ibid., Ziad Jarrah.

52. *was to purchase knives to be used in the attacks,* FBI Penttbom Briefing, Knife Purchases.

52. *FAA regulations at the time allowed,* Statement of James C. May, president and CEO of the Air Transport Association of America, Second hearing of the National Commission on Terrorist Attacks on the United States, May 22, 2003. According to the statement, "Under pre-9/11 FAA regulations, only 'knives with blades four inches long or longer and/or knives considered illegal under local law' were prohibited."

52. *flew north from Fort Lauderdale to Newark,* FBI Miami, Timeline Pertaining to South Florida.

53. *having flown from Miami to Baltimore,* USA vs. Moussaoui, Chronology of Events for Hijackers, 8/16/01–9/11/01, Mohamed Atta. Atta flew from Fort Lauderdale to Baltimore on September 7 and flew from Baltimore to Boston on September 9.

53. *The trooper described him as "extremely calm and cooperative,"* http://edition.cnn.com/2002/US/01/09/inv.hijacker.traffic.stops, "Another Hijacker Was Stopped for Traffic Violation," January 9, 2002; http://transcripts.cnn.com/TRANSCRIPTS/0201/08/se.01.html, "Maryland State Police Release Videotape of Traffic Stop of One of Hijackers," January 8, 2002.

53. *checked out of the Marriott . . . and herded the others into two rooms at the nearby Days Inn,* USA vs. Moussaoui, Chronology of Events for Hijackers, 8/16/01–9/11/01, Ziad Jarrah.

53. *"He said he had even bought a new suit for the occasion,"* Elizabeth Neuffer, Hijack Suspect Lived a Life, or a Lie," *Boston Globe,* September 25, 2001.

53. *Jarrah was heard addressing Atta as "boss,"* Statement for the Record, FBI Director Robert S. Mueller III.

54. you will see the result, and everybody will be happy, CBC News, The Fifth Estate, "The Pilot," October 10, 2001.

Chapter Six: Just Living Their Lives

Background information on the passengers and crew in this chapter was compiled primarily from three sources: Jere Longman's *Among the Heroes;* a special section of the *Pittsburgh Post-Gazette* from October 28, 2001; and "Brief Biographies: Passengers and Crew of Flight 93" from the Flight 93 National Memorial website (http://nps.gov/flni/historyculture/upload/Biographies -Passenger-Crew.pdf). Additional sources for this chapter were books written by the wives of Todd Beamer, Tom Burnett, Jeremy Glick, and LeRoy Homer and a profile of Mark Bingham, all listed in the bibliography. Some specific instances, and other sources, are noted here.

55. *to start a new life with her daughter,* Author interview with Carole O'Hare, January 2013.
55. *"bear, here we come,"* Longman, *Among the Heroes,* pp. 71–74.
56. *"I wouldn't have been surprised if they'd seen each other in school, maybe even talked,"* Author interview with Alice Hoglan, April 2013.
57. *He became a "standards captain,"* www.dahlfund.org.
57. *Air Force Aircrew Instructor of the Year,* www.leroywhomerjr.org.
58. *He had been an all-state wrestler and captain of the soccer team at Saddle River Day School,* Adrian Wojnarowski, "Glick Lost His Life but Won His Final Bout," www.espn.com, September 17, 2001.
59. *"He was like a guided missile,"* Longman, *Among the Heroes,* p. 135.
59. *hit a game-winning home run,* Lisa Beamer with Ken Abraham, *"Let's Roll!"* p. 35.
60. *opening a gash that required 140 stitches,* Author interview with Kenny Nacke, September 2012.
61. *"He loved the United States,"* Oral history transcript with Yachiyo Kuge and Naoya Kuge, Flight 93 National Memorial, interview conducted by Kathie Shaffer (Haruko Konno-George, translator).
61. *"let herself loose,"* "Passenger: Waleska Martinez," *Pittsburgh Post-Gazette,* October 28, 2001.
62. *John Talignani was born in Italy,* "Brief Biographies: Passengers and Crew of Flight 93" from the Flight 93 National Memorial website (http://nps.gov/flni/ historyculture/upload/Biographies-Passenger-Crew.pdf).
62. *"I know your game,"* Longman, *Among the Heroes,* p. 51.
62. *"Oh, she was feisty,"* Oral history transcript with Elizabeth (Betty) Kemmerer, Flight 93 National Memorial, interview conducted by Kathie Shaffer.

Chapter Seven: Zero Hour

64. *At 5:01 a.m. on the morning of September 11,* FBI Timeline of 9-11 Hijacker Activity and Movements, Boston Investigative Summary, p. 7.
64. *"and at no time appeared conspicuous,"* INTELWIRE, Federal Bureau of Investigation, Translation of the interview conducted by German authorities of the girlfriend of Ziad Jarrah, September 18, 2001.

64. *had driven more than one hundred miles to Portland, Maine,* Fouda and Fielding, *Masterminds of Terror,* p. 141.

65. *"at least one group had a chance of getting through,"* Ibid.

65. *Nawaf al Hazmi and Majed Moqed each set off two alarms,* Staff Statement No. 3 ("The Aviation Security System and the 9/11 Attacks"), pp. 9–10.

65. *swiped by an explosive trace detector,* Ibid., p. 10.

65. *"they had defeated all the security layers that America's civil aviation system then had in place,"* National Commission on Terrorist Attacks Upon the United States, *The 9/11 Commission Report,* p. 4.

65. *The strategic seating arrangements were determined in advance,* Fouda and Fielding, *Masterminds of Terror,* p. 144. Binalshibh said the general plan was to have "two members sitting as close as possible to the cockpit door to break in at a certain point of time and two at the back to keep the passengers at bay." The seating charts of all four planes indicate that there always was a two-man team of muscle hijackers seated near the front. However, because of the different layouts of a 757 (one aisle) and a 767 (two aisles, more maneuverability), the overall seating arrangements were slightly different. On the 757s, which were used for Flights 77 and 93, the hijacker pilots (Hanjour and Jarrah, respectively) sat in the first row of first class for the easiest access to the cockpit. On the 767s, which were used for Flights 11 and 175, the pilots (Atta and Shehhi, respectively) sat a few rows behind the break-in team.

65. *featured two aisles and allowed more room to maneuver,* Staff Statement No. 4 ("The Four Flights"), p. 3.

65. *A two-man team was assigned to sit side by side near the front,* Fouda and Fielding, *Masterminds of Terror,* p. 144; Staff Statement No. 4, p. 3.

66. Each brother knew exactly what he was supposed to do, Fouda and Fielding, *Masterminds of Terror,* p. 144.

66. *"among their forces and soldiers with a small group of nineteen,"* Ibid., p. 142.

66. *with ninety-two people on board,* USA vs. Moussaoui, Government Exhibit ST00001, 01-455-A, p. 4.

67. *"turn twenty degrees right,"* Ibid. p. 1.

67. *Wail and Waleed al Shehri, seated in 2A and 2B,* Ibid., p. 82.

67. *used AT&T airphones to report,* National Commission on Terrorist Attacks Upon the United States, *The 9/11 Commission Report,* p. 5.

67. *had "jammed" their way into the cockpit,* Ibid.

67. *passenger Daniel Lewin,* Ibid. Daniel Lewin was seated directly in front of hijacker Satam al Suqami. Flight attendant Amy Sweeney reported that a man in first class had his throat slashed. Although Lewin and Suqami weren't technically in first class, they were in business class in the front third of the plane. There was no other specific report of a passenger being stabbed on Flight 11.

67. *"I don't know, I think we're getting hijacked,"* Ibid.

68. *he hit the wrong button and communicated instead to air traffic control,* USA vs. Moussaoui, Government Exhibit ST00001, 01-455-A, p. 3.

68. *"We have some planes,"* Ibid.

68. *"you'll endanger yourself and the airplane,"* Ibid.

68. *Amy Sweeney, called the American Flight Services Office in Boston,* National Commission on Terrorist Attacks Upon the United States, *The 9/11 Commission Report,* p. 6.

68. *and that one spoke "excellent English,"* Memorandum for the Record, Interview with Michael Woodward, American Airlines Flight Service Manager.

68. *"Because the hijackers showed me a bomb,"* Gail Sheehy, "Stewardess ID'd Hijackers Early, Transcripts Show," *New York Observer,* February 16, 2004.

69. *"Oh my God, we are way too low,"* National Commission on Terrorist Attacks Upon the United States, *The 9/11 Commission Report,* pp. 6–7.

69. *At 8:46 a.m., American Airlines Flight 11 rammed into the North Tower,* USA vs. Moussaoui, Government Exhibit ST00001, 01-455-A, p. 4.

69. *the prevailing sentiment in the aviation industry was that domestic hijackings were largely a thing of the past,* Staff Statement No. 3, p. 1.

69. *78 percent of respondents cited poor aircraft maintenance as "a greater threat to airline safety" than terrorism,* Ibid.

70. *known as the Common Strategy,* Staff Statement No. 4, p. 1.

70. *"optimize actions taken by a flight crew to resolve hijackings peacefully,"* Ibid., p. 4.

70. *The last major terrorist attack on a US-flagged airliner had been thirteen years earlier,* Staff Statement No. 3, p. 5.

70. *the Computer-Assisted Passenger Prescreening Program (CAPPS),* Ibid., p. 6.

70. *were not required to undergo additional screening,* USA vs. Moussaoui, Government Exhibit ST00001, 01-455-A, p. 109.

70. *Nine of the nineteen hijackers were singled out by CAPPS,* Staff Statement No. 3, pp. 6–7.

70. *including Ahmed al Haznawi of Flight 93,* Ibid., p. 7.

71. *"Bin Laden Threats Are Real,"* Staff Statement No. 10 ("Threats and Responses in 2001"), p. 2.

71. *"patterns of suspicious activity in this country consistent with preparations for hijackings,"* "Bin Laden Determined to Strike in US," Declassified and Approved for Release April 10, 2004.

71. were likely to be successful in hijacking a US domestic aircraft, Staff Statement No. 3, p. 11.

71. *rumbled down Boston's Logan Airport runway that morning at 8:14,* National Commission on Terrorist Attacks Upon the United States, *The 9/11 Commission Report,* p. 7.

72. *contacted air traffic control to report hearing "a suspicious transmission,"* USA vs. Moussaoui, Government Exhibit ST00001, 01-455-A, p. 5.

72. *The hijackers attacked at about 8:42,* National Commission on Terrorist Attacks Upon the United States, *The 9/11 Commission Report,* p. 7.

72. *Fayez Banihammad and Mohand al Shehri, seated in 2A and 2B, respectively, likely crashed the cockpit,* USA vs. Moussaoui, Government Exhibit ST00001, 01-455-A, p. 83.

72. *reported that a flight attendant had been stabbed,* Ibid., p. 5.

72. *flight attendant Robert Fangman contacted the United Airlines office in San Francisco,* National Commission on Terrorist Attacks Upon the United States, *The 9/11 Commission Report,* pp. 7–8; Staff Statement No. 4, p. 2.

72. *He said the plane had been hijacked and was making "strange moves,"* National Commission on Terrorist Attacks Upon the United States, *The 9/11 Commission Report,* p. 7; Memorandum for the Record, Department of Justice Briefing on cell and phone calls from UA Flight 175, p. 3.

72. *passenger Brian Sweeney called his mother,* National Commission on Terrorist Attacks Upon the United States, *The 9/11 Commission Report,* p. 8; Memorandum for the Record, Department of Justice Briefing on cell and phone calls from UA Flight 175, p. 3.

72. *and former football player at Boston University,* www.goterriers.com/genrel/091401aad.html, "Memorial Service Set for Former Gridder Brian Sweeney"; http://business.highbeam.com/3972/article-1G1-86242817/hero-wife-proud-honor-husband-memory, "Hero's Wife Proud to Honor Husband's Memory," *Boston Herald,* May 24. 2002.

72. *from a phone just across the aisle in row thirty-two,* Memorandum for the Record, Department of Justice Briefing on cell and phone calls from United Flight 175, p. 3.

72–73. *Bailey, age fifty-three, had played ten seasons in the National Hockey League,* www.hockeydb.com/ihdb/stats/pdisplay.php?pid=169.

73. *Mark Bavis, age thirty-one, had spent three seasons in hockey's unforgiving minor leagues,* www.hockeydb.com/ihdb/stats/pdisplay.php?pid=249.

73. *Peter Hanson placed a second call to his father in Connecticut at 9:00 a.m.,* National Commission on Terrorist Attacks Upon the United States, *The 9/11 Commission Report,* p. 8.

73. *"Don't worry, Dad. If it happens, it'll be very fast,"* Ibid.

73. *ripped into the South Tower of the World Trade Center,* Ibid.

74. *took off from Washington's Dulles Airport at 8:20 a.m.,* USA vs. Moussaoui, Government Exhibit ST00001, 01-455-A, p. 6.

74. *reached its normal cruising altitude of 35,000 feet at 8:46,* Ibid.

74. *The hijackers gained control of the plane by at least 8:54,* Ibid.

74. *Nawaf al Hazmi and his brother, Salem, seated in 5E and 5F,* Ibid., p. 84.

74. *flight attendant Renee May and passenger Barbara Olson,* Ibid., p. 7.

74. *One said the "pilot" had made an announcement that the plane was hijacked,* National Commission on Terrorist Attacks Upon the United States, *The 9/11 Commission Report,* p. 9.

74–75. *Ted Olson was solicitor general of the United States,* Ibid.

75. *he had argued the case for George W. Bush before the US Supreme Court,* www.gibsondunn.com/lawyers/tolson.

75. *the Boeing 757 was about thirty-eight miles west of the nation's capital,* USA vs. Moussaoui, Government Exhibit ST00001, 01-455-A, p. 8.

75. *Hanjour began a severe 330-degree turn,* Ibid.

75. *At 9:37 a.m., American Airlines Flight 77,* Ibid.

75–76. *thousands of commuters streamed past the sixty-four-story USX Tower,* From his office at One Chatham Center in Pittsburgh, the author observed commuters flocking to their cars parked at Mellon Arena and in nearby lots.
76. *unaware of the danger lurking just a few thousand feet above their heads,* National Transportation Safety Board, Office of Research and Engineering, Flight Path Study, United Airlines Flight 93, February 19, 2002. According to the flight path study, Flight 93 was near Pittsburgh shortly before 10:00 a.m.

Chapter Eight: Mayday

77. *"I'm on the eight o'clock instead of the nine-twenty,"* Longman, *Among the Heroes,* pp. 12–13.
77. *"Screw it,"* Lyz Glick and Dan Zegart, *Your Father's Voice,* p. 188.
77. *Tom Burnett and Donald and Jean Peterson all had tickets for later departures,* Longman, *Among the Heroes,* pp. 8, 116.
77. *just to get to San Francisco on her way home to Honolulu,* Ibid., p. 12.
78. *Christine Snyder changed her itinerary three times,* Ibid., p. 54.
78. *Patricia Cushing and Jane Folger decided several days earlier to make the switch,* Ibid., p. 35.
78. *Bingham considered flying to the coast on September 10,* Ibid., p. 28.
78. *Nicole Miller missed her connection,* Ibid., p. 55.
78. *but opted to try standby,* www.washtimesherald.com/weekend-features/ x601175145/9-11-SERIES-Families-of-victims-tell-oral-history-of-Flight-93, Randy Griffith, CNHI, "9/11 Series: Families of Victims Tell Oral History of Flight 93," September 6, 2011.
78. *just learned the night before of a work issue in California that required his attention,* Longman, *Among the Heroes,* p. 124.
78. *to get to a business meeting on the West Coast,* Ibid., p. 194.
78. *wanted to spend more time with his two boys,* Ibid., p. 201.
78. *Wanda Green had been scheduled for duty on September 13,* Ibid., p. 23.
78. *Debbie Welsh was filling in for another flight attendant,* Ibid., p. 25.
78. *Captain Jason Dahl switched to Flight 93,* Ibid., p. 1.
78. *Haznawi and Ghamdi boarded together at 7:39,* National Commission on Terrorist Attacks Upon The United States, Third Staff Monograph, "The Four Flights and Civil Aviation Security," released by the National Archives on September 13, 2005, p. 35.
78. *entering the Jetway at 7:48,* Ibid.
79. *the 6'1", 220-pound judo champ,* Size descriptions of the passengers were found throughout Longman's *Among the Heroes* and the October 28, 2001, special edition of the *Pittsburgh Post-Gazette,* which profiled the passengers and crew. Additional information about Mark Bingham was found in Jon Barrett's *Mark Bingham, Hero of Flight 93,* p. 12.
79. How many small groups beat big groups by the will of God, www.theguardian .com/world/2001/sep/30/terrorism.september113, "Last Words of a Terrorist," *The Guardian/The Observer,* September 30, 2001.

79. *pulled back from the gate at 8:01 a.m.*, www.nps.gov/flni/historyculture/upload/Timeline_flight_93.pdf.

80. *on an aircraft that could hold 182*, Ibid., p. 36.

80. *It was the lightest load by far of the four targeted flights*, National Commission on Terrorist Attacks Upon the United States, *The 9/11 Commission Report*, pp. 4–11.

80. *finally took off at 8:42*, Ibid., p. 10.

80. *As it was, Captain Jason Dahl banked sharply*, NTSB animation of flight path.

80. *all ten of the passengers in their seating area*, Flight 93 seating chart, USA vs. Moussaoui, Prosecution Trial Exhibits, Exhibit No. P200055.

80. *"GOOD MORNIN',"* www.nps.gov/flni, Flight 93 Timeline, p. 7; Third Staff Monograph, p. 37.

81. *the kind that pilots describe as "severe clear,"* www.nps.gov/flni, Flight 93 Timeline, p. 2.

81. *asked United to relay a text message to her husband*, Third Staff Monograph, p. 37.

81. *and at 9:27:30 a.m. the pilots responded*, National Transportation Safety Board, Vehicle Recorders Division, *Air Traffic Control Recording, Transcript of ATC communications with a Boeing B-757 (United Airlines flight 93) which crashed near Shanksville, PA on September 11, 2001*, Specialist's Report by Joseph A. Gregor, December 21, 2001. Aircraft-to-Ground Communication, p. 7.

81. *tied red bandanas around their heads*, Third Staff Monograph, p. 40.

81. *plummeted dramatically at that point*, NTSB animation of flight path. Times and altitudes are included throughout the animation. Flight 93 dropped rapidly from an altitude of 34,995 feet to 34,315 feet before stabilizing—a total of 680 feet.

81. *At 9:28:16 a.m., Cleveland air traffic control heard the first chilling sounds*, NTSB, *Air Traffic Control Recording*, p. 7.

81. *"get out of here!"* Ibid.

81. *"just some guttural, guttural sounds,"* Oral history transcript with John Werth, Flight 93 National Memorial, interview conducted by Kathie Shaffer.

82. *Werth made seven attempts to contact Flight 93*, Ibid., pp. 7–8; www.nps.gov/flni, Flight 93 Timeline, p. 8.

82. *"We have a bomb on board. So, sit."* INTELWIRE, www.intelwire.com, CVR (Cockpit Voice Recorder) from UA Flight #93, 10862.adv.doc, original September 2002, major review December 4, 2003, p. 2, http://intelfiles.egoplex.com/2003-12-04-FBI-cockpit-recorder-93.pdf.

82. *and a "protection team" to deal with the passengers*, Fouda and Fielding, *Masterminds of Terror*, p. 144.

83. *"once inside, he would not have been visible to the passengers,"* National Commission on Terrorist Attacks Upon the United States, *The 9/11 Commission Report*, p. 12.

83. *with a steady ascent over Ohio*, NTSB animation of the flight path.

83. *took the plane up to 40,700 feet*, Ibid.

84. *"Don't move! Shut up,"* CVR from UA Flight #93, p. 2.

84. *"please, don't hurt me . . . Oh, God!"* Ibid., p. 3.

84. *believe this was one of the first-class flight attendants,* Summers and Swan, *The Eleventh Day,* p. 49.

84. *from aboard American Flight 11 indicate that two of the flight attendants were stabbed,* National Commission on Terrorist Attacks Upon the United States, *The 9/11 Commission Report,* pp. 6, 13. Amy Sweeney, a flight attendant on Flight 11, reported that two flight attendants had been stabbed. At least one caller from Flight 93 reported that a flight attendant had been stabbed.

85. *"I don't want to die. I don't want to die,"* CVR from UA Flight #93, p. 3.

85. *"Everything is fine. I finished,"* Ibid., p. 4.

85. *At 9:39 a.m., he made his second attempt,* Ibid.

85. *"We have a bomb aboard and we are going back to the airport,"* Ibid.

85. *twelve people on board made a total of thirty-five phone calls,* Memorandum for the Record, Department of Justice briefing on cell and phone calls from UA Flight 93, May 13, 2004. Many of the original media reports described the phone calls made from Flight 93 as cell phone calls. Assistant US attorney Dave Novak and his team provided a briefing following an "exhaustive" study of GTE Airfone records and an examination of phone records of passengers and crew who used cell phones. It was determined that passengers and crew made thirty-five calls from Airfones on Flight 93. There were only two calls made on cell phones and both came late in the flight—at 9:58 a.m.—when the plane was at a lower altitude. Of the thirty-five Airfone calls, nineteen were connected for seven seconds or less (two of these were misdials) and one was connected for fourteen seconds. The other fifteen calls got through and resulted in conversations or recorded messages to people on the ground. The twelve passengers and crew making Airfone calls were Todd Beamer, Mark Bingham, Sandy Bradshaw, Marion Britton, Tom Burnett, Joe DeLuca, Jeremy Glick, Lauren Grandcolas, Linda Gronlund, CeeCee Lyles, Waleska Martinez, and Elizabeth Wainio. In addition, passenger Ed Felt and Lyles made cell phone calls. In all, records show that thirteen passengers and crew made a total of thirty-seven calls from Flight 93.

86. *to report what one called "a little problem,"* Longman, *Among the Heroes,* p. 128.

86. *placed a series of brief phone calls to his wife, Deena,* Phone Calls from Flight 93 Crew and Passengers, Flight 93 National Memorial, p. 2. This report of the phone calls is a compilation of information from FBI interviews, from USA vs. Moussaoui trial evidence, and from the Third Staff Monograph of the 9/11 Commission. The first Airfone call from Flight 93 was made by Tom Burnett in row twenty-four (A-B-C) at 9:30 a.m. There are records of three Airfone calls from Tom. Deena says she received four calls. She believes the first was from Tom's cell phone (Memorandum for the Record, Deena Burnett interview by Commission staffers John Raidt and Lisa Sullivan, April 26, 2004). There was, however, no record of such a call from Tom on his cell phone bill, according to the memorandum.

86. *ready for her first day of preschool,* Deena Burnett with Anthony Giombetti, *Fighting Back,* p. 59.

86. *"Tom, are you ok?"* Ibid., p. 61.

86. *"the hijackers have already knifed a guy,"* Ibid. According to Deena, Tom also said during the first call that one of the hijackers had a gun. But Tom never mentioned a gun again, and no other caller made reference to a gun. Jeremy Glick specifically told his wife, Lyz, that the hijackers did not have a gun. No evidence of firearms was discovered at the Flight 93 crash site. Almost certainly, if the hijackers were in possession of a gun, they would have used it against the passengers and crew during the final battle for control of the plane. Despite Tom's initial statement in the frenzy of the takeover, it is not believed that the al-Qaeda terrorists on Flight 93 had a gun.

86. *She called a Speed Dial Fix number from row thirty-three,* Phone Calls from Flight 93 Crew and Passengers, Flight 93 National Memorial, p. 2.

87. *"shockingly calm,"* Ibid.

87. *two other passengers made contact with loved ones in the first ten minutes,* Memorandum for the Record, Department of Justice Briefing on cell and phone calls from UA 93, p. 2. Bingham's call was connected at 9:37:03 a.m., Glick's at 9:37:41 a.m. The hijacking started at 9:28 a.m. So calls by Burnett, Bradshaw, Bingham, and Glick all took place within the first ten minutes after the terrorists struck.

87. *Bingham, calling from row twenty-five, spoke first to his aunt,* Phone Calls from Flight 93 Crew and Passengers, Flight 93 National Memorial, p. 3; Longman, *Among the Heroes,* pp. 129–30; Barrett, *Mark Bingham, Hero of Flight 93,* pp. 156–58. Bingham knew that his mother, Alice Hoglan, was at the home of her brother, Vaughn, and Vaughn's wife, Kathy. Alice later changed the spelling of her last name from Hoglan to Hoagland, but it was Hoglan on September 11, 2001. For consistency, it is used as Hoglan throughout the book.

87. *"Thank God it's you,"* Glick and Zegart, *Your Father's Voice,* p. 189.

88. *"three Iranian guys took over the plane. They put on these red headbands,"* Ibid.

88. *"not completely irrational but on the cusp,"* Ibid.

88. *"whatever decisions you make in your life, no matter what, I'll support you,"* Ibid., pp. 190–91.

88. *informing her that the passenger who had been knifed was now dead,* Burnett with Giombetti, *Fighting Back,* p. 64.

88. *Mickey had been seated in 5B,* Flight 93 seating chart, USA vs. Moussaoui, Prosecution Trial Exhibits, Exhibit No. P200055.

89. *"they are hijacking planes all up and down the East Coast,"* Burnett with Giombetti, *Fighting Back,* p. 64.

89. *"It's a suicide mission!"* Ibid.

Chapter Nine: "We're Going to Do Something"

90. *"Honey, are you there?"* Longman, *Among the Heroes,* p. 128.

90. *attempted seven more calls in the next four minutes,* Memorandum for the Record, Department of Justice briefing on cell and phone calls from UA Flight 93, p. 2. Lauren made a total of eight calls between 9:39:21 and 9:43:44 a.m.

90. *technology allowed only eight calls to be placed from one airplane at the same time,* USA vs. Moussaoui, testimony of Sgt. Ray Guidetta of the New Jersey State Police, April 11, 2006.

90–91. *Joe DeLuca, Linda Gronlund's traveling companion, called his father from row twenty-six,* Ibid., p. 2.

91. *"It's Lynn. Um, I only have a minute,"* Phone Calls from Flight 93 Crew and Passengers, Flight 93 National Memorial, p. 7.

91. *She was sitting across the aisle from passenger Todd Beamer,* Memorandum for the Record, Department of Justice briefing on cell and phone calls from UA Flight 93, pp. 2–3. Beamer called from the Airfone in row thirty-two D-E-F. Lyles called from row thirty-two A-B-C.

92. *"I hope to be able to see your face again, baby. I love you. Good-bye,"* Phone Calls from Flight 93 Crew and Passengers, Flight 93 National Memorial, p. 7.

92. *"Ok, that's United ninety three calling?"* NTSB, *Air Traffic Control Recording,* p. 7. These five transmissions from air traffic control in Cleveland to Flight 93 were made between 9:39:19 and 9:41:01 a.m.

92. *At 9:41 a.m., he attempted to make their job more difficult by turning off the transponder,* National Commission on Terrorist Attacks Upon the United States, *The 9/11 Commission Report,* p. 29.

92. *ordered all commercial and private aircraft in US airspace to land at the nearest airport,* Ibid., p. 42.

93. *"Order everyone to land!"* Summers and Swan, *The Eleventh Day,* p. 51.

93. *guide an estimated 4,500 planes all over the country to new destinations,* Ibid., pp. 51–52. By 12:16 p.m., the FAA reported that the order had been successfully carried out. More than 4,500 flights had been landed safely or directed away from US airspace.

93. *"United ninety three, do you hear Cleveland center?"* NTSB, *Air Traffic Control Recording,* p. 7. These five transmissions were made between 9:45:29 and 9:48:39 a.m.

93. *Todd attempted four calls in rapid succession,* Memorandum for the Record, Department of Justice briefing on cell and phone calls from UA Flight 93, p. 2.

94. *transferred the call to supervisor Lisa Jefferson,* Lisa Jefferson and Felicia Middlebrooks, *Called,* pp. 29–30.

94. *"Can you explain to me in detail exactly what's taking place?"* Ibid., p. 33.

94. *"That's how I'm getting my information,"* Ibid., pp. 34–36.

94. *Todd said that two people were lying on the floor,* Ibid., pp. 36–37.

94. *"Oh my God, we're going down!"* Ibid., p. 44.

95. *He asked Lisa to recite the Lord's Prayer with him,* Ibid., p. 47.

95. *descended more than 20,000 feet,* NTSB animation of the flight path.

96. *"Should we let the guys in?"* CVR from UA Flight #93, p. 5.

96. *"Bring the pilot back,"* Ibid.

96. *someone described as a "low-pitch native English-speaking male" had said, "Oh, man!"* Ibid. This took place at 9:41 a.m., about thirteen minutes after the hijackers attacked the pilots in the cockpit.

96. *another more gradual descent*, NTSB animation of the flight path.

96. *"I bear witness that there is no other God but Allah,"* Ibid.

96. *both remained on the phone until the moment they charged the cockpit*, Memorandum for the Record, Department of Justice Briefing on cell and phone calls from UA Flight 93, pp. 2–3.

97. *"Where are the kids?"* Burnett with Giombetti, *Fighting Back*, pp. 66–67.

97. *"They know your plane has been hijacked,"* Ibid., p. 67.

97. *"If I don't make it through this, will you do me a favor?"* Jefferson and Middlebrooks, *Called*, p. 47.

97. *Among then were Waleska Martinez and Marion Britton*, Memorandum for the Record, Department of Justice briefing on cell and phone calls from UA Flight 93, p. 3.

97. *"they've slit two people's throats already,"* Bryan Burrough, "Manifest Courage," *Vanity Fair*, December 2001.

98. *"What was I gonna say?"* Ibid.

98. *Marion, using the Airfone in row thirty-three A-B-C*, Memorandum for the Record, Department of Justice briefing on cell and phone calls from UA Flight 93, p. 3. Marion's call lasted 232 seconds.

98. *urging her to call her family*, Longman, *Among the Heroes*, p. 168. Longman and others speculated that it was Lauren Grandcolas who handed the phone to Elizabeth. That may have been because their original ticketed seats on the flight were in the same row—Lauren in 11D and Elizabeth in 11F. However, the hijackers had moved the passengers to the rear of the plane immediately after attacking the cockpit. The DOJ briefing of phone calls determined that Lauren made her calls from row twenty-three D-E-F. Both Marion and Elizabeth called from the Airfone in row thirty-three A-B-C. Elizabeth's call began about half a minute after Marion's ended. It would have been Marion who handed the phone to Elizabeth.

98. *She reached her stepmother, Esther Heymann*, Longman, *Among the Heroes*, pp. 167–72; Phone Calls from Flight 93 Crew and Passengers, Flight 93 National Memorial, p. 8.

98. *"Elizabeth, I've got my arms around you,"* Longman, *Among the Heroes*, p. 168.

98. *"how much harder this is going to be on you than it is for me,"* Ibid., p. 171.

98. *Sandy described the hijackers as three men with dark skin wearing red bandanas*, Phone Calls from Flight 93 Passengers and Crew, Flight 93 National Memorial, p. 8.

98. *"We were talking about the kids, and I think she knew she was going to die,"* Oral history transcript with Philip Bradshaw, Flight 93 National Memorial, interview conducted by Barbara Black.

99. *"They just hit the Pentagon,"* Burnett with Giombetti, *Fighting Back*, p. 65.

99. *Lyz Glick told Jeremy*, Glick and Zegart, *Your Father's Voice*, p. 193.

99. *"We have to do something,"* Burnett with Giombetti, *Fighting Back*, p. 66.

99. *"I'm going to take a vote,"* Glick and Zegart, *Your Father's Voice*, p. 193.

99. *"I still have my butter knife from breakfast,"* Ibid.

99. *"A few of us passengers are getting together. I think we're going to jump the guy with the bomb,"* Jefferson and Middlebrooks, *Called*, p. 52.

99. *"I'm going to have to go out on faith,"* Ibid., p. 53.

100. *fifteen minutes longer than any of the other flights*, National Commission on Terrorist Attacks Upon the United States, *The 9/11 Commission Report*, pp. 4–11. Flight 93 took off at 8:42 a.m. and the hijacking began forty-six minutes later at 9:28 a.m. By contrast, Flight 11 was hijacked fifteen minutes after takeoff (p. 4); Flight 175 was hijacked approximately twenty-eight minutes after takeoff (p. 7); and Flight 77 was hijacked approximately thirty-one minutes after takeoff (p. 8).

100. *"and they put the ax into it. So, everyone will be scared,"* CVR from UA Flight #93, p. 6. The discussion about the ax took place at 9:53 a.m.

101. *"No one will ever take me down without a fight,"* Longman, *Among the Heroes*, p. 123.

101. *could bench-press 350 pounds,* Ibid., p. 121.

101. *described by a friend as a "sleeping volcano,"* Ibid., p. 48.

101. *who played American football in Japan,* Oral history transcript with Yachiyo Kuge and Naoya Kuge, Flight 93 National Memorial, interview conducted by Kathie Shaffer (Haruko Konno-George, translator).

101. *Don Greene had a license to fly small planes,* Longman, *Among the Heroes*, pp. 182–86.

101. *Sonny Garcia, a former air traffic controller for the California Air National Guard,* Ibid., p. 182.

101. *preparing hot water to throw on the hijackers,* Third Staff Monograph, p. 44.

101. *Some investigators believe they also commandeered a food cart,* Longman, *Among the Heroes*, pp. 206–7.

101. *"I'm going to put the phone down,"* Glick and Zegart, *Your Father's Voice*, p. 194.

102. *"I'll be home for dinner,"* Burnett with Giombetti, *Fighting Back*, p. 67.

102. *"Let's roll,"* Jefferson and Middlebrooks, *Called*, p. 53.

102. *The counterattack began at 9:57,* CVR from UA Flight #93. The hijackers in the cockpit heard a commotion and began to wonder if there was a fight going on. This was the beginning of the passenger/crew revolt.

102. *Never before in the history of commercial aviation,* Burrough, "Manifest Courage," *Vanity Fair,* December 2001.

102. *"They're getting ready to break into the cockpit,"* Phone Calls from Flight 93 Crew and Passengers, Flight 93 National Memorial, p. 8.

102. *"Everyone's running to first class. I've got to go. Bye,"* Oral history transcript with Philip Bradshaw.

102. *"Is there something? . . . A fight?"* CVR from UA Flight #93, pp. 6–7.

102. *The final two phone calls from Flight 93 were made at 9:58,* Memorandum for the Record, Department of Justice briefing on cell and phone calls from UA Flight 93, p. 3. Both calls were from cell phones.

102. *when the plane was barely at 5,000 feet,* NTSB animation of the flight path.

102. *Felt provided the basic details of the hijacking,* Phone Calls from Flight 93 Crew and Passengers, Flight 93 National Memorial, p. 9. There had been one early media report that Felt said he heard an explosion and saw white smoke coming from the plane, but it has been discounted. Author Jere Longman, in his book *Among the Heroes,* spoke with John Shaw, the 911 dispatcher who took the call; Shaw said Felt never mentioned an explosion or smoke. "Didn't happen," Shaw said (Longman, p. 264). Felt's wife, Sandra, heard the tape of her husband's call and confirmed Shaw's version of events to Longman. In addition, Gordie Felt, Ed's brother, told me his brother did not mention an explosion or smoke on the tape. "Absolutely not," Gordie said. It is important to remember that Ed Felt's call was made a full five minutes before the plane crashed. The written transcript indicates that Felt repeatedly said "Hijacking in progress," said he was calling from a bathroom, identified the flight as United 93, and said the plane was a 757 heading from Newark to San Francisco.

103. *"they're forcing their way into the cockpit,"* Longman, *Among the Heroes,* p. 180.

103. *began jerking the yoke,* NTSB animation of the flight path.

103. *most likely Burnett,* Burnett with Giombetti, *Fighting Back,* p. 203. Deena Burnett described hearing a passenger shout, "In the cockpit! In the cockpit!" when families were allowed to listen to the cockpit voice recorder in 2002. "It was Tom," she wrote. "It was so clearly, so unmistakably his voice. As soon as I heard it, I sat straight up."

103. *"There are some guys. . . . All those guys,"* CVR from UA Flight #93, p. 7. This was at 9:59:18 a.m. Much of the remainder of the narrative in this chapter is drawn from pages 7–10 of the cockpit voice recorder as well as the NTSB animation of the flight path.

103. *Three times in a period of five seconds,"* Ibid., p. 8. The transcript indicates that an Arabic-speaking male shouted "Ah!" on three occasions between 9:59:53 and 9:59:58 a.m.

103. *Atta had told Ramzi Binalshibh that he would crash his plane,"* National Commission on Terrorist Attacks Upon the United States, *The 9/11 Commission Report,* p. 244.

103. *"When they all come, we finish it off,"* CVR from UA Flight #93, p. 8. This statement came at 10:00:09 a.m.

104. *"Up, down. Saeed, up down!"* Ibid. This was at 10:00:37 a.m.

104. *"Is that it? . . . I mean, shall we pull it down?"* Ibid., p. 9. This was at 10:01:08 a.m.

104. *"Cut off the oxygen! Cut off the oxygen!"* Ibid. This was at 10:01:16 a.m.

104. *"Turn it up!"* Ibid. This was at 10:02:17 a.m.

105. *turning upside-down in midair,* NTSB animation of the flight path; NTSB, Office of Research and Engineering, Flight Path Study, United Airlines Flight 93, February 19, 2002.

105. *At 10:03:09 a.m., one of the hijackers said in a whisper,* CVR from UA Flight #93, p. 10.

Chapter Ten: Where Is the Plane?

106. *when the walls started to shake,* Oral history transcript with Paula Pluta, Flight 93 National Memorial, interview conducted by Kathie Shaffer.

106. *Diamond T strip mine,* www.nps.gov/flni, Flight 93 Timeline, p. 15. The local name for the area is "Diamond T." It refers to the job name of the strip mine that had operated at the site for many years. It was no longer in operation in 2001 and had been filled in, or "reclaimed."

106. *"The house started to vibrate and things started rattling and shaking,"* Oral history transcript with Paula Pluta.

106. *"There was an airplane crash here!"* Transcription of calls to Somerset County Emergency Management Agency, September 11, 2001.

107. *It might have been in the flight path,* Flight 93 was heading in the general direction of the Shanksville-Stonycreek School when it crashed. The crash site was less than three miles from the school. It is impossible to project the precise flight path, especially since Jarrah was rocking the wings as the passengers attacked the cockpit.

107. *"I stood around and was looking and there just . . . there wasn't anything to see,"* Oral history transcript with Paula Pluta.

107. *"I knew there wasn't anything that we could do,"* Oral history transcript with Cathy and David Berkebile, Flight 93 National Memorial, interview conducted by Kathie Shaffer.

107. *a cooling unit that was maybe eight inches by twelve inches,* Ibid.

108. *"big pile of charcoal,"* Bob Batz, Tom Gibb, Monica L. Haynes, Ernie Hoffman, Ginny Kopas, Cindi Lash, and James O'Toole, "The Crash in Somerset: 'It Dropped Out of the Clouds,'" *Pittsburgh Post-Gazette,* September 12, 2001.

108. *"clothes hanging from the trees,"* Ibid.

108. *'I just pointed and screamed,"* Ibid.

108. *'they're coming to get us,'* Ibid.

108. *Ida's, he said, was a "busy little place for a small, little town,"* Oral history transcript with Rick King, Flight 93 National Memorial, interview conducted by Kathie Shaffer.

109. *"Rick," she said, "I hear a plane!"* Ibid.

109. *"I mean, I could hear the engine screaming,"* Ibid.

109–110. *'I'm convinced it was a commercial airliner. I want additional departments,'* Ibid.

110. *Keith Custer, Merle Flick, and Robert Kelly,* Ibid.

110. *"there's pieces of metal and debris laying everywhere,"* Ibid.

110. *"And they kept coming back with . . . no signs of anybody,"* Ibid.

111. *"I saw a window out of the plane. I saw a seat, a piece of a seat,"* Ibid.

111. *Flight 93 was traveling at 563 mph,* NTSB, Flight Path Study, United Airlines Flight 93.

111. *at 10:03:11 a.m.,* Ibid.

111. *died instantly of blunt-force trauma,* Author interview with Wally Miller, September 2012.

111. *More than 5,500 gallons of jet fuel,* The NTSB determined there were 5,564 gallons of fuel on board when Flight 93 crashed. Original reports put the total at more than 7,000 gallons.
111. *crater that early eyewitnesses estimated to be thirty feet wide,* www.nps.gov/flni, "Sources and Detailed Information."
112. *"It looked like what you see after a tornado or hurricane goes through,"* Cindi Lash, "Flight 93 Crash Shook His House like a Tornado," *Pittsburgh Post-Gazette,* September 14, 2001.
113. *"A lot of people lost their lives in my backyard,"* Judy D. J. Ellich, "The Hoovers: Walking the Whole Way Through," *Somerset Daily American,* September 10, 2011.
113. *Coroner Wally Miller's phone rang,* Author interview with Wally Miller, September 2012.
113. *"twin engines or single-engine jobs,"* Ibid.
114. *"there were about eighteen inches of jet fuel pooled up at the bottom,"* Ibid.
114–115. *"Anything that wasn't connected to bone or sinew just got obliterated,"* Ibid.
115. *more than one thousand people representing seventy federal, state, and local agencies,* www.nps.gov/flni, Sources and Detailed Information.
116. *Twelve other members of the little Shanksville Fire Department,* www.nps.gov/flni, Flight 93 Timeline, p. 18.
116. *"Of course, I had to go,"* Author interview with Wally Miller, September 2012.

Chapter Eleven: One Big Family

117. *"We are getting reports,"* www.youtube.com/watch?v=l98AVR_YvUg; http://transcripts.cnn.com/TRANSCRIPTS/0109/11/bn.or.html, CNN Breaking News, "America Under Attack," aired September 11, 2001—10:30 a.m., p. 3.
117. *Lyz had passed the phone,* Glick and Zegart, *Your Father's Voice,* pp. 194–96.
117. *knees buckled and she began to sob,* Burnett and Giombetti, *Fighting Back,* p. 72.
117. *"Release the phone line,"* Jefferson and Middlebrooks, *Called,* pp. 54–55.
118. *"we don't know—if this is somehow connected to what has gone on in New York and Washington,"* www.youtube.com/watch?v=l98AVR_YvUg; http://transcripts.cnn.com/TRANSCRIPTS/0109/11bn.08.html, CNN Breaking News, "America Under Attack," aired September 11, 2001—10:45 a.m., p. 1.
118. *"Dad, what is going on?" she said. "Where's Richard?"* Oral history transcript with Lori Guadagno, Flight 93 National Memorial, interview conducted by Kathie Shaffer.
119. *'He's going to be coming out any minute,'* Ibid.
119. *The phone rang that morning and it was a neighbor. Where was Jason?* Oral history interview with Sandy Dahl, Flight 93 National Memorial, interview conducted by Kathie Shaffer.

120. *"Where's Dad?"* Ibid.

120. *"Sandy, I have to tell you bad news,"* Ibid.

120. *In Danville, California, Carole O'Hare was up early,* Author interview with Carole O'Hare, January 2013.

121. *had arrived at her new address in Danville,* Ibid.

121. *Family and friends left forty-four messages,* Barrett, *Mark Bingham, Hero of Flight 93,* pp. 9, 19, 35, 151, 165; Julia Prodis Sulek, "Messages for Flight 93 Passenger Capture Fear, Resolve on Sept. 11," *San Jose Mercury News,* September 11, 2011.

123. *At first Kenny was in denial about Joey being on the plane,* Author interview with Kenny Nacke, September 2012.

124. *"Nope, no way! I'm not going,"* Beamer with Abraham, *Let's Roll,* pp. 227–33.

125. *Beamer left an Oracle pen,* Ibid., p. 232.

125. *a "Got Milk?" poster,* Glick and Zegart, *Your Father's Voice,* p. 25.

125. *Kuge brought a Japanese flag,* Longman, *Among the Heroes,* p. 240.

125–126. *Rick King and other volunteer firemen in dress uniforms,* Oral history transcript with Rick King, Flight 93 National Memorial, interview conducted by Kathie Shaffer; author interview with Rick King, November 2012.

126. *'This is not the way I thought my mother would die,'* Oral history transcript with Elizabeth (Betty) Kemmerer, Flight 93 National Memorial, interview conducted by Kathie Shaffer.

126–127. *John Talignani was already in despair,* Longman, *Among the Heroes,* pp. 16–17, 241.

127. *services for Tom Burnett in both California and Minnesota,* Burnett with Giombetti, *Fighting Back,* pp. 130, 136.

127. *Martinez in Puerto Rico,* Longman, *Among the Heroes,* p. 240.

127. *where LeRoy and Melodie were married,* Homer, *From Where I Stand,* p. 39.

127. *celebrate the life of Georgine Corrigan,* Longman, *Among the Heroes,* p. 242.

127. *nationally televised address to a joint session of Congress,* Beamer with Abraham, *Let's Roll,* p. 243.

127. an exceptional man named Todd Beamer, www.washingtonpost.com/wp-srv/nation/specials/attacked/transcripts/bushaddress_092001.html, George W. Bush, *Address to a Joint Session of Congress and the American People,* United States Capitol, September 20, 2001.

128. *"we felt an obligation to our loved ones to make sure their stories were told,"* Author interview with Gordie Felt, September 2012.

Chapter Twelve: The FBI Investigates

129. *largest investigation ever undertaken,* www.fbi.gov/about-us/history/famous-cases/9-11-investigation, *Famous Cases and Criminals, 9/11 Investigation (PENTTBOM).* According to the report, "At the peak of the case, more than half of our agents worked to identify the hijackers and their sponsors and, with other agencies, to head off any possible future attacks."

129. *"Flight 93 was the most important aspect of the 9/11 investigation,"* Todd McCall, *The Criminal Investigation: Searching for Evidence at the Flight 93 Crash Site,* Flight 93 National Memorial, Learning Center Without Walls, September 9, 2012. FBI agents McCall, John Larsen, and Jack Shea took part in a panel discussion at the memorial to commemorate the eleventh anniversary of the attacks.

129. *"accordioned" onto the middle,* Oral history transcript with William Robert "Bob" Craig, Flight 93 National Memorial, interview conducted by Kathie Shaffer. Craig described his own observations as well as the explanation he received from the National Transportation Safety Board (NTSB).

130. *to Indian Lake, about a mile and a half downwind,* Ibid.; Jere Longman and Jo Thomas, "Recovered Recorder May Give Clues of a Struggle for Control," *New York Times,* September 14, 2001. FBI special agent Bill Crowley noted that "pieces of light debris, like nylon and paper, had landed as far away as New Baltimore." This was downwind from the crash site.

130. *Wells Morrison . . . was among the first to arrive that morning,* Jack Shea, *The Criminal Investigation: Searching for Evidence at the Flight 93 Crash Site,* Flight 93 National Memorial, Learning Center Without Walls, September 9, 2012.

130. *FBI Evidence Response Teams,* Oral history transcript with Bob Craig.

130. *"We had an airplane that flew into the ground and the earth that had fallen on top of that,"* Glenn J. Kashurba, *Courage after the Crash,* pp. 110–11.

131. *nose axle . . . landing just beyond the banks of a sediment pond,* Pennsylvania State Police, *Forensic Mapping of United Airlines Flight 93 Crash Site.*

131. *thousand-pound engine fan,* http://edition.cnn.com/2001/US/09/24/inv.pennsylvania.site/index.html, "FBI Finished with Pennsylvania Crash Site Probe," September 24, 2001.

131. *The largest was a piece of the fuselage,* Ibid.

131. *The tragedy hit a little closer to home for Veitz than most,* Oral history transcript with Louis Veitz, Flight 93 National Memorial, interview conducted by Kathie Shaffer.

131. *"You start finding personal belongings, you start to put faces to the people that used to be in that airplane,"* Ibid.

132. *"I've never seen the amount of shrapnel,"* Oral history transcript with Mark Trautman, Flight 93 National Memorial, interview conducted by Kathie Shaffer.

132. *'you have a good cry once in a while, it helps you out,'* Ibid.

133. *McCall remembers driving past an elementary school,* Todd McCall, *The Criminal Investigation: Searching for Evidence at the Flight 93 Crash Site,* Flight 93 National Memorial, Learning Center Without Walls, September 9, 2012.

133. *"We're at war,"* National Commission on Terrorist Attacks Upon the United States, *The 9/11 Commission Report,* p. 326.

133. *reported "with near certainty,"* Bob Woodward, *Bush at War,* p. 26.

134. *"Investigators found a Lebanese passport,"* FBI UA Flight 93 Investigative Team, *Search Evidence.*

134. *Jarrah's passport was extensively charred,* U.S. Department of Justice Memorandum, John J. Ross, Jr., Supervisory Forensic Document Examiner, September 20, 2001.

134. *Other items located nearby,* Pennsylvania State Police, *Forensic Mapping of United Airlines Flight 93 Crash Site.*

134. *fourteen pieces of knives,* FBI Report, *Knives Found at the UA Flight 93 Crash Site (from items submitted to the FBI Lab);* National Commission on Terrorist Attacks Upon the United States, *The 9/11 Commission Report,* p. 457, note 82.

134. *first page of a handwritten letter in Arabic,* FBI UA Flight 93 Investigative Team, *Crime Scene Evidence,* Lab no. 010912013.

134. *Similar letters were found in connection to two other flights,* www.fbi.gov, *Facts and Figures 2003,* p. 2.

134. *Atta's suitcase never made it,* Memorandum for the Record: Review of investigation conducted by the FBI of Atta's suitcases at Boston, Mass., February 10, 2004.

135. *On September 14, the FBI officially released the names of all nineteen hijackers,* FBI National Press Office, "FBI Announces List of 19 Hijackers," September 14, 2001.

135. *Jarrah's rented red Mitsubishi Galant . . . was found in the parking lot at the Newark Airport,* Ibid.; FBI UA Flight 93 Investigative Team, *Search Evidence.*

135. *The first breakthrough came at 4:20 p.m.,* Longman and Thomas, "Recovered Recorder May Give Clues of a Struggle for Control," *New York Times,* September 14, 2001.

135. *"digging down, digging down,"* Oral history transcript with Bob Craig.

135. *Reagan National Airport into the aircraft's flight computer,* National Commission on Terrorist Attacks Upon the United States, *The 9/11 Commission Report,* p. 457, note 85.

136. *None of the black boxes were recovered from Flights 11 and 175,* National Park Service, *Sources and Detailed Information,* Flight 93 National Memorial, www.nps.gov/flni/historyculture/sources-and-detailed-information.htm.

136. *They did not have to wait long,* Matthew P. Smith, "Flight 93 Voice Recorder Found in Somerset County Crash Site," *Pittsburgh Post-Gazette,* September 15, 2001; Oral history transcript with Bob Craig.

136. *landed mysteriously in Cleveland,* Theory proposed in the video *Loose Change, 2nd Edition,* by Dylan Avery and Korey Rowe.

137. *until four minutes after it was already down—10:07 a.m.,* Third Staff Monograph, p. 46. "The call was the first notification the military—at any level—received about Flight 93"; Staff Statement No. 17 ("Improvising a Homeland Defense"), p. 17. "NEADS first received a call about United 93 from the

military liaison at Cleveland Center at 10:07. Unaware that the aircraft had already crashed, Cleveland passed to NEADS the aircraft's last known latitude and longitude. NEADS was never able to locate United 93 on radar because it was already in the ground."

137. *wasn't issued from the White House bunker until at least 10:10,* Staff Statement No. 17, pp. 24–25. At this point, in the confusion, Cheney was given a report that the aircraft was eighty miles out—even thought it had already crashed.

137. *recorded in his notes that the president told him at 10:20 a.m. he had given shoot-down authoritzation,* National Commission on Terrorist Attacks Upon the United States, *The 9/11 Commission Report,* p. 41.

137. *did not reach NEADS until 10:31,* Staff Statement No. 17, p. 19.

137. *(Flight 1989 eventually* did *land in Cleveland),* Ibid., p. 14.

137. *"continued well into the afternoon and evening,"* Michael Bronner, "9/11 Live: The NORAD Tapes," *Vanity Fair,* August 2006.

137. *requesting some sort of military assistance as early as 9:36 a.m.,* Staff Statement No. 17, p. 15.

138. *It was not until thirteen minutes later, at 9:49 a.m.,* Ibid., p. 16.

138. Uh, ya know everybody just left the room, Ibid.

138. *briefly lost track of Flight 93 somewhere over Pittsburgh,* Ibid.

138. *"waving his wings,"* Ibid.

138. *the following transmission at 10:15,* Ibid., pp. 17–18.

139. *125 miles from Washington, DC,* Ibid., p. 16.

139. *Two armed F-16 fighter jets,* Ibid., p. 28.

139. *had not been briefed on details of the threat,* Ibid. According to the staff statement, "But the Langley pilots were never briefed about the reason they were scrambled. As the lead pilot explained, 'I reverted to the Russian threat. . . . I'm thinking cruise missile threat from the sea. You know you look down and see the Pentagon burning and I thought the bastards snuck one by us. . . . (Y)ou couldn't see any airplanes, and no one told us anything.' The pilots knew their mission was to identify and divert aircraft flying within a certain radius of Washington, but did not know that the threat came from hijacked commercial airliners."

139. *"negative clearance to shoot,"* Ibid. pp. 17–19.

139. an unprecedented challenge they had never before encountered and had never trained to meet, National Commission on Terrorist Attacks Upon the United States, *The 9/11 Commission Report,* p. 45.

139. *Dassault Falcon 20 business jet,* Staff of *Popular Mechanics* magazine, *Debunking 9/11 Myths: Why Conspiracy Theories Can't Stand Up to the Facts,* p. 111.

140. *C-130H cargo plane,* National Commission on Terrorist Attacks Upon the United States, *The 9/11 Commission Report,* pp. 25–26, 30.

140. *"If they were fighting with the hijackers . . . I guarantee it happened right here,"* Longman and Thomas, "Recovered Recorder May Give Clues of a Struggle for Control," *New York Times,* September 14, 2001.

140. *made its final fatal dive into the open field,* Longman, *Among the Heroes,* pp. 212–14.

140. *"The plane was not shot down,"* Ibid., p. 264.

141. *"There was no debris in the flight path until the crash site,"* Author interview with Wally Miller, September 2012.

141. *to see if there was anything "suspicious,"* Oral history transcript with Bob Craig.

141. *shoulder-to-shoulder sweep,* Ibid.

141. *"The facts just didn't support their position,"* Jack Shea, *The Criminal Investigation: Searching for Evidence at the Flight 93 Crash Site,* Flight 93 National Memorial, September 9, 2012.

142. *more than twice the size to eighty-five feet,* Environmental Resources Management (ERM), *Final Closure Report, Flight 93,* September 3, 2002, p. 8.

142. *"until there is nothing to be found,"* Oral history transcript with Bob Craig.

142. *The FBI concluded its investigation . . . recovered 95 percent of the Boeing 757,* www.cnn.com, "FBI Finished with Pennsylvania Crash Site Probe," September 24, 2001.

142. *signed over at that point to the local coroner,* Oral history transcript with Bob Craig.

Chapter Thirteen: The "Hick" Coroner

143. *"I do know a little about grief,"* Author interview with Wally Miller, September 2012.

143. *"nearest thing to a hero the crash investigation had produced,"* Glick and Zegart, *Your Father's Voice,* p. 137.

144. *"an absolutely fierce advocate for the families,"* Author interview with Gordie Felt, September 2012.

144. *"expecting an answering machine,"* Oral history transcript with Melodie Homer, Flight 93 National Memorial, interview conducted by Kathie Shaffer.

144. *was about 7,700 pounds,* Author interview with Wally Miller, September 2012.

144. *fingerprints on file,* Ibid.

144. *temporary morgue was set up,* Pennsylvania Emergency Management Agency, Statewide Terrorist Activities (incident summary), September 12, 2001.

144. *Armed Forces Institute of Pathology's DNA identification laboratory,* Cindi Lash, "Flight 93 Victim Identification Long, Arduous," *Pittsburgh Post-Gazette,* September 25, 2001.

145. *"I think you understand what the scenario is,"* Tom Gibb, "Four Flight 93 Victims Identified," *Pittsburgh Post-Gazette,* September 22, 2001.

145. *"a young, shaven version of Abe Lincoln,"* Peter Perl, "Hallowed Ground," *Washington Post,* May 12, 2002.

145. *"a jawbone with four or five teeth in it,"* Author interview with Wally Miller, March 2013.

146. *an additional 150 pounds of remains,* Ibid.

146. *"pop rivet holding two pieces of aluminum,"* Gibb, "Latest Somerset Crash Site Findings May Yield Additional IDs," *Pittsburgh Post-Gazette,* October 3, 2001.

146. *cover it with six inches of topsoil,* Author interview with Wally Miller, March 2013.

146. *asked Miller how close they could get to the impact site,* Ibid.

146. *"poured a little, tiny bit in each glass,"* Oral history transcript with Sandy Dahl, Flight 93 National Memorial, interview conducted by Kathie Shaffer.

147. *Lorne Lyles's home late on the evening of September 23,* Oral history transcript with Lorne Lyles, Flight 93 National Memorial, interview conducted by Kathie Shaffer.

147. *Melodie Homer received her call,* Homer, *From Where I Stand,* p. 50.

148. *"This is just my mommy's room now,"* Beamer with Abraham, *Let's Roll,* p. 178.

148. ALL MY LOVE, 8-2-69, Steve Levin, "Flight 93 Victims' Effects to Go Back to Families," *Pittsburgh Post-Gazette,* December 30, 2001.

148. *"we had chosen for our wedding ceremony,"* Homer, *From Where I Stand,* p. 56.

148. *once belonged to Hilda Marcin's husband, Edward,* Oral history transcript with Elizabeth (Betty) Kemmerer, Flight 93 National Memorial, interview conducted by Kathie Shaffer.

149. *"especially when there's so little that you have,"* Oral history transcript with Lori Guadagno, Flight 93 National Memorial, interview conducted by Kathie Shaffer.

149. *when analysts positively identified the remains of the last passenger,* Author interview with Wally Miller, September 2012.

149. *Miller had wanted to bring family members together in one large setting,* Ibid.

149. *"I was surprised at my own curiosity,"* Glick and Zegart, *Your Father's Voice,* p. 105.

150. *"things we didn't know,"* Oral history transcript with Sandy Dahl.

150. *"You can't even imagine the emotion,"* Author interview with Debby Borza, November 2012.

150. *"might turn up at the mouth of the hole,"* Glick and Zegart, *Your Father's Voice,* pp. 106–7.

150. *"They wanted to hear the cockpit voice recorder,"* Author interview with Wally Miller, September 2012.

151. *"The terrible thing was losing my husband and having to live with it,"* Glick and Zegart, *Your Father's Voice,* pp. 108–9.

151. *to travel to Somerset County to appear on NBC's* Today *show,* Ibid., p. 135.

152. *"So what am I getting back?"* Ibid., p. 139.

Chapter Fourteen: The Tape

153. *"I wanted to hear the tape for myself,"* Burnett with Giombetti, *Fighting Back,* p. 193.

153. *"I believed their concern to be insulting,"* Ibid.

153. *a jarring experience on November 15, 2001,* Homer, *From Where I Stand,* pp. 100–1.

154. *Until then, it is very arrogant of you or your agency to presume anything,* Ibid. pp. 101–3.

154. *Deena received a voice mail on the afternoon of March 21,* Burnett with Giombetti, *Fighting Back,* p. 194.

154. *Melodie got the same message,* Homer, *From Where I Stand,* p. 104.

154. *was scheduled from 1:30 to 5:30,* Burnett with Giombetti, *Fighting Back,* p. 200.

154. *It was Meredith Rothenberg,* Ibid., p. 199.

155. *"achieve an end without violence,"* Ibid.

155. *required to pass through a metal detector,* Longman, *Among the Heroes,* p. 276.

155. *had to be placed on a long table,* Glick and Zegart, *Your Father's Voice,* p. 144.

155. *"uncomfortable blue chairs,"* Ibid.

155. *opened the proceedings with an explanation of what they were about to hear,* Burnett and Giombetti, *Fighting Back,* p. 200.

155. *"they weren't going to let us have copies of the transcript,"* Author interview with Debby Borza, November 2012.

155. *Tom's voice shouting, "In the cockpit!"* Burnett with Giombetti, *Fighting Back,* p. 203.

155. *Jeremy's "judo grunt,"* Glick and Zegart, *Your Father's Voice,* p. 145.

155. *"It was pure rage,"* Author interview with Kenny Nacke, September 2012.

156. *"This was as close as I could be to my daughter in her final moments,"* Sam Leith, "Cockpit Tape Confirms Courage of Terrorist Victims on Flight 93," *The Telegraph,* April 20, 2002.

156. *"They sounded like the heroes people are saying they were,"* Ibid.

157. *"It was a sustained assault that went on for several minutes,"* Author interview with Alice Hoglan, April 2013.

157. *"I think it was a story of extreme bravery,"* Oral history transcript with Meredith Rothenberg, Flight 93 National Memorial, interview conducted by Kathie Shaffer.

158. *"she probably was just calming these people down,"* Oral history transcript with Elizabeth (Betty) Kemmerer, Flight 93 National Memorial, interview conducted by Kathie Shaffer.

158. *"I just needed to be alone. And scream,"* Author interview with Lyz Glick, February 2013.

159. *they stemmed from his inexperience in dealing with the national news media,* Author interview with Wally Miller, March 2013.

160. *"Of course there was no blood,"* Ibid.

160. *"I still thought it made sense for the families to organize,"* Ibid.

161. *"to an interim board of directors,"* www.familiesofflight93.org.

161. *"He gave us the strength to form an organization,"* Author interview with Kenny Nacke, September 2012.

161. *she found a "strange peace" as she gazed across the rural landscape,* Burnett with Giombetti, *Fighting Back,* p. 212.

161. *the fortitude and fearlessness of the soldiers who fought at Gettysburg in July 1863,* Ibid., p. 18.

162. *"which so fascinated and inspired him,"* Ibid., p. 212.

162. *"they made that conscious choice,"* Author interview with Wally Miller, March 2013.

Chapter Fifteen: "A Common Field One Day . . ."

163. *to ask if she could take a picture of the fire truck,* Craig Fehrman, "The Forgotten Memorial, How 9/11 Changed Shanksville, Pennsylvania," *New Republic,* August 24, 2011.

164. *the lawn of her home on Bridge Street,* Memorial Timeline, Flight 93 National Memorial, p. 4.

164. *"Whoever needs us, we're there for them,"* Ibid.

164. *"even if they couldn't really see anything yet,"* Author interview with Donna Glessner, Flight 93 National Memorial staff, April 2013.

164. *placed by the congregation of the Somerset Alliance Church,* Memorial Timeline, Flight 93 National Memorial, p. 2.

164–165. *The County Commissioners held a meeting on October 10,* Ibid., p. 6; Author interview with Barbara Black, Chief of Interpretation and Cultural Resources at the Flight 93 National Memorial, April 2013.

165. *The experience was very personal,* Author interview with Barbara Black, April 2013.

165. *"We'll never know what or why,"* Ibid.

166. *On November 2, 2001,* Memorial Timeline, Flight 93 National Memorial, p. 7.

166. *Instead, she would be there for several hours, answering questions, listening to stories,* Author interview with Barbara Black, April 2013.

166. *overheard a few onlookers talking about the crash,* Author interview with Donna Glessner, April 2013.

167. *"no one was even greeting them,"* Author interview with Barbara Black, April 2013.

167. *'we can't have people coming to our community and not be taken care of,'* Glenn J. Kashurba, *Quiet Courage,* p. 206.

167. *The first training session was held on January 26, 2002,* Memorial Timeline, Flight 93 National Memorial, p. 7; Author interview with Donna Glessner, April 2013.

167. *Chuck later became the unofficial photographer,* Author interview with Barbara Black, April 2013.

167. *created forty slate angels,* Ibid.

167. *while paying their respects,* Ibid.

168. *"A Field of Honor Forever,"* Ibid.; *Tribute Items,* Flight 93 National Memorial.

168. by members of the 19th Special Forces, Ibid.

168. *sounded like a worthwhile project for his firm to explore,* Author interview with Paul Murdoch, architect of the Flight 93 National Memorial, April 2013.

169. *gone canoeing at Ohiopyle State Park and visited Frank Lloyd Wright's architectural masterpiece at Fallingwater,* Ibid.

169. *It also meshed with the project's mission statement,* www.nps.gov/flni/ parknews/upload/07-30-04ApprovedMissionStatementDocs-2. "Flight 93 National Memorial Mission Statement."

169. *drew interest from forty-eight states and twenty-seven countries,* www.nps .gov/flni/parkmgmt/designquestions.htm, "Questions About the Design."

169. *"we wanted to create an open dialogue about what the memorial could be,"* Author interview with Jeff Reinbold, National Park Service, February 2013.

170. *would bear the names of the forty passengers and crew,* Paul Murdoch Architects, *The Design;* author interview with Paul Murdoch, April 2013.

170. *"was very much rooted in the land there,"* Author interview with Paul Murdoch, April 2013.

170. *design professionals, project partners, local residents, and nine family members of the passengers and crew,* www.nps.gov/flni/parkmgmt/intldesigncomp.htm, "International Design Competition," Stage I and Stage II juries, Flight 93 National Memorial.

170. *regiments who helped repel Pickett's Charge,* Author interview with Ed Root, May 2013. Root is coauthor of the book *Isn't This Glorious,* about the 15th, 19th, and 20th Massachusetts regiments.

171. *"I thought that made it worthy of an excellent memorial,"* Ibid.

171. *one of five entries selected for the final stage,* www.nps.gov/flni/parkmgmt/ intldesigncomp.htm, "International Design Competition."

171. *"gave a standing ovation to the design,"* www.nbcnews.com, "Flight 93 Memorial Design Selected," Associated Press, September 7, 2005.

171. *"to retain its simplicity,"* Ibid.

171. *"really harnesses the spirit of our forty heroes,"* Ibid.

171. *Someone alerted Murdoch to a blog,* Author interview with Paul Murdoch, April 2013.

172. *they had dismissed it as nonsensical,* Author interviews with Ed Root and Jeff Reinbold, May and February 2013.

172. *"Everyone sort of rolled their eyes,"* Author interview with Ed Root, May 2013.

172. *who openly questioned the design,* Anne C. Mulkern, "Trancredo Rips Sept. 11 Memorial," *Denver Post,* September 14, 2005.

172. *creating a website and writing a book,* Alec Rawls, www.crescentofbetrayal .com.

172. *the best way to confront the hysteria was to meet it head on,* www.nps.gov/flni, *White Paper: Prepared by the Fight 93 National Memorial Project Partners,* October 23, 2007.

172. *They contacted religious and academic experts to examine Rawls's claims,* www .nps.gov/flni, Memorial Design Evaluation: Daniel A. Griffith, January 5, 2007; Memorial Design Assessment, Dr. Kevin Jaques, February 27, 2007. Other documents also available under "Flight 93 Memorial Partners Support Design."

172. *"The landform of that bowl at the crash site, that* circle, *is what we always were working with,"* Author interview with Paul Murdoch, April 2013.

173. *"all but the fanatical fringe,"* Ibid.

173. *"It's an insult to my son and all the others,"* Sean D. Hamill, "Design of a Memorial to Flight 93 Fuels Tension between Families," *New York Times,* May 4, 2008.

173. *"It's actually offensive,"* Author interview with Gordie Felt, September 2013.

173. *unanimous vote of the board of directors,* Families of Flight 93, "Letter to Honorable Tom Tancredo, House of Representatives," November 9, 2007.

173. *"we have found no merit in their claims,"* Statement from Gordon Felt, president of the Families of Flight 93, May 2, 2008.

174. *"it really didn't set us back at all,"* Author interview with Joanne Hanley, former superintendent of Flight 93 National Memorial, May 2013. At one point, Tom Burnett Sr. asked that his son's name not be included in the memorial. But Hanley said that the National Park Service and the project partners would move forward with the design that was approved by the Department of the Interior, which included all forty names of the passengers and crew.

174. *playing among the hemlock trees,* Author interview with Tim Lambert, landowner, May 2013.

174. *"but those are* our *trees,"* Ibid.

175. *"I was struck by the magnitude of what happened there,"* Judy D. J. Ellich, "The Hoovers: Walking the Whole Way Through," *Somerset Daily American,* September 10, 2011.

175. *"to close my involvement in the case,"* "Owners to Get 9/11 Field in Pa. Back," Associated Press, July 29, 2005.

175. *The first large parcel of more than 900 acres was purchased,* Sean D. Hamill, "Flight 93 Memorial Effort Gains Over 900 Acres," *New York Times,* March 19, 2008.

175. *controlled 275 acres,* Daniel Lovering, "Flight 93 Memorial Land in Dispute," Associated Press, June 6, 2007; Richard Robbins, "Five Flight 93 Land Buys Nearly Done," *Pittsburgh Tribune-Review,* August 2, 2009; Martha T. Moore, "Flight 93 Memorial Deal Is Struck," *USA Today,* August 31, 2009.

176. *when Secretary of the Interior Ken Salazar visited Somerset County,* NPS press release, "National Park Service Signs Agreement with Owners on Land for Flight 93 Memorial," August 31, 2009.

176. *"if a national tragedy occurs on your land,"* Author interview with Tim Lambert, May 2013.

176. *On August 31, Salazar announced,* NPS press release, "National Park Service Signs Agreement with Owners on Land for Flight 93 Memorial," August 31, 2009.

176. *which owned the Rollock scrap yard,* Vicki Rock, "Agreement Near for Flight 93 Property," *Somerset Daily American,* July 31, 2009.

176. *allowing the courts to establish fair compensation,* NPS press release, "National Park Service Signs Agreement with Owners on Land for Flight 93 Memorial," August 31, 2009; Sean D. Hamill, "Land Deal Is Reached for a Flight 93 Memorial," *New York Times,* January 18, 2009.

176. *would pay more than nine million dollars,* Martha T. Moore, "Flight 93 Memorial Deal Is Struck," *USA Today,* August 31, 2009.

177. *"walking on your own property and you feel you are trespassing,"* Judy D. J. Ellich, "The Hoovers: Walking the Whole Way Through," *Somerset Daily American,* September 10, 2011.

177. *who helped ceremonially turn the dirt,* Mary Pickels, "Flight 93 National Memorial Event to Honor Heroes," *Pittsburgh Tribune-Review,* November 6, 2009.

177. *'Those young people are the future of this memorial,'* Author interview with Debby Borza, December 2012.

177. *"we were creating a small town of our own,"* Author interview with Jeff Reinbold, February 2013.

177. *was estimated to cost sixty million dollars,* Ibid.

178. *"many people thought the funds would just pour in,"* Ibid.

178. *"a testament to the actions of the people on board Flight 93,"* Tom Ridge and Ed Rendell, "A Call to Service from Flight 93," *Washington Post,* November 7, 2009.

179. *"Pearl Harbor didn't ask to be bombed,"* Kashurba, *Quiet Courage,* p. 239.

Chapter Sixteen: Ten Years Later

180. *traffic extended well more than a mile,* The author sat in that traffic on September 10, 2011.

180. *780 family members of the passengers and crew,* Vicki Rock, "Obamas Visit Flight 93 National Memorial Site," *Somerset Daily American,* September 12, 2011. The number was attributed to Gordie Felt, president of the Families of Flight 93.

181. *"You feel the sky,"* www.youtube.com, "Flight 93 National Memorial," *Herald Standard Media,* September 8, 2011.

181. *"'but it can never forget what they did here,'"* www.youtube.com, *Dedication of the Flight 93 National Memorial,* September 10, 2011. The speeches also received extensive media coverage, but this is a video of the entire dedication ceremony.

182. a legacy of bravery and selflessness that will always inspire America, Ibid., George W. Bush speech.

183. all because ordinary people, given no tide to decide, did the right thing, Ibid., Bill Clinton speech.

183. *no stranger to personal tragedy,* Larry McShane, "Joe Biden Beats Odds after Wife, Daughter Killed," *New York Daily News,* August 24, 2008; "A Timeline of U.S. Sen. Joe Biden's Life and Career," Associated Press, August 22, 2008.

184. "If they mean to have a war, let it begin here," www.youtube, *Dedication of the Flight 93 National Memorial,* September 10, 2011, Joe Biden speech.

184. *raised the first flag at the national memorial,* Author interview with Jeff Reinbold, National Park Service, June 2013.

184. *"this isn't for us, is it?"* Mackenzie Carpenter, Sean D. Hamill, Ann Rodgers, and Bill Toland, "Thousands Visit Flight 93 Site for Dedication of Memorial," *Pittsburgh Post-Gazette,* September 11, 2011.

185. *"for this encounter with tragedy and evil,"* Author interview with Tom Ridge, February 2013.

185. *took the governor's career down a path he never anticipated,* Tom Ridge, *The Test of Our Times,* pp. 19–24.

186. Or a unique combination? Ridge Global Security, *Remarks by the Honorable Tom Ridge, Flight 93 National Memorial Service of Remembrance,* September 11, 2011.

186. *"as much to the families as the memorial itself,"* Joe Mandak, "Grief, Reflection Mark Flight 93 Memorial Ceremony," Associated Press, September 11, 2011.

186. with the memory and guidance of forty good shepherds, Ridge Global Security, *Remarks by the Honorable Tom Ridge, Flight 93 National Memorial Service of Remembrance,* September 11, 2011.

187. *Wally Miller had to choke back tears,* Randy Griffith, "10 Years of Emotions: Memorial Marks Crash of Flight 93," *Johnstown (PA) Tribune-Democrat,* September 11, 2011.

187. *"Take your time, Wally,"* Author interview with Jeff Reinbold, Flight 93 National Memorial, June 2013.

187. *President Barack Obama arrived to place a wreath at the crash site,* Tahman Bradley, "Obama Visits Flight 93 National Memorial," abcnews.co.com, September 11, 2011; www.youtube.com, *President Obama, September 11, Flight 93 National Memorial, 10th anniversary,* September 11, 2011. Obama had visited the World Trade Center site earlier that morning. He visited the Pentagon later in the day.

187. *"speech for the ages,"* Cip Minemyer, "Ridge Embraces 40 Heroes in Classic Oration," *Johnstown (PA) Tribune-Democrat,* September 11, 2011.

187. *"where the aircraft hit the ground,"* Author interview with Wally Miller, March 2013.

188. *"We could share that moment among ourselves,"* Author interview with Debby Borza, November 2012.

188. *"I wouldn't have it any other way,"* Author interview with Wally Miller, March 2013.

189. *"including mine,"* Ibid.

189. *"right down to shoveling dirt on the graves,"* Ibid.

190. *"a phone call or a text away if they need me,"* Ibid.

Chapter Seventeen: Legacy

191. *"Things did not need to turn out the way they did. Choices matter,"* George Will, "After 150 Years, the Choices Made at Gettysburg Still Reverberate," *Washington Post,* June 30, 2013.

192. *"Destroyer of the American Spirit,"* "AQ Celebrates 9/11 Hijackers," http://hotair.com/archives/2006/09/10/video-aq-celebrates-the-911-hijackers, September 10, 2006.

192. *"What appears to be a hole in the ground is truly a monument of heroism,"* Gerry Dulac, "Prayer Service for the Victims of Attack Moves Steeler Family," *Pittsburgh Post-Gazette,* September 15, 2001.

193. *"It was a disturbed harmony,"* Oral history transcript with Jack Grandcolas, Flight 93 National Memorial, interview conducted by Barbara Black.

193. *"they gave it unconditionally,"* Ibid.

193. *LeRoy W. Homer Jr. Foundation,* Homer, *From Where I Stand,* p. 87; www.leroywhomerjr.org.

193. *Captain Jason Dahl Scholarship Fund,* www.dahlfund.org.

193. *to finish the book Lauren had started,* Lauren Catuzzi Grandcolas, Vaughn Catuzzi Lohec, and Dara Catuzzi Near, *You Can Do It!: The Merit Badge Handbook for Grown-Up Girls,* available at www.amazon.com.

193. *Ride with the 40,* Matthew B. Stannard, "Flight 93 Memorial Rolls from Sea to Shining Sea," *San Francisco Chronicle,* September 11, 2009.

193. *Thomas Burnett Day of Service,* Kelly Smith, "Bloomington Schools Honor 9/11 Hero," *Minneapolis Star-Tribune,* September 13, 2011.

194. *Deora Bodley Alumni Award,* www.ljcds.org/page.cfm?p=2557.

194. *Honolulu Community College (HCC) dedicated a memorial,* 9/11 Living Memorial, www.voicesofseptember11.org.

194. *"That's not really a good place for me,"* Oral history transcript with Lori Guadagno, Flight 93 National Memorial, interview conducted by Kathie Shaffer.

194. *"something that can teach, can inspire, can transition,"* Lori Guadagno, *9/11 and the Next Generation,* Flight 93 National Memorial, Learning Center Without Walls, September 8, 2012.

195. *"very anxious, uncomfortable dagger feeling in my heart,"* Author interview with Lyz Glick, February 2013.

195. *"I was on the phone with him while it was happening,"* Ibid.

196. *"I'm sure she will someday—when she's ready,"* Ibid.

196. *"silver lining to a very gray cloud of September 11,"* Oral history transcript with Jack Grandcolas.

197. *"His hand was shaking, but his voice was calm,"* Nicole Eickhoff, "A Grateful Nation: Stories from the U.S. Capitol," Flight 93 National Memorial, Learning Center Without Walls, September 9, 2012.

197. *"Evacuate immediately!"* Nellie Neumann, "A Grateful Nation: Stories from the U.S. Capitol," Flight 93 National Memorial, Learning Center Without Walls, September 9, 2012.

197. *"For all I knew, it was the last look I would have at anything,"* Ibid.

198. I thank them, and I have made a vow to live my life in gratitude of their sacrifice, Nicole Eickhoff, "A Grateful Nation: Stories from the U.S. Capitol," Flight 93 National Memorial, Learning Center Without Walls, September 9, 2012.

199. *"Had they not taken the action that they did that day, we would not be standing here at the Capitol,"* Nellie Neumann, "A Grateful Nation: Stories from the U.S. Capitol," Flight 93 National Memorial, Learning Center Without Walls, September 9, 2012.

199. *Mohammed Atef, al-Qaeda's military commander,* Khaled Dawoud, "Mohammed Atef (obituary)," *The Guardian,* November 18, 2001; www.telegraph.co.uk/news/obituaries/1362754/Mohammed-Atef.html, "Mohammed Atef," *The Telegraph,* November 19, 2001.

199. *Ramzi Binalshibh, the plot's key facilitator,* Fouda and Fielding, *Masterminds of Terror,* pp. 15–21; Cam Simpson and John Crewdson, "Terror Suspects Arrested," *Chicago Tribune,* September 14, 2002.

200. *Khalid Sheikh Mohammed, the mastermind,* McDermott and Meyer, *The Hunt for KSM,* pp. 244–48.

200. *subjected to extensive waterboarding,* US Justice Department, Memorandum for John A. Rizzo, Senior Deputy Counsel, Central Intelligence Agency, May 30, 2005, p. 8.

200. *"justice has been done,"* www.cnn.com/2011/POLITICS/05/02/bin.laden.white.house, "Obama Tells Families of 9/11 Victims That 'Justice Has Been Done,'" May 2, 2011.

200. *Beverly Burnett, Tom's mother, praised SEAL Team Six,* Steve Karnowski, "Family of Minn. 9/11 Hero Praises US Forces," *Minneapolis Star-Tribune,* May 2, 2011.

201. *Richard Reid, who tried to ignite explosives in his shoe,* Michael Elliott, "The Shoe Bomber's World," *Time,* February 16, 2002.

201. *who tried to light explosives in his underwear,* David Ariosto and Deborah Freyerick, "Christmas Day Bomber Sentenced to Life in Prison," www.cnn.com, February 17, 2012.

201. shall come to this deathless field, to ponder and dream, www.joshualawrencechamberlain.com, *Dedication of the Maine Monuments at Gettysburg,* October 3, 1889.

202. *"I caught just a quick flash of light,"* Oral history transcript with Val McClatchey, Flight 93 National Memorial, interview conducted by Kathie Shaffer.

202. *"Oh, jeez, it's just smoke rising over the barn and the hillside,"* Ibid.

203. *Washington Post, Newsweek, Time,* Ibid.

203. *"conspiracy theorists . . . call me and harass me,"* Sean D. Hamill, "Picture Made on 9/11 Takes a Toll on Photographer," *New York Times,* September 10, 2007.

203. *Outstanding Achievement for Amateur Photography,* Judy D. J. Ellich, "'End of Serenity' Photo Will Be Displayed aboard USS *Somerset,*" *Somerset Daily American,* June 19, 2013.

203. *'I'm still here to see it. A blink of an eye and I wouldn't be,'* Oral history transcript with Val McClatchey.

204. *without mentioning that he had been one of the first people to reach the crash site,* Craig Fehrman, "The Forgotten Memorial: How 9/11 Changed Shanksville, Pennsylvania," *New Republic,* August 24, 2011.

204. *"they were still probably going to die, but they did it anyway,"* Oral history transcript with Rick King, Flight 93 National Memorial, interview conducted by Kathie Shaffer.

204. *"They tried to overcome evil. They didn't just take it,"* Oral history transcript with Joyce Dunn, Flight 93 National Memorial, interview conducted by Kathie Shaffer.

GENERAL BIBLIOGRAPHY

Books

Barrett, Jon. *Mark Bingham, Hero of Flight 93.* Los Angeles: Advocate Books, 2002.

Beamer, Lisa, with Ken Abraham. *Let's Roll! Ordinary People, Extraordinary Courage.* Carol Stream, IL: Tyndale House Publishers, 2002.

Burnett, Deena, with Anthony Giombetti. *Fighting Back: Defining Moments in the Life of an American Hero, Tom Burnett.* Longwood, FL: Advantage Books, 2006.

Fouda, Yosri, and Nick Fielding. *Masterminds of Terror: The Truth Behind the Most Devastating Terrorist Attack the World Has Ever Seen.* New York: Arcade Publishing, 2003.

Glick, Lyz, and Dan Zegart. *Your Father's Voice: Letters for Emmy About Life with Jeremy—And Without Him After 9/11.* New York: St. Martin's Griffin, 2004.

Homer, Melodie. *From Where I Stand: Flight #93's Pilot's Widow Sets the Record Straight.* Minneapolis: Langdon Street Press, 2012.

Jefferson, Lisa, and Felicia Middlebrooks. *Called: "Hello, My Name Is Mrs. Jefferson. I Understand Your Plane Is Being Hijacked."* Chicago: Northfield Publishing, 2006.

Kashurba, Glenn J. *Courage after the Crash: Flight 93 Aftermath—An Oral and Pictorial Chronicle.* Somerset, PA: SAJ Publishing, 2002.

———. *Quiet Courage.* Somerset, PA: SAJ Publishing, 2006.

Longman, Jere. *Among the Heroes: United Flight 93 and the Passengers and Crew Who Fought Back.* New York: HarperCollins, 2002.

McDermott, Terry. *Perfect Soldiers: The 9/11 Hijackers: Who They Were, Why They Did It.* New York: HarperCollins, 2005.

McDermott, Terry, and Josh Meyer. *The Hunt for KSM: Inside the Pursuit and Takedown of the Real 9/11 Mastermind, Khalid Sheikh Mohammed.* New York: Little, Brown and Company, 2012.

Miniter, Richard. *Mastermind: The Many Faces of the 9/11 Mastermind, Khalid Shaikh Mohammed.* New York: SENTINEL, published by the Penguin Group, 2011.

National Commission on Terrorist Attacks Upon the United States. *The 9/11 Commission Report.* New York: W. W. Norton & Company, 2004.

Ridge, Tom, with Larry Bloom. *The Test of Our Times: America Under Siege . . . And How We Can Be Safe Again.* New York: Thomas Dunne Books, 2009.

Smerconish, Michael A., with Kurt A. Schreyer. *Instinct: The Man Who Stopped the 20th Hijacker.* Guilford, CT: Lyons Press, 2009.

Soufan, Ali, with Daniel Freedman. *The Black Banners: The Inside Story of 9/11 and the War Against al-Qaeda.* New York: W. W. Norton & Company, 2011.

Staff of *Der Spiegel* magazine. *Inside 9-11: What Really Happened.* New York: St. Martin's Press, 2002.

Staff of *Popular Mechanics* magazine, David Dunbar and Brad Reagan, eds. *Debunking 9/11 Myths: Why Conspiracy Theories Can't Stand Up to the Facts.* New York: Hearst Books, 2011.

Summers, Anthony, and Robbyn Swan. *The Eleventh Day: The Full Story of 9/11 and Osama bin Laden.* New York: Ballantine Books, 2011.

Woodward, Bob. *Bush at War.* New York: Simon & Shuster, 2003.

Wright, Lawrence. *The Looming Tower: Al-Qaeda and the Road to 9/11.* New York: Vintage Books, 2006.

Magazines

Bronner, Michael, "9/11 Live, The NORAD Tapes," *Vanity Fair,* August 2006, www.vanityfair.com.

Burrough, Bryan, "Manifest Courage," *Vanity Fair,* December 2001, www.vanityfair.com.

Fehrman, Craig, "The Forgotten Memorial: How 9/11 Changed Shanksville, Pennsylvania," *New Republic,* September 15, 2011.

Weaver, Mary Anne, "The Indecisive Terrorist," *London Review of Books,* September 8, 2011.

Zeman, Ned, and David Wise, David Rose, and Bryan Burrough, "The Path to 9/11: Lost Warnings and Fatal Errors," *Vanity Fair,* November 2004, www.vanityfair.com.

Newspapers

Boston Globe, Chicago Tribune, The Guardian, Johnstown (PA) Tribune-Democrat, Los Angeles Times, New York Times, Pittsburgh Post-Gazette, San Francisco Chronicle, San Jose Mercury News, Somerset (PA) Daily American, Star-Ledger (Newark), The Telegraph, Wall Street Journal, Washington Post. The special section published by the *Pittsburgh Post-Gazette* on October 28, 2001, was especially helpful.

Websites

www.cnn.com, www.dahlfund.org, www.familiesofflight93.org, www.leroywhomerjr .org, www.nps.gov/flni, www.philly.com, www.co.somerset.pa.us, www.tomburnettfoundation.org, www.venice-fla.com.

Oral Histories—Flight 93 National Memorial

Ed Ballinger—United Airlines flight dispatcher

Cathy and David Berkebile—Somerset County residents who rushed to the crash site

Philip Bradshaw—Husband of flight attendant Sandy Bradshaw

William Robert "Bob" Craig—FBI, Senior Team Leader, Pittsburgh Division Evidence Response Team

Sandy Dahl—Wife of Captain Jason Dahl
Joyce Dunn—First-grade teacher, Shanksville-Stonycreek School
Lloyd and Joan Glick—Parents of passenger Jeremy Glick
Jack Grandcolas—Husband of passenger Lauren Grandcolas
Lori Guadagno—Sister of passenger Richard Guadagno
Melodie Homer—Wife of First Officer LeRoy Homer
Betty Kemmerer—Daughter of passenger Hilda Marcin
Rick King—Assistant Fire Chief, Shanksville Volunteer Fire Department
Arne Kruithof—Owner, Florida Flight Training Center
Yachiyo and Naoya Kuge—Mother and brother of passenger Toshiya Kuge
Lorne Lyles—Husband of flight attendant CeeCee Lyles
Paula Pluta—Somerset County resident who rushed to the crash site
Meredith Rothenberg—Wife of passenger Mark "Mickey" Rothenberg
Mark Trautman—Arborist, Penn State University
Louis Veitz—Pennsylvania State Police
John Werth—Air Traffic Controller, Cleveland Air Route Traffic Control Center

Author Interviews

Lyz (Glick) Best—Wife of passenger Jeremy Glick
Barbara Black—Chief of Interpretation and Cultural Resources, Flight 93
    National Memorial
Debby Borza—Mother of passenger Deora Bodley
Beverly Burnett—Mother of passenger Tom Burnett
Gordie Felt—Brother of passenger Ed Felt; president, Families of Flight 93
Donna Glessner—Flight 93 National Memorial staff
Joanne Hanley—Former superintendent, Flight 93 National Memorial
Alice Hoglan—Mother of passenger Mark Bingham
Rick King—Assistant Fire Chief, Shanksville Volunteer Fire Department
Tim Lambert—Landowner at the crash site; radio reporter
Wally Miller—Somerset County coroner
Paul Murdoch—Designer, Flight 93 National Memorial
Kenny Nacke—Brother of passenger Louis "Joey" Nacke
Carole O'Hare—Daughter of passenger Hilda Marcin
Jeff Reinbold—Superintendent, National Parks of Western Pennsylvania,
    Flight 93 National Memorial
Governor Tom Ridge—Governor of Pennsylvania on September 11, 2001;
    First Secretary, US Department of Homeland Security
Ed Root—Cousin of flight attendant Lorraine Bay; former president, Families
    of Flight 93
Patrick White—Cousin of passenger Louis Nacke; former vice president,
    Families of Flight 93

Public Presentations—Flight 93 National Memorial

Glessner, Donna, Nicole Eickhoff, Nellie Neumann, "A Grateful Nation: Stories from the U.S. Capitol," Learning Center Without Walls, September 9, 2012.

Knepp, Joy, Lori Guadagno, Dr. Mary Margaret Kerr, "9/11 and the Next Generation," Learning Center Without Walls, September 8, 2012.

Shea, John A., Todd McCall, John Larsen, FBI agents, "The Criminal Investigation: Searching for Evidence at the Flight 93 Crash Site," Learning Center Without Walls, September 9, 2012.

Documents

INTELWIRE, www.intelwire.com, CVR (Cockpit Voice Recorder) from UA Flight #93, 10862.adv.doc, original September 2002, major review December 4, 2003. http://intelfiles.egoplex.com/2003-12-04-FBI-cockpit -recorder-93.pdf.

INTELWIRE, www.intelwire.com, Federal Bureau of Investigation, Translation of the interview conducted by German authorities of the girlfriend of Ziad Jarrah, September 18, 2001.

Memorandum for the Record, Department of Justice briefing on cell and phone calls from UA Flight 93, May 13, 2004.

National Commission on Terrorist Attacks Upon the United States, Staff Statements No. 1 ("Entry of the 9/11 Hijackers into the United States"), No. 3 ("The Aviation Security System and the 9/11 Attacks"), No. 4 ("The Four Flights"), No. 10 ("Threats and Responses in 2001"), No. 16 ("Outline of the 9/11 Plot"), No. 17 ("Improvising a Homeland Defense").

National Transportation Safety Board, Office of Research and Engineering, Flight Path Study, United Airlines Flight 93, February 19, 2002.

National Transportation Safety Board, Vehicle Recorders Division, *Air Traffic Control Recording, Transcript of ATC communications with a Boeing B-757 (United Airlines flight 93) which crashed near Shanksville, PA on September 11, 2001*, Specialist's Report by Joseph A. Gregor, December 21, 2001.

Statement for the Record, FBI Director Robert S. Mueller III, Joint Intelligence Committee Inquiry.

United States of America vs. Zacarias Moussaoui, United States District Court for the Eastern District of Virginia, Government Exhibit ST00001, 01-455-A (111 pages plus attachments).

USA vs. Moussaoui, Chronology of Events for Hijackers, 8/16/01–9/11/01.

USA vs. Moussaoui, Defendant's Exhibit 941, "Substitution for the Testimony of Khalid Sheikh Mohammed."

USA vs. Moussaoui, Indictment of Zacarias Moussaoui.

USA vs. Moussaoui, Prosecution Trial Exhibits, various (as identified).

9/11 and Terrorist Travel, Staff Report of the National Commission on Terrorist Attacks Upon the United States.

9/11 Commission Briefing, Flight Training, January 13, 2004, by John Allen, Deputy Director, Flight Standards Service.

9/11 Report: Joint Congressional Inquiry, Report of the Joint Inquiry into the Terrorist Attacks of September 11, 2001, by the House Permanent Select Committee on Intelligence and the Senate Select Committee on Intelligence, July 24, 2003.

Index